The Next Big Earthquake
in the Pacific Northwest

FULL RIP 9.0

SANDI DOUGHTON

SASQUATCH BOOKS
SEATTLE

To my family of friends: RB, CB, PB, CD, BH, JJ,
MM, DM, DR, AS, SS, JV, Patu & Six-Thirty

Printed in the United States of America
Published by Sasquatch Books
17 16 15 14 13   9 8 7 6 5 4 3 2 1

Editor: Gary Luke
Project editor: Michelle Hope Anderson
Cover design: Anna Goldstein
Interior design and composition: Sarah Plein
Cover photograph: Seattle Skyline © Newleaf/Veer.com
                Glass © Smit/Veer.com
Copy editor: Sue Mann

Library of Congress Cataloging-in-Publication Data is available.
ISBN: 978-1-57061-789-8

Sasquatch Books
1904 Third Avenue, Suite 710
Seattle, WA 98101
(206) 467-4300
www.sasquatchbooks.com
custserv@sasquatchbooks.com

Certified Chain of Custody
SUSTAINABLE Promoting Sustainable Forestry
FORESTRY
INITIATIVE   www.sfiprogram.org
             SFI-01268

SFI label applies to the text stock

CONTENTS

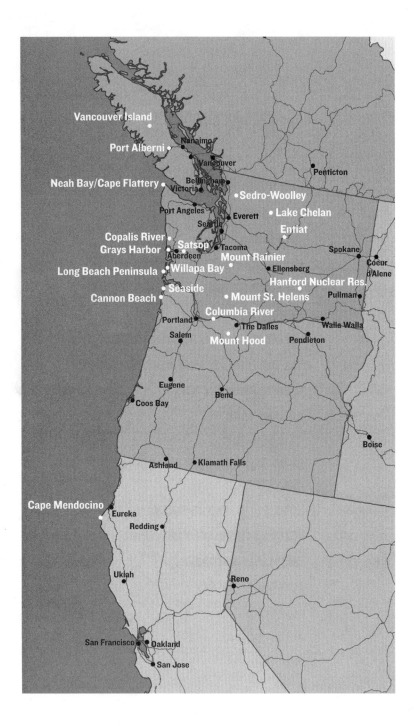

INTRODUCTION:

A WARNING FROM THE PAST

STORIES PASSED DOWN FROM THAT NIGHT don't tell us if dogs howled a warning. Huddled together in the cold, the animals might have sensed the first faint vibrations while the people slept.

A quarter moon hung in the sky.

Far offshore, where only the boldest whalers paddled their canoes, a seven-hundred-mile-long gash on the ocean floor was shifting. Masses of rock thrust past each other, grinding and buckling and jerking as if the planet were being torn apart.

People jolted awake in their longhouses. The motion pounded out a staccato rhythm, like a woodpecker hammering a tree. Cedar planks rattled and timbers groaned. In those first moments, it might have seemed as if a gale were sweeping in off the Pacific. But how could the wind rock the ground? Children cried out in fear. Men and women stumbled toward doorways.

The ground began to roll like the sea. People dropped to their hands and knees, felled by shaking so intense, cedar-bark baskets flew into the air. Ancient spruce trees whipped back and forth like saplings, raining branches onto the forest floor. The people lucky enough to make it outside clung in darkness to a world that seemed intent on casting them off.

As the seam in the seafloor continued to rip, the shaking swept along the western edge of North America. Under its thick blanket of mud, the margin of a great geologic plate shuddered and slid westward, pulling the continent with it. Shock waves raced out in all directions, traveling miles in seconds and rattling the shores of the inland sea many coast-dwellers had heard of, and some had visited. The people who live there today call it Puget Sound.

One minute passed.

Hillsides where condominiums now command million-dollar views trembled and sloughed off cascades of mud and stones. Deer and elk stampeded blindly, but couldn't escape the unearthly shaking. Nor could the people. From the Haida in the far north, to the Quileute on the Washington coast and the Yurok of California's redwood forests, the tribes of the Pacific Northwest felt the earth reshaping itself beneath their feet.

Two minutes.

Carved posts that had supported plank buildings for generations crashed to the ground. It was January and the people were gathered in lowland camps for the winter. The river mouths where many longhouses clustered were the first to turn to jelly and spout geysers of watery sand. At the confluence where Portland would later spring up, sandbars vibrated into a slurry. Fountains spurted from spruce swamps along the Columbia River. The tide flats of the Duwamish River, today the busy port of Seattle, trembled and split. In the night, no one saw the undulations. Only later would people notice strange patterns left behind in the sand and silt.

Three minutes.

Forested slopes gave way, rushing downhill in a tumult. River valleys and shorelines quivered and dropped by several feet. Stands of cedar that had sprouted centuries ago were suddenly below sea level. Some of the gray-haired elders had felt the earth shake before; this time they wondered if it would ever stop.

The year was 1700.

When earthquakes strike urban areas, they give off a dull roar like a jet passing overhead. The din rises from thousands of structures vibrating and grating against each other. What would the sound have been like centuries ago, when there was just the thrashing of forests and the wrenching of miles-thick chunks of crust?

Four minutes.

The only signs of humanity were scattered native settlements. Imagine the scene today. What highway would remain passable after being tossed like a ship on the high seas? How many bridges and office towers could twist for four minutes and still stand? Pipelines that carry water, gasoline, and oil to fuel a modern economy run through the same valleys that dissolved under the shaking so long ago. Power poles march over slopes that were scarred by landslides and littered with fallen trees.

Five minutes.

Like a storm with its strength spent, the maelstrom in the earth subsided. The edge of the underwater plate ground to a halt, perhaps fifty feet from where it started. Along seven hundred miles of wild coastline, tribal communities who had never encountered each other rode out the final throes in tandem. In the stillness that followed, survivors must have felt as if they had slipped the clutches of an angry god. They couldn't have known the most awful blow was yet to come.

Triggered by the upheaval on the ocean floor, swells were hurtling toward the coast faster than any fish could swim. Would the sliver of moon have cast enough light to reveal the sea pulling back? Surely people heard the thunder as the surge neared shore and gathered height.

The ocean stampeded across the land like a tide gone mad. No longhouse could stand up to the rush. Beaches where hundreds of thousands of tourists now fly kites and race three-wheelers on sunny days were swallowed by waves no man or beast could outrun. Uprooted trees became battering rams. Caught up in the icy water, people flailed desperately for anything to grab onto, anything to keep them afloat. Entire villages were swept away in a matter of moments.

The earthquake that lashed the Pacific Northwest in 1700 ranks among the mightiest the Earth can yield. Scientists today call it a megaquake—a magnitude 9 monster that ripped the full length of the offshore fault where seafloor and continent collide, and unleashed a killer tsunami. Only a handful of seismic disasters in modern times have approached the same level of fury.

No one who saw the videos from the 2004 Indian Ocean megaquake and tsunami will ever forget the wall of water that pulverized cities and muscled through resorts as if they were made of cardboard. More than two-hundred thousand people died. The force of the fault rupture made the Earth wobble on its axis.

In March 2011, an offshore fault ripped loose off Japan. The magnitude 9 quake shoved the island of Honshu eight feet to the east and triggered a tsunami that reached the closest shores in twenty minutes. A nation whose leaders thought they were prepared for the worst watched in horror as waves poured over seawalls and swept nearly twenty thousand people to their deaths. Nuclear reactors crippled by the flood melted down and spewed enough radiation to turn the surrounding countryside into a no-man's-land.

For Northwesterners, the images from Japan of doomed men and women running from the waves and tall buildings engulfed by water resonated in a visceral way. Even the world's most earthquake-ready nation was no match for the kind of blow that had struck the Pacific Northwest more than three centuries ago—and which geologists now know will strike again someday. When it does, it will roil a human landscape that has undergone a tectonic shift of its own. The region called Cascadia is now home to more than fifteen million people and several of North America's most vibrant cities, businesses, and ports.

"The 'Big One' in the Pacific Northwest has the potential to be the most costly and destructive disaster in the history of the United States, both in terms of loss of life and economic damage," said James Lee Witt, former director of the Federal Emergency Management Agency (FEMA). "The long-term economic impact could alter our entire economy."

Analyses from Oregon put the state's possible death toll at five thousand or more.

Rough estimates of economic losses in Oregon and Washington approach $80 billion, without factoring in damage from Northern California and British Columbia.

But the realization that the Cascadia region is vulnerable to the world's most formidable earthquakes and tsunamis was slow in coming.

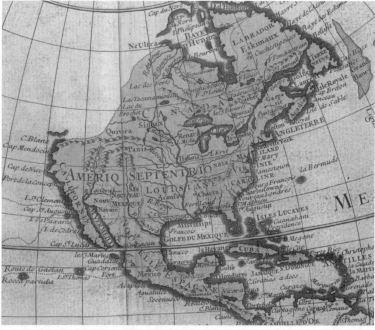

In 1700, world maps showed a void north of California.

When the 1700 megaquake struck, the Pacific Northwest didn't exist in the eyes of the world. Most maps of North America showed a void above California. England's colonies were thriving on the continent's eastern shore, but explorers didn't begin to chart the coastlines of the Northwest with their snow-capped peaks and impenetrable forests until the end of the century. It was the mid-1800s before European and American settlers began arriving in large numbers.

By then, more than seven generations had passed since 1700. Some of the region's indigenous people retained their collective memories of the cataclysm, but an onslaught of outsiders drowned out the native voices. The story of a night when earth and sea convulsed was lost to history.

If the newcomers paused to consider earthquakes, as they must have after San Francisco was reduced to a smoldering wreck in 1906, it was to congratulate themselves for living in a more *solid* place than California. In the 1920s, a geology professor named Collier Cobb surveyed the Puget Sound area and pronounced it earthquake-proof. "Los Angeles may shimmy with earthquakes and San Francisco may get another one," he said, "but Seattle, set on the deepest glacial drift yet discovered, has a shock absorber which makes the city immune for all time." The Chamber of Commerce & Commercial Club liked the quote so much they featured it in national newspaper ads.

It wasn't until the mid-1980s that a young scientist digging in marshes along the Washington coast uncovered the first solid evidence of upheaval in the past. The rediscovery of the 1700 quake and tsunami is one of geology's most remarkable detective stories. The finding ignited a revolution in earth science that's still under way, still yielding insights into the forces responsible for both the region's breathtaking beauty and its seismic perils. Once considered a backwater, the Pacific Northwest has been the epicenter of some of the world's most exciting seismological research for nearly thirty years.

Piece by piece, scientists have re-created a history fraught with mayhem. If there's one thing geologists grasp more fully than most people, it's that what happened before will happen again. "People look upon the natural world as if all motions of the past had set the stage for us and were now frozen," said geologist Eldridge Moores, in John McPhee's *Annals of the Former World*. "To imagine that turmoil is in the past and somehow we are now in a more stable time seems to be a psychological need. . . . [But] the time we're in is just as active as the past. The time between events is long only with respect to a human lifetime."

Scientists now understand that the Northwest is even more seismologically complex than California, subject to three distinct types of earthquakes: deep, shallow, and 1700s-style giants. California may rock more often, but it can't rock as hard or in so many ways. The 1700 megaquake was sixty times as powerful as the quake that destroyed San Francisco.

Despite its outsized risks, the Pacific Northwest lags in its ability to cope with a restless Earth. Californians have had nearly two centuries to come to terms with the shaky ground they inhabit. In Japan people have been adapting to life with earthquakes for more than a thousand years. Northwesterners are still getting used to their region's status as a seismic hot spot. For many, the discoveries of the past few decades have been nothing but bad news.

But the work of a generation of geoscientists has given the region the gift of foresight. It's better to know what's coming than to be caught off guard. Geologists may never be able to predict earthquakes, but they have been able to map out the Northwest's seismic destiny in a level of detail that hasn't been matched in many other parts of the world. Without having suffered through a great earthquake in modern times, the Pacific Northwest has been granted the chance to get ready before the next one strikes.

The new insights began to dawn in the 1960s, when geologists developed a comprehensive theory that for the first time made sense of why and where earthquakes occur. By the early 1970s, scientists strongly suspected the existence of an offshore fault—the fault that turned out to be responsible for the 1700 quake. But then they made the mistake of shrugging it off.

CHAPTER I:

QUIET AS KANSAS

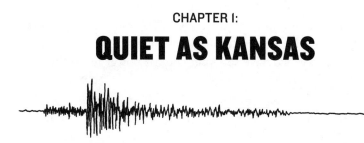

ON A MISTY MORNING in October 2011, the Satsop nuclear plant's cooling towers floated like twin mirages above Washington's Chehalis River valley. Traffic was heavy on the highway that connects Olympia to the Pacific Coast. One after another, flatbed trucks, vans, and pickups exited onto a back road and wound their way to the plant's hilltop perch.

The parking lot was already packed. Men in cowboy hats and Carhartts prowled a warehouse the size of a football field, inspecting the items that were up for grabs. Pallets piled high with circuit breakers and heaps of rusted cable filled one corner. Fuses as big as flashlights spilled out of cardboard boxes like leftovers from Dr. Frankenstein's laboratory. An emergency eyewash station leaned against metal lockers stamped "Property of WPPSS."

"It's basically a bunch of spare parts," explained Stan Ratcliff. When Ratcliff hired on with the Washington Public Power Supply System (WPPSS) in 1981, he was one of more than five thousand workers at the Satsop site. If all had gone according to the utility consortium's plans, a pair of pressurized-water reactors would be humming atop this ridge, thirty miles from the state capital. Instead, Ratcliff was overseeing a final fire sale to clear out odds and ends he squirreled away for decades.

Bargain hunters gathered around as auctioneers kicked off the daylong marathon. Metal shelves fetched ten bucks. A contractor carted off three transformers at $400 apiece. Bidding was brisk on bins filled with nuts and bolts, though one man joked that he ought to scan the merchandise with a Geiger counter. The plant's marquee components—the reactor vessels, steam generators, and condensers—had been sold off for scrap years ago.

What remained were the towers, each nearly as tall as the Space Needle, and a sprawl of unfinished structures. The site is a business park now. One tenant fabricates steel tanks in the cavernous building where turbines would have spun out enough power to run the city of Seattle.

The plant never produced a watt.

The Satsop reactors were among five WPPSS set out to build in the early 1970s, at a time when the atom's promise seemed limitless and analysts warned that the Northwest would need twenty nuclear plants just to keep the lights on. Other utilities caught the fever, proposing reactors on the Oregon coast, the Columbia River, and in the Skagit valley north of Seattle. The threat of earthquakes barely factored into the equation, though why would it? This wasn't California.

It was economics, not seismicity, that toppled the WPPSS nuclear house a decade later and earned it the nickname "Whoops." When construction costs ballooned more than fivefold and power shortages failed to materialize, the consortium defaulted on $2.25 billion in bonds. The debacle left a lingering distaste for nuclear energy in the Northwest and jacked up power bills to pay off the debt.

But WPPSS left a scientific legacy too, one that's still playing out across the region. The prospect of nuclear proliferation inspired the first hard look at the Northwest's seismic nature. Armed with insights from a new field called plate tectonics, a handful of geologists started asking questions neither the nuclear industry nor much of the scientific establishment wanted to hear.

The Cessna banked right and Tom Heaton squinted to make out the coastline through ribbons of fog. The plane was flying low, only a few hundred feet above the bluffs. The pilot warned he'd have to pull up fast or risk crashing into a headland if the cloud ceiling lowered. The previous day had been windy and clear, but Heaton still hadn't spotted what he was looking for along the rim of the Northwest. The year was 1983 and he was on a mission for the Nuclear Regulatory Commission (NRC). Construction at the Satsop plant was in full swing. Experts hired by WPPSS had assured the NRC that its reactors were designed to ride out the worst possible earthquake, but the NRC wanted a second opinion.

Heaton was an unlikely choice to provide it. Just thirty-two years old, he was the newest hire at the U.S. Geological Survey's (USGS) Pasadena office. His previous job was a one-year stint advising Exxon on earthquakes and offshore oil rigs. The son of a mathematician and a music teacher, Heaton never intended to go into geology. He wanted to play guitar. A pragmatic assessment of his prospects in the music industry quashed that plan, and a bad head for memorization bounced him out of chemistry, his second choice. He switched to physics, but the employment prospects were grim. At least there were jobs in the earth sciences.

As a doctoral student at Caltech, he earned a reputation for cockiness—even among a group who considered themselves the Bronx Bombers of geoscience. NRC officials took note when Heaton challenged several top professors, all on the nuclear payroll, at a workshop on reactor safety. He thought they were exaggerating their ability to predict how the ground would shake during an earthquake. "They were using a lot of big words," recalled Heaton, one of the only students in attendance. "But I thought it was a bit of a snow job, and I said so."

Heaton learned the hard way to question his own assumptions as well. In his first solo scientific paper, he used a mathematical trick to tease out an apparent correlation between tides and earthquakes. When he collected more data, he realized he was wrong. In one of the most humbling exercises for a scientist, he had to correct the record.

"I really hated it," Heaton recalled. "I realized I hadn't been critical enough of my own thinking."

Even colleagues who called Heaton arrogant admired his willingness to poke at authority. The NRC probably figured it would take a touch of arrogance to step into the nuclear arena, where billions of dollars and political careers were at stake. At least the agency knew it hadn't hired a yes man.

One of the first things Heaton did after accepting the assignment was to charter the Cessna and fly nearly six hundred miles of coastline from Northern California to the Strait of Juan de Fuca. He was looking for evidence of giant earthquakes in a place where most geologists insisted they could never happen.

Before he took to the air, Heaton spent several bleary-eyed days in his office slogging through reams of paperwork on the Satsop project. Despite reading a decade's worth of seismic studies on the plant site and its environs, he was struck by how little was really known about earthquake risks in the Northwest.

Professor Cobb's earthquake-proof cushion had long since proved bogus. The region was not immune to damaging quakes. In 1949 a magnitude 7.1 earthquake north of Olympia rattled an area nearly the size of Texas and killed eight people. A quake south of Seattle in 1965 knocked every pier on the waterfront askew and caused more than $85 million of damage in today's dollars. Hundreds of tiny quakes struck across the region every year. But few rose to the level of California-style disasters, and the scientific response was a collective yawn. There just wasn't enough action to make it interesting.

WPPSS reviewed the historical records, which went back about 150 years, and reached the logical conclusion: What's past is prologue. The middling quakes since settlers arrived in the mid-1800s were what the region could expect in the future. The consortium added a margin of safety and for the Satsop plant set its worst-case scenario at a magnitude 7.5 quake near Olympia.

As he tracked the logic through the documents, Heaton's BS meter started to buzz. "I was there to be the devil's advocate," he recalled. "If they were making claims, I asked, 'What's the basis of those claims?'"

Heaton knew 150 years is less than a gnat's wing beat on geologic time scales. He also knew that geology itself had been turned upside down since WPPSS started planning the Satsop plant in the early 1970s. But the new thinking hadn't budged the utility's seismic bottom line.

As late as 1975, some textbooks still ridiculed the notion that the planet's crust was divided into plates that float like bumper cars on a cushion of semimolten rock. Most geoscientists Heaton's age remember trying to make sense of the convoluted theories their professors offered to explain why California was jittery and Iowa wasn't. One idea blamed quakes on stress in the Earth's crust caused by the weight of mountain ranges. Another theory said the Earth's surface was cooling from its fiery origins and wrinkling like the skin of a baked apple. The wrinkles were mountains, and cracks in the shriveling crust were earthquakes.

The old ideas persisted so long because there was nothing better to replace them. They weren't much closer to reality than Benjamin Franklin's notion that earthquakes were caused by a subterranean sea jostling the planet's shell. In the third century BC, Aristotle invoked a kind of planetary flatulence caused by air currents that reverberate through caverns like the "wind in our bodies . . . [that] can cause tremors and throbbings." In truth, early earthquake science was as frustrating as medicine before the discovery of germs. Earthquakes happened, and nobody knew why.

That didn't stop geologists from defending their flawed theories as ferociously as mother bears defend their cubs when German meteorologist Alfred Wegener suggested in 1912 that many of the mysteries could be explained by continents that drift. American scientists were particularly vicious. "Utter, damned rot," declared the president of the American Philosophical Society. But within a few decades, seafloor surveys were turning up a lot of things that didn't fit the old world view. Among them were canyons deep enough to swallow Mount Everest and underwater mountain ranges that girdled the globe like seams on a baseball.

Some of the most pivotal evidence came from surveys off the Northwest coast. In the mid-1950s, British geophysicist Ronald Mason and marine engineer Arthur Raff of the Scripps Institution of Oceanography convinced the U.S. Navy to let them tag along on a series of hydrographic cruises. The scientists modified a magnetic sensor used to detect enemy subs and towed it behind the ship. What they found was a pattern of zebra stripes on the ocean floor that proved to be the key to a major puzzle: if continents drifted, what was the driving force?

The stripes, tens of miles wide, revealed that molten rock is oozing up along underwater ridges to create new seafloor. As the magma flows outward and solidifies, its crystals align with the Earth's magnetic field like compass needles. But the magnetic field flips every few hundred thousand years. The stripes on the seafloor were a record of those reversals stretching back through time. They also provided a yardstick by which to measure the seafloor's annual expansion of an inch or two. Multiplied over millennia, that conveyor-belt motion was what nudged the continents—or more precisely, the huge slabs of rock called tectonic plates in which continents are embedded.

For geologists it was as if somebody finally switched on the light. "Plate tectonics really set us free and flying," said Tanya Atwater in *Annals of the Former World*. Atwater was a graduate student as the revolution dawned and used the new theory to explain the forces that created the San Andreas Fault. "It is a wondrous thing to have the random facts in one's head suddenly fall into the slots of an orderly framework," she said.

That framework divides the globe into ten major plates and more than a dozen smaller ones. Made up of crust and a portion of the mantle below, the plates can be more than sixty miles thick. They slide atop a layer where heat and pressure give solid rock the consistency of Silly Putty.

When geologists overlaid their new tectonic grid on maps of the world, they could instantly see that the action occurs at the boundaries where plates meet. Mountain ranges like the Himalayas are the crumpled fenders of head-on collisions. The North American and Pacific Plates grind past each other side by side to form the San Andreas Fault. But the most volatile boundaries of all are subduction zones: the places where the ocean floor plows into a continent. The land rides up over the seafloor like an Abrams tank rolling over a line of Mini Coopers. In what could be called the ultimate recycling process, the oceanic plate sinks—or subducts—back into the hot interior of the Earth.

ACTIVE VOLCANOES, PLATE TECTONICS, AND THE RING OF FIRE

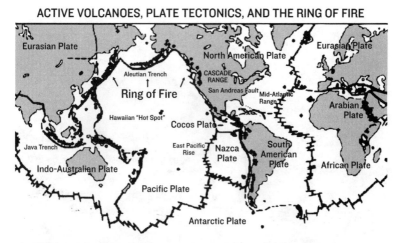

The planet's surface is made up of ten major plates and dozens of smaller ones, all in motion. The Pacific Ring of Fire, where plates collide around the ocean basin, is where the majority of the world's earthquakes and volcanic eruptions occur.

The world's biggest earthquakes—the monsters that jolt the planet on its axis—all originate from subduction zones. Long before plate tectonics, the Pacific Ring of Fire was infamous for being home to three-quarters of the Earth's volcanoes and 90 percent of earthquakes. Now the reason was clear as geologists traced out the plate boundaries that circle the Pacific basin.

By the early 1980s, WPPSS couldn't ignore the fact that the Pacific Northwest sits squarely on that ring, just inland from the boundary where a chunk of ocean floor called the Juan de Fuca Plate dives under North America. The nuclear plant proponents just didn't think it was anything to worry about.

During his aerial reconnaissance, Heaton saw ample evidence of a landscape shaped by tectonic forces. As the Cessna skirted Washington's wild beaches, the massifs of the Olympic Mountains crowded the horizon. Oregon's coves and sandy beaches blended into a backdrop of rumpled hills. The collision of plates could account for that kind of buckling. To the east the Cascade volcanoes dotted the skyline

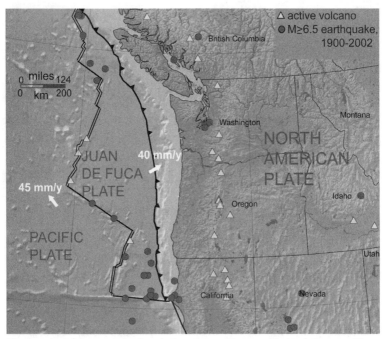

The Cascadia Subduction Zone, where the Juan de Fuca Plate meets the North American Plate, lies offshore and stretches seven hundred miles from Vancouver Island to Northern California. The plates converge at a rate of about forty mm per year. The adjacent Pacific Plate moves northward at forty-five mm per year. The toothed line represents the plate boundary.

like a string of giant pearls. Volcanic arcs are a by-product of subduction. They form as molten blobs of the recycled plate rise through cracks and vents. It was clear the Northwest's offshore subduction zone, called Cascadia, had been active in the past. But was it still capable of causing trouble?

Despite the bravado of youth—"I thought I was a hotshot," Heaton recalled with a chuckle—he realized he needed help. Luckily, he didn't have to go far to find it. The clapboard colonial that housed the USGS Pasadena office sat across the street from Caltech's Division of Geological and Planetary Sciences and the office of Hiroo Kanamori. No one knew more about subduction zones at that time than the Japanese-born scientist, and it's probably still true. "I'm not sure I could have pulled it off without him around," Heaton said.

Kanamori was the first to delve into the subset of earthquakes so powerful they blew the needle off the Richter scale. The replacement he devised, called the moment magnitude scale, is universally accepted today, though Richter's name still sticks. Kanamori is also a nice guy in a discipline in which egos can soar off the charts. Heaton can be brusque; Kanamori is gracious. Yet the two scientists share a probing intellect that drew them together, first as student and mentor, then as colleagues.

It was Kanamori who suggested Heaton fly the coast. In parts of Japan, subduction zone quakes jerk up shorelines several feet at a time. After thousands of years and dozens of quakes, some Japanese coasts look like stair steps. Heaton chartered the Cessna in Eugene, Oregon, and scanned cliffs and headlands from Cape Mendocino to Cape Flattery for these uplifted terraces. He didn't find many.

He and Kanamori later spent two weeks in an SUV driving the region with colleagues from Japan. Nothing they saw screamed out a history of giant quakes. Maybe WPPSS was right in arguing that the Cascadia Subduction Zone was in a class by itself: an earthquake-free class.

The power consortium wasn't alone in that assessment. Most geologists agreed. Even Heaton's employer considered Cascadia unworthy of mention in the national earthquake hazard maps. The USGS scientist in charge of mapping at the time dismissed any suggestion of subduction zone quakes as antinuclear propaganda.

At a time when geologists were just beginning to get the hang of their new paradigm, Cascadia didn't seem to fit the mold. Subduction zones are usually seismically noisy places. Slabs of rock more than five hundred miles long and hundreds of miles wide don't grind past each other easily. They stick in spots, build up pressure, then slip. Each slip makes an earthquake. Japan, which sits at the boundary of four plates, experiences tiny temblors every five seconds and more than one thousand quakes a year big enough to be felt.

The Northwest had occasional quakes, but they weren't on the subduction zone. The Cascadia plate boundary was "quiet as Kansas," as Bob Yeats put it. The Northwest's elder statesman of seismology, Yeats moved to Oregon from California in 1977 and counted himself among the most adamant skeptics of Cascadia's menace.

Scientists concocted a grab bag of theories to explain the subduction zone's silence. One even suggested the Juan de Fuca and North American Plates were pulling apart, not converging. Another group pointed out that Cascadia lacks the deep offshore trench characteristic of many active subduction zones.

Several scientists argued that size matters. Compared to the world's major tectonic slabs, the Juan de Fuca Plate is little more than a postage stamp—though it didn't start out that way.

When subduction began along the Northwest coast about 200 million years ago, the oceanic plate offshore was gigantic. Geologists call this tectonic ancestor the Farallon Plate. Much of the modern Northwest landscape originated in a succession of volcanic islands and microcontinents that rode the conveyor belt of the subducting Farallon Plate until they collided with North America. Too bulky to be crammed down into the Earth's interior, these chunks of land fused with the continent. Each arrival extended the Northwest coastline westward from its original position near Idaho's border with Washington and Oregon.

The Okanogan Highlands latched on about 175 million years ago, followed by the Blue and Wallowa Mountains. The North Cascades docked about 95 million years ago, and were crushed, folded, and fractured in the impact. Vancouver Island and much of Northwestern British Columbia arrived the same way. Scientists estimate the Farallon Plate delivered at least fifty chunks, called terranes, over its long history.

But in the process, the plate itself was largely consumed as it subducted under North America. All that remains is the Juan de Fuca Plate and another nub called the Cocos Plate off the coast of Central America. Someday, even those vestiges will be swallowed up completely. So it didn't seem unreasonable for geologists to speculate that the subduction process had already run out of steam.

The first studies on the Satsop plant flatly stated that subduction sputtered to a halt half a million years ago. Even the 1980 eruption of Mount St. Helens didn't change many minds. It takes a long time to stop a tectonic train, Cascadia skeptics pointed out. The fact that residual blobs of magma were popping up in volcanoes didn't mean the subduction zone was still active.

The newest Satsop studies in Heaton's pile presented a different argument. Cascadia would never rank among the planet's seismic bad boys, WPPSS argued, because the plates were slipping past each other as smoothly as skis over snow. No sticking. No buildup of tension. No earthquakes. The reasons were a mystery, but sediments from the Columbia River might be acting as a lubricant to grease the skids.

Heaton considered the arguments from every angle he could think of, asking himself whether the evidence justified the conclusions. The WPPSS case struck him as a house of cards balanced on a skimpy historical record. "It was almost like reading a legal case instead of a scientific case," he recalled. Heaton and Kanamori discussed a more ominous explanation for Cascadia's silence—one that WPPSS chose to discount.

The reason subduction zones produce the most powerful quakes is a simple matter of geometry. The bigger the fault, the bigger the quake. Subduction zones are a kind of fault—a boundary along which rock layers move past each other. No other faults, not even the mighty San Andreas, can match them for size. Subduction zones can extend for 600 miles or more, but it's not just their length that makes them treacherous. The interface where rocks jerk past each other in a quake, called the rupture zone, is immense. A magnitude 9 subduction zone quake can rupture an area bigger than the state of Maine.

Subduction zones are at their most dangerous when the down-going plate and the overriding plate lock up along their entire length. When the pressure reaches the breaking point, the result is what scientists call a megathrust quake. Japan's 2011 disaster was a megathrust. So was the 2004 giant that triggered the Indian Ocean tsunami and Alaska's 1964 magnitude 9.2 monster.

Was it possible the entire Cascadia Subduction Zone was locked up tight? That would explain the lack of smaller quakes. The subduction zone could be building toward its next rupture. In that case the passage of 150 quake-free years didn't mean the region was safe. It just meant that not enough time had passed for the fault to reach its breaking point.

BIGGER FAULT = BIGGER QUAKE

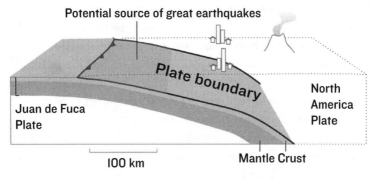

Subduction zone quakes are the world's biggest because they involve a huge surface area.

On his final Cessna flight, Heaton felt uneasy. He had seen the damage done when subduction zone quakes rocked the coastlines of Alaska and Chile: roadways buckled, towns turned upside down, communities awash. The landscape unfurling beneath him was so reminiscent of those places that he could imagine similar mayhem visited upon the quiet fishing towns and harbors of the Northwest. "I was struck by a deep sadness," he recalled. "I thought, 'What a tragedy it would be if it happened here.'"

While Heaton was surveying the coast, WPPSS's finances were already starting to implode. The last thing the project needed was a seismic bogeyman.

The difference between the type of quake the Satsop plant was designed to withstand and a coastwide megathrust is like the difference between twenty-five atomic bombs and twenty-five thousand. Ground shaking can last ten times longer—up to five minutes. How much more would it cost to build a nuclear plant to stand up to something that big?

Many scientists had staked their reputations on a quiet Cascadia. Several of the country's most famous geologists were on contract with the nuclear industry, as was the chairman of the University of Washington (UW) Geology Department. UW geology professor Eric

Cheney went up against his boss and an army of consultants when he sided with a citizens' coalition of teachers, hippies, and farmers challenging Puget Sound Power & Light's plan to build two reactors near the Skagit River community of Sedro-Woolley. "At every meeting there were ten of them—and infinitely more money—against one of me," Cheney recalled.

Like Heaton, Cheney didn't think the plants' seismic analyses passed the smell test. The proponents made claims based on scant evidence. He challenged them to explain how they could be so sure when seismic studies had barely scratched the region's surface.

Cheney eventually helped uncover a previously unknown fault running through the hills above the reactor site. It was the final straw for a project staggering under cost overruns and fierce opposition.

The WPPSS plants at Satsop never attracted the same kind of protest as the Skagit plants. Hammered by the decline of the timber industry and far removed from the state's urban corridor, the mill towns of southwest Washington welcomed the jobs. But a battle was brewing behind the scenes even before Heaton climbed into his rented airplane. A few clues had trickled in that the Northwest coast might be on the move, rising and tilting in perplexing ways.

Geologists at the consulting firm WPPSS hired to analyze earthquake risks were concerned the motion might be a sign the subduction zone was locked and building toward a megaquake. They raised the issue innocently and weren't prepared for the fallout from WPPSS and its prime contractor. "They sort of went crazy," recalled geologist David Schwartz, one of the leaders of the consulting team.

The contractor called a hasty meeting to lecture the upstarts on the reasons Cascadia wasn't a threat. For Schwartz it was the beginning of a year of agony. His job was to finesse the final report in a way the client would accept while remaining true to the science. No wonder it read like a legal document to Heaton.

"They didn't want any changes that might upset the NRC and kill the project," said Schwartz. At one meeting he got into a shouting match with an eminent geologist who represented WPPSS. Heaton attracted his share of flak, too. An angry Oregon official suggested the USGS find something else for the young scientist to work on.

Heaton and Kanamori paid no attention to the politics. They were busy compiling seismic rap sheets on the world's subduction zones to compare with Cascadia. No one had taken such a big-picture view, and what the scientists saw was disturbing. Far from being an outlier, Cascadia seemed to be in good company with some of the planet's most notorious seismic actors.

Size didn't matter with the tiny oceanic plate off the coast of Mexico that triggered killer quakes. Japanese records that date back before the samurai era show quiet periods lasting two hundred years or more between quakes on the infamous Nankai subduction zone offshore from Tokyo. To Heaton, the southern coast of Chile provided the most striking parallel to Cascadia. The topography is nearly identical to the Pacific Northwest. The two subduction zones are about the same length, and neither has an obvious seafloor trench. The ocean floor off both coasts is young and warm, which makes it more likely to stick to the overriding plate.

To their regret, South American scientists in the late 1950s had drawn the same conclusion as their Northwest counterparts, reporting that seismic risks along Chile's southern coast were slight. A few years later, a magnitude 9.5 quake—the biggest ever recorded—struck the area and triggered a giant tsunami. More than 1,700 people died and 2 million were left homeless. The quake also set off a volcanic eruption.

"The more we looked at the data, the more similar Cascadia looked to places that have had really large earthquakes," Heaton said. In their final report, he and Kanamori warned there was no reason to assume the subduction zone off the Northwest coast wasn't poised to spring with the same force that slammed Chile.

Published in 1984, the report was more of a landmark for geologists than for the nuclear industry. To the Satsop plants, it was like a leaky faucet on the *Titanic*. WPPSS was already sinking. The consortium stopped construction on the twin reactors even before Heaton finished writing. His parents were among the 75,000 investors who watched WPPSS bonds evaporate from their pension funds and portfolios. The consortium scrambled for years to bring at least one of the

Satsop plants online. When that effort failed, it tried to peddle the reactor parts to China, but the communists declined. Scrap dealers paid pennies on the dollar to cart off equipment worth millions.

But as the Northwest's nuclear era fizzled, the fuse was lit for an explosion in seismological research. All of a sudden, the region didn't seem so boring anymore. "That report really got everybody's attention," recalled seismologist Steve Malone, who expanded earthquake monitoring at the University of Washington. News reports introduced Northwesterners to a new term—*subduction*—and the unwelcome news that they might not be able to thumb their noses at Californians anymore. Community leaders and government officials scratched their heads and wondered how seriously to take the prospect of megaquakes on their turf. Scientists were always changing their minds. Was this real or just a sidetrack?

Heaton couldn't say. His case was flimsy, and he knew it. Cascadia wasn't convicted, merely suspect. Despite the time spent flying and driving the coast, he and Kanamori hadn't found a scrap of evidence that the subduction zone had ever generated great earthquakes. They had no idea when—or if—earthquakes might strike. Heaton doubted that the truth about Cascadia's nature would be resolved during his career. The mystery might be solved only if—or when—the subduction zone decided it was time.

CHAPTER 2:
WRITTEN IN MUD

IT WAS BRIAN ATWATER'S THIRD DAY IN NEAH BAY, and the rain hadn't stopped once. The tiny outpost on the Strait of Juan de Fuca is home to Washington's Makah people, for whom blustery weather is as much a part of life as sea otters and the tides. But Atwater was a recent transplant to the Northwest. Even his fisherman's sweater, hand knit from thick wool, couldn't keep the March chill from seeping into his bones.

The year was 1986. Clouds shrouded the rocky headland of Cape Flattery, the northwestern-most point of the contiguous United States. Atwater's destination was a line of hills to the south overlooking a sweep of Pacific beach. He thought he might find evidence there to prove Tom Heaton wrong.

But bushwhacking the highlands would be tough enough when the ground was dry. While he waited for the weather to clear, Atwater decided to poke around in the small valley that angles like an emerald boulevard between the strait and the ocean.

According to a story told by Makah elders, seawater once surged across this boggy neck of land and turned the cape into an island. Atwater had heard the tale but wasn't sure what to make of it. The Connecticut native had joined the tiny USGS contingent in Seattle only a year earlier. His career until then was spent mostly in California. Atwater didn't study earthquakes, though. His specialty was mud.

He spent those first soggy days in Neah Bay probing the lowland with a core barrel—a metal pipe with a T-bar handle on top. Over and over he plunged the barrel into the ground and cranked. The cylinders of muck he extracted were as big around as broom handles and about as interesting. Each core was a window into the marsh's geologic history, which looked uneventful. He screwed three-foot-long extensions onto the barrel to probe deeper underground and further back in time.

Atwater's solo expedition was inspired by a USGS workshop he attended in Seattle six months earlier. After Heaton and Kanamori had disturbed the region's seismic complacency, the USGS invited earthquake experts from across North America to put their heads together on the Cascadia question. Heaton traveled from California to lay out his concerns. Skeptics made their case. All that was missing were facts.

"It really was a matter of opinion at the time," recalled John Adams, of the Geological Survey of Canada. "The evidence wasn't very good one way or another."

Atwater wanted to attend the closed-door sessions where detailed discussions took place, but the organizer turned him away. What would a guy who spent his time mucking around in swamps have to contribute? So the young scientist sat with local politicians, business owners, and emergency responders in a hotel ballroom while Heaton presented an overview for the public.

The jittery audience wanted answers, but Heaton explained that he didn't have any. Cascadia looked like it might be dangerous, but there was no smoking gun to prove it. The only field data came from tide gauges and highway surveys, and scientists couldn't agree if the news was good or bad.

Gauges to track tidal fluctuations and sea level had been installed up and down the West Coast beginning at the turn of the twentieth century. The data were messy, complicated by seasonal variations and storms and broken instruments. Still, scientists thought they could make out a trend. The Northwest shoreline appeared to be rising by increments so tiny they took decades to show up. Adams and others found similar creep when they compared highway leveling surveys from 1900 with measurements eighty years later. If they squinted to factor out the fuzziness, it looked like coastal mountain ranges were slowly tilting to the east.

If the gauges and surveys were telling the truth—a big *if* in pre-GPS days—then the ocean floor must be shoving under the continent exactly as expected at an active subduction zone. One camp of geologists argued that the motion proved the plates were slipping smoothly and the subduction zone was toothless. Heaton and others saw the bulge as a red flag, a sign that the plates were locked and building to disaster.

As Heaton described the ground motions for the Seattle audience, Atwater jotted notes. He might not know much about earthquakes, but he thought he knew a way to settle the debate.

At Neah Bay the coastline seemed to be rising about a tenth of an inch a year. Geologic processes may be slow, but they grind on for eons. If the Juan de Fuca Plate was slipping harmlessly under North America with no earthquakes, Atwater reasoned, then the coast would have been rising for a very long time. A shoreline at sea level three thousand years ago would be nearly thirty feet higher today.

"I figured that was something I ought to be able to see," he recalled. He picked as his target a couple of ponds in the hills behind Neah Bay. He would push cores around the pond margins and pick apart the mud layers in search of saltwater plants and other signs that the ponds had been lifted up from sea level by a benign subduction zone. If he found them, the region could relax.

It's just as well Atwater didn't get the chance to explain his plan to the experts assembled in Seattle. They might have fallen out of their chairs laughing. Mud was something you wiped off your boots at the door to the seismology lab. Earthquake scientists spent their time indoors, analyzing squiggles recorded on a drum as vibrations reverberated through the ground.

The notion that it was possible to learn something about earthquakes by digging into the ground was so new it had only just been given a name: paleoseismology. One of the pioneers, Kerry Sieh, got a failing grade from his thesis committee at Stanford when he proposed to trench a section of the San Andreas Fault and look for evidence of past movement in the soil layers. Sieh would go on to validate the approach and make the case that paleoseismology was the only way to figure out what a fault had done in the distant past—and what it was likely to do in the future.

But in the 1980s, field geology was still largely the province of hardrock men. Many got into the business because they wanted to climb mountains and hike the high country. Their mission was to map the Earth's ancient bones in search of mineral deposits. Mud, dirt, and anything else that stood between them and bedrock were just crud.

But Atwater knew the crud had stories to tell. It was as an undergraduate at Stanford, where he overlapped briefly with Sieh, that he learned to read mud the way other people read novels.

Atwater's interest in geology was ignited by a field trip to the Grand Canyon and nurtured by the part-time job he landed at USGS headquarters in the Bay Area suburb of Menlo Park. He spent weekends sorting through hundreds of sediment cores extracted from San Francisco Bay in preparation for bridges, some of which were never built. Stored in Mason jars and brass tubes, the cores held a ten-thousand-year record of the bay's history that no one had fully deciphered.

To read that record, Atwater learned what the layers had to say about the bay's ancient past. He tracked the way barren mud flats could grow into lush marshes as sediments deposited by rivers built up over time. He learned to recognize the signature of landscapes drowned thousands of years ago when sea level rose. For his doctoral research, Atwater studied the evolution of the Sacramento–San Joaquin River Delta. He immersed himself in his subject, living fifteen feet below sea level in a mouse-infested trailer.

That background would prove ideal for stalking earthquakes in the Northwest, but it didn't seem that way in the unrelenting rain of Neah Bay. He hadn't found much of anything, and he was sick of being wet.

It was a melancholy time for the young scientist. He and his wife were mourning the death of their youngest daughter, Sarah. Born with Down syndrome and a weakened immune system, she was the reason the family moved to Seattle. The University of Washington had a special program for kids like Sarah, and she did well there. But just before her second birthday she succumbed to an infection.

Atwater stayed close to home during those years, giving up most fieldwork in favor of office projects. Neah Bay was one of his first trips since Sarah's death and he was eager to head home. But he hated to leave a job half done. There was one more place to look.

A small river called the Waatch meanders through the valley where Atwater was getting doused. As long as he was there, he figured he ought to check out its banks.

Field geology is a struggle to suss out what lays hidden below the ground without benefit of a bulldozer or X-ray vision. Atwater's cores were helpful, but they sampled only isolated spots. Like swinging blindfolded at a piñata, it was possible to miss the good stuff. But if cores are snapshots, stream cuts are panoramas—and the water has already done the digging.

By late afternoon the outgoing tide lowered the water level enough for Atwater to hop over the lip of the stream and drop into the channel. Feet sloshing in the water, he pulled out his World War II–vintage folding shovel and scraped away at the riverbank. A few strokes revealed a thick brown band running through the mud like a chocolate layer in the middle of a vanilla cake. Roots and other bits of vegetation identified the dark band as peat: a soil layer that had once luxuriated in the sun, thick with the same plants that cover the valley today.

"What do we have here?" Atwater murmured to himself, smoothing the surface. Something in the past had caused the ancient marsh to abruptly drop from above sea level to underwater. After the dunking, the river and tides gradually delivered enough silt to build a new marsh atop the old one.

Atwater thought back to the Seattle meeting. Heaton hadn't found uplifted terraces along the coast, but he told the group that didn't necessarily rule out subduction zone quakes. Although shorelines jerked upward in some parts of Japan, other coastal areas dropped during megathrust ruptures. Atwater also remembered hearing about coastlines in Alaska that fell below sea level in 1964.

He wondered if what he was seeing in the banks of the Waatch River could be the missing link in the Cascadia story: proof that the Earth had been jolted in the past.

As the light faded, he loaded his gear into the back of his government-green pickup and drove into town. At Neah Bay's only store, Atwater bought a postcard. He jotted a few lines describing what he had uncovered and addressed the card to Heaton.

The two researchers barely knew each other, but Atwater felt a connection. "If I wanted to share what I had just seen, who on the planet would be most interested?" Atwater recalled. "The only person I could think of was Tom."

It wouldn't be long before the entire region took note.

On a chilly morning in November 2011, Atwater pulled his truck off a gravel road and jumped out to admire a ditch clogged with ferns and moss-covered branches. Water flowed beneath the tangle, burbling but unseen.

"The mighty Niawiakum," he said with a grin. "I do love this river."

Nearly two hundred miles south of Neah Bay, the Niawiakum had been Atwater's next stop in the spring of 1986. Twenty-five years later snow dusted the ground as he drove the back road from South Bend, to revisit the modest waterway that yielded so many stunning insights into the Northwest's seismic heritage.

The Niawiakum (nee-uh-WYE-uh-kum) runs a scant five miles from its source in the Willapa Hills of Southwest Washington before merging into Willapa Bay, the shallow estuary that is the nation's top producer of farmed oysters. By the time Atwater punched his first core there, he wasn't working blind anymore. The mud wizard had schooled himself on great earthquakes and the strange ways they distort coastlines.

It was hard to picture how a single type of quake could produce such a mix of effects. In Alaska, parts of Kodiak Island were shoved thirty feet skyward in the 1964 earthquake, the likes of which the United States had never seen. But near Anchorage the hamlets of Portage and Girdwood lost more than six feet of elevation in an instant. Cook Inlet flowed into houses and swamped spruce forests. Crews had to rebuild the Seward Highway to lift it back above sea level. Chile was wracked by a similar mix of ups and downs after its 1960 megathrust quake.

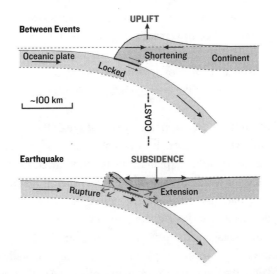

SIMPLIFIED EARTHQUAKE CYCLE

The Northwest coast bulges upward between earthquakes when the Cascadia Subduction Zone is locked. The land drops abruptly when the fault ruptures, flooding marshes and leaving clues to a history of tectonic upheaval.

Before they could explain the patterns, scientists had to deconstruct the way a subduction zone quake plays out. Fieldwork after the Alaska quake was invaluable, as were early computer simulations.

On a subduction zone that's locked tight, the researchers discovered, the descending seafloor snags the leading edge of the continental plate and pulls it down like a twenty-pound steelhead tugging on the tip of a fishing pole. Behind the leading edge, the continental plate bulges up as the two masses of rock bear down on each other.

Another way to visualize the process is to hold one edge of a playing card in each hand and bend it into an upside down U. As the edges pull down, the middle of the card bulges up. Let go of one edge, and it whips up while the bulge flattens out.

That's essentially what happens in a megathrust rupture: The leading edge of the continental plate, which is always offshore, jerks upward, lifting a vast column of water and triggering a tsunami. Behind the leading edge, the ground drops. When scientists figured out the sequence, they saw that whether a particular chunk of land rose or fell depended on its location relative to the plate boundary. The parts of Kodiak Island that sat closest to the leading edge of the continental plate jerked upward. Portage dropped because it was farther away.

Atwater suspected the Northwest coast was riding the bulge of a locked subduction zone like Portage before 1964. That would account for the rising coast and tilting mountains. When the fault ruptured the coast would drop, as it apparently had at Neah Bay.

But he couldn't leap to conclusions based on a single observation. There were other possible explanations for the buried marsh. Maybe storms flooded the Waatch Valley or sea level spiked for some reason in the past. A small quake might have jiggled the ground hard enough to pack down the soil and allow the tide to wash in.

In Chile and Alaska, expanses of coastline hundreds of miles long sank all at once. A Cascadia megaquake would have rocked the entire region and left its fingerprints in many places. Atwater set out to search for them.

"I went after the Niawiakum because it has a tiny drainage basin," he said, hopping back into the truck. The bumpy road makes a series of curves as it descends from the stream's hilly birthplace to a prairie fringed by spruce and fir. Now recognizable as a river, the Niawiakum has carved hairpin turns through marsh grass burnished by the pale sun. Atwater pulled the truck to a stop by a concrete bridge and stepped out to survey the familiar scene. The only sounds were the rush of water and the rustle of grass.

"It's almost completely natural," he said. The landscape remains unchanged from his first visit and uniquely suited to capture a history of cataclysm.

A geologist could waste a lot of time in the Northwest searching for the tracks of earthquakes that struck hundreds or thousands of years ago. On the open coast, pounding waves scrub away clues. It's equally futile to prowl the banks of rivers regularly scoured by winter floods. Forested uplands are so tangled with vegetation that in 1889 it took a party of explorers half a year to claw its way across the Olympic Peninsula. Atwater's experience in the backwaters of California taught him that some of nature's best recorders of land-level changes are the tributaries of quiet bays.

Rivers like the Niawiakum meander through marshes barely above sea level. Slam those marshes with an earthquake that lowers the ground a few feet and they're underwater. Eventually, the tides will wash in enough sediment to raise the ground above sea level again and a new marsh is born. But a record of the old one is preserved like a buried ruin. The Niawiakum's compact basin doesn't funnel enough rain to generate floods that could muddle the picture, Atwater explained. He unfolded a map and traced the outline of the watershed with his finger. "It's wonderfully small."

Atwater's destination that November morning was a stretch of river upstream from the Goose Point Oyster plant, where workers stacked wire baskets on the dock for the next day's harvest. Beyond the plant stretched the watery expanse of Willapa Bay, a "misted, spongy, oozeful kind of place," in the words of writer Ivan Doig. A log truck roared by on Highway 101 as Atwater suited up for a slog in the mud.

Sitting on the tailgate of the truck, he threaded his legs into the neoprene chest waders that are his cold-weather garment of choice. They're warm and, unlike rubber boots, resist being sucked off by mud that grabs like wet concrete. He pulled on a lime-green parka encrusted with grime and a fluorescent orange vest, its pockets stuffed with notebooks and tools. A red toque topped off the ensemble. Oystermen changing shifts stared as Atwater hefted his backpack, shovel, and core barrel and crunched through pickleweed to the river's edge.

A great blue heron glided to a landing on the opposite bank and lowered into a crouch. Like the bird, Atwater is tall and lean with a tendency to hunch. His high-profile profession forced him to overcome shyness, but his preference is to blend into the background. Ask friends to describe him and the words *quirky* and *humble* come up again and again.

With a string of seminal discoveries and membership in the elite National Academy of Sciences, Atwater could claim the prerogatives of a celebrity scientist these days. Or, as one friend put it, "If Brian was an asshole, that would be normal." Instead, he still wedges himself into the back seat so students can sit up front during field trips.

When he first explored the margins of Willapa Bay in 1986, Atwater was an outsider to earthquake science. He didn't know if his suspicions about giant quakes would fizzle or bear fruit. The Niawiakum changed that, he explained, plopping on his butt and sliding into the riverbed. The water was low enough to expose a four-foot slice of history. Atwater chopped at the surface with his folding shovel and rocked back on his heels. "It really just knocks you out," he said, beaming at the riverbank as if at an old friend.

Atwater found one buried marsh at Neah Bay. This stretch of riverbank holds four. The topmost layer is peaty and stubbled with bits of plants preserved like flies in amber. As the layers march back in time, they become thinner and less distinct. At another spot along the river, Atwater pulled cores in 1986 that contained nine buried soil layers. It seemed far-fetched at the time to think each one could represent a great earthquake. Then Atwater found something so startling it convinced him he was on the right track.

Leaning closer to the cutbank, he shaved the surface smooth with a blade and pointed out faint white tracings that lay like filigree atop several of the buried peat layers. He plucked a pinch and rubbed it between his fingers. Sand.

The sand came from the bottom of Willapa Bay. And there was only one force Atwater could think of capable of flinging it this far inland. He pulled out a battered field notebook and flipped to his original entry from April 1986. "Sand layers may each represent a tsunami wave," he read.

He closed the book. "That really made an impression on me."

This tiny creek seemed to tell of a turbulent history marked not only by repeated megaquakes but also by devastating waves of a type the modern world would not comprehend until the 2004 Indian Ocean disaster swept more than two hundred thousand people from the face of the earth.

Atwater knew he would need a mountain of proof if he was going to rewrite the region's seismic narrative. In 1986 he set up camp in a

KOA near the shores of Willapa Bay, the first of many such outposts over the next several years.

Fieldwork is a side of science the public rarely sees, filled with tedium and, sometimes, terror. The team that discovered magnetic zebra stripes on the bottom of the Pacific sailed on twelve cruises and made thousands of transects, towing their instrument back and forth. At Mount St. Helens geologists dashed through a hail of flying rocks to grab magma samples from the crater. Atwater's work wasn't as dangerous, but it was much filthier.

Former USGS scientist Wendy Grant Walter, who worked with Atwater on the Niawiakum, recalled trying to navigate in mud up to her boot tops. "It took all my strength just to yank one leg out," she said. "Then that would push the other leg in deeper." Three or four steps and she was soaked in sweat. Sometimes it took the combined strength of two people to pound the core barrel through marsh grass as fibrous as a doormat.

Atwater's frugality—a heritage of his Yankee upbringing—ensured that the government got its money's worth. Base camp was a 1950s trailer that looked like an aluminum bread box. The floor was falling out when Atwater inherited it from a hard-rock geologist nearing retirement. The single axle made the rig so tippy that Atwater would haul it only on back roads. There was no bathroom, but the kitchen had an apartment-size stove. Ten people could squeeze in for dinner on a rainy night.

Atwater would bake bread most evenings and serve it in the morning with hot chocolate, said Boyd Benson, who was a student at UW when he started working with Atwater. "I learned how to cook in that trailer," Benson added.

Atwater's work vehicle was a 1978 Dodge pickup, another USGS hand-me-down. Students called it the "beast" for its balky steering and the way it rattled when the speedometer nudged past 50 mph. His personal vehicle was even worse. The 1962 Mercury Comet station wagon cost less than his canoe, an aluminum Grumman he picked up in the late 1970s at a cut rate because of the gouge in its side. More than thirty years later, he still has the canoe. He drove the Comet until the roof was so rusted it wouldn't hold a patch.

Brian Atwater points out evidence of a megaquake and tsunami in the banks of the Niawiakum River during a 2007 field trip.

Both car and canoe came in handy on the Niawiakum, where Atwater hit on the technique that he would use up and down the coast. When the tide was down and the riverbanks exposed, he launched the Grumman into the upper reaches of the waterway. As he drifted downstream, he stopped to scrape and scrutinize the mud layers. By the time he neared the river's mouth, the rising tide would provide a free ride back to his starting point. He called it lazy. Colleagues rolled their eyes.

"Brian would be out there digging like crazy, doing the work of three people," Benson recalled. "So I would try to at least do the work of two." Catching tides meant early mornings, and Atwater was always the first person up. In the evenings he was the one who didn't want to stop brainstorming around the kitchen table.

Atwater also drew nonscientists into the search, inviting locals along on his expeditions and picking their brains about promising places to explore. "Some people with doctorates speak a language only known to other scientists," said John Shulene, a retired schoolteacher who volunteered with Atwater for thirteen years. "Brian is a down-home guy."

That inclusiveness makes Atwater a rarity: a scientist with a fan club. Members include retired engineers with time on their hands, earthquake junkies, and amateur naturalists. "Brian is willing to sit down with odd ducks," said his old friend and collaborator David Yamaguchi, a forester who considers himself part of that flock.

After finishing its work on the Niawiakum, Team Atwater shifted north to Grays Harbor, another large bay on the Washington coast. Next they prowled inlets in the estuary of the Columbia River. On every river, in every bay, the scientists found the same buried layers in the same relative order. "I didn't really catch on to how important it was at first," Wendy Grant Walter recalled. "But once we started finding the evidence everywhere, things got pretty exciting."

For Atwater the excitement was tinged with nerves. He was challenging long-held assumptions, and he knew skeptics would pounce on any flaws in his fieldwork or logic. He checked and rechecked his data and interpretations. What if there were another explanation that he was missing? "He knew he had to get it right, to get all the details down," said his wife, Frances DeMarco. A single-minded focus gripped her husband, as it always does when he prepares his scientific reports. "It takes up all his energy. We just step back and let him be."

In May 1987, Atwater laid out his findings: Over the past seven thousand years, Washington's coastline had dropped abruptly at least six times, by as much as six feet in places. He allowed as to how there might be an innocuous explanation, but his money was on the seven-hundred-mile-long subduction zone sleeping like a dragon offshore.

Atwater doesn't do a lot of fieldwork on the Northwest coast anymore, but he spends a lot of time retracing his steps. Visiting scientists ask to see the buried marshes for themselves, and Atwater obliges. Teachers, city council members, and geology clubs request field trips, and Atwater says sure. In May 2011, he led a group up the Copalis River on the central Washington coast. Among the party were a pair of television journalists, an anthropologist, and the fire chief of Hoquiam, a nearby mill town that was just coming to grips with the damage a tsunami could do to its waterfront.

The Copalis is one of Atwater's favorite showcases for the Cascadia story. It's got multiple buried marshes. It's got layers of tsunami sand. But the exceptional thing about this river is the way it helped him zero in on the two questions emergency planners, builders, and community leaders across the Northwest started asking as soon as Atwater's report about past megaquakes hit the press: How big? And when's the next one?

The Grumman was lashed to the roof of a new government SUV. The hybrid vehicle had separate heating controls for the driver's and passenger's sides, power windows, and a smooth ride. Atwater hated it. The USGS declared the "beast" obsolete and made him relinquish it. He was still bereft. "I had an emotional attachment to that truck," he said, untying the canoe and sliding it carefully to the ground so as not to scratch the SUV's paint.

Pacing the cobbled shore, Atwater dispensed life jackets, then offered a quick paddling lesson. The flotilla straggled upstream and passed under a coastal highway bridge, rebuilt after the tsunami from Alaska's 1964 megaquake swept logs up the Copalis and knocked out the old span.

The tide was low, and Atwater maneuvered his canoe around sandbars and snags. In 1987, his report kicked up a scientific furor, but he was too busy to pay much attention. "I don't know what people really thought," he recalled as he paddled. Bob Yeats, then the geology chairman at Oregon State University, was in the thick of the debate. "There was a lot of surprise and consternation among the ranks," he said. At a national conference, one of the nation's top geophysicists cautioned his colleagues not to jump on Atwater's bandwagon.

Skeptics continued to hold sway at some universities. One geologist was warned by a friend not to mention his interest in Cascadia when he interviewed for an academic job in 1989. "It could be career threatening to go up against the big boys," he recalled. WPPSS was still hoping to salvage one of the Satsop reactors. The consortium surveyed geologists after Atwater's report was published, and found them deeply divided over the subduction zone's menace.

BIRTH OF A GHOST FOREST

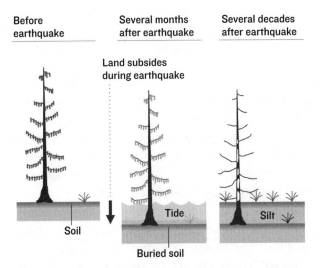

Before earthquake

Several months after earthquake

Several decades after earthquake

Land subsides during earthquake

Soil

Tide

Buried soil

Silt

Coastal subsidence in a subduction zone quake can drown forests and marshes and leave a lasting record of the earthquake's occurrence.

But there was no holding back the tide of discovery. Atwater's report set off a stampede of fieldwork across the Northwest. Geologists and graduate students headed to their closest stretch of coastline to look for similar signs and found them in abundance.

In Oregon, researchers discovered six buried marshes in Netarts Bay. An estuary on the Columbia yielded signs of a tsunami that traveled more than five miles upstream. Scientists digging on the Fraser River delta near downtown Vancouver, British Colombia, uncovered sand that boiled to the surface during fierce ground shaking. By 1995, a summary report listed eighty-six studies blanketing the coast from the tip of Vancouver Island to Cape Mendocino—all pointing toward a long history of quakes.

As he signaled the canoes to follow him to the other side of the Copalis River on the 2011 field trip, Atwater recalled the pressure he felt to put dates on past earthquakes, particularly the most recent one. "There was a lot of interest," he said. It's impossible to predict when the next quake will strike, but knowing how frequently a fault has snapped in the past is the next best thing. Solid dates could also address the size question, Atwater explained. If marshes up and down the coast were buried at the same time, that meant Cascadia had unleashed a full-rip 9 monster that ruptured the entire fault. If not, the worst case might be a series of 8s, separated by decades or even centuries. "We felt an urgency to figure out how long a stretch of coast was involved," he said, nosing his canoe up against the muddy bank and stepping into the thigh-high water.

The rest of the party clustered around as Atwater hacked out a section of riverbank with his trenching tool, revealing the familiar layer-cake of mud. He unsheathed a Japanese weeding hoe, called a *nejirigama*, and plucked out a hunk of several-hundred-year-old vegetation killed during the last megaquake. It was silverweed, a plant that grows on the surrounding marshes. "You can see the bracts on the base of the stem," Atwater explained, teasing apart the stub with gloved fingers. That the bracts are so well preserved is proof the ground dropped in an instant, he told the group.

Atwater climbed back into his canoe and led the expedition upstream.

When he first discovered fossil plants and tree roots in the buried marshes, Atwater was hopeful radiocarbon dating could reveal the timing of past earthquakes. But the early results proved as blurry as next month's weather forecast. Atwater could see that the most recent quake hit sometime between the 1600s and the 1800s, but he couldn't narrow the window. Earlier quakes stretched back in time from roughly one thousand years ago, when Viking raiders terrorized Europe, all the way back to the reign of the Pharaohs in 1400 BC. The intervals between quakes appeared to range from a few centuries to nearly a thousand years. But with uncertainties of two centuries or more, it was hard to say for sure. Atwater chafed at the imprecision.

Then, as happened so many times over the years, he got lucky.

"I first found this place in 1987," he said, leaning on his paddle to round the Grumman through a broad curve in the river. A spectral scene appeared in the distance. Towering trunks of long-dead cedars, bleached white as bone, stood sentinel in a meadow fringed with spruce.

"The ghost forest of the Copalis." Atwater said.

Atwater beached the canoe and scrambled up the bank onto ground thick with huckleberry, salal, and sharp-bladed grass. Channels that fill with brackish water when the tide is high snaked among the spongy hassocks. The marsh had the feel of an old battlefield—hushed now, but the battered trunks testifying to great violence in the part.

It hit suddenly, Atwater explained. During the last great earthquake, this riverfront forest shuddered and dropped. Trees that took root during the Middle Ages drowned, their roots suddenly submerged. The trunks were still upright after so long only because cedar is resistant to rot.

When he first saw those ghosts, Atwater didn't know what to make of them. He had seen roots of Sitka spruce in buried marshes along with silverweed and other plants. But the tree trunks had rotted away long ago. "I was confused by standing trees," he recalled, circling a dead giant that measured six feet across. It was David Yamaguchi, the forester, who helped figure out what those silent witnesses could say about the upheaval that claimed their lives.

The two researchers had met by chance when Atwater presented a lunchtime seminar at Mount St. Helens. In the wake of its colossal outburst, the volcano was swarming with "more scientists than flies on bear turds," Yamaguchi recalled. He was the one who didn't fit in, a chatty biologist surrounded by geologists who preferred the company of rocks. The USGS hired him on a temporary basis because his knack for tree rings turned out to be useful. By analyzing forests killed or damaged in previous eruptions, Yamaguchi was able to fill in some of the blanks in the volcano's eruptive history.

In the field he peppered the geologists with questions: What did they see when they looked at the landscape? How could they tell one type of lava flow from another? In return he taught them how to distinguish hemlock from fir and how to read the vegetation for clues about the underlying soil and rock.

As he munched his sandwich and listened to Atwater bemoan his mushy carbon dates, Yamaguchi raised his hand.

"I know someone who can help you," he said.

"Who?" Atwater asked.

"Me."

Tree-ring dating works best in places like the desert Southwest, where it was developed. Wide seasonal swings in rainfall create ring-width patterns so varied and crisp they pop out to the naked eye. Dendro-chronologists have a harder time of it in the Pacific Northwest, where one year is just as soggy as the next. Worst of all are the coastal rain forests, where nature delivers up to 170 inches of precipitation a year and timber grows faster than anywhere else in the world.

"The happier trees are, the less distinctive their ring patterns," Yamaguchi explained. Despite his confident declaration, he wasn't sure he could use trees to figure out when the last megaquake struck.

Yamaguchi's first visit to the ghost forest raised his hopes. A fresh cedar aroma wafted into the air as his chain saw bit into the trunks. He sliced out pie-shaped wedges. The bark was gone and the outer rings rubbed away by time and weather. But the interior patterns were clear and varied. "That was exciting," Yamaguchi recalled. "If the rings had been uniform, I didn't have a chance."

That's because counting rings in the ghost cedars alone couldn't tell him when the latest earthquake hit. He had no way of knowing which ring corresponded to which year. What Yamaguchi needed were reference sequences from trees where the date of death was known. The reference cedars had to come from the same neck of the Northwest woods, because trees that experience similar weather patterns will have similar ring patterns: wide during wet years, skinny during years with less rainfall. The patterns are like bar codes. If Yamaguchi could find good reference trees, he could compare their bar codes to those in the quake-killed cedars and look for overlapping sequences. That would allow him to anchor the ghost forest in time and zero in on the trees' final years of life.

But in the late-1980s, old-growth cedars along the Washington coast were as rare as spotted owls. Lowland forests were the first to fall in the logging frenzy that gathered steam after World War I and continued chugging for seven decades. Museums had cross-sections of some of the grandfather trees, but getting permission to work with

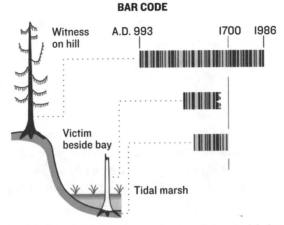

BAR CODE

Scientists compared the bar code–like ring sequences from trees that survived the last Cascadia megaquake with trees killed by the quake to estimate an approximate date.

them and verify the dates would be tough. It was Yamaguchi's turn for a stroke of luck.

In the summer of 1987, he and Atwater drove the region's back roads and paddled streams in search of more ghost forests. One day the scientists spotted a scene that looked like something from the heyday of the timber barons. On a tiny island at the south end of Willapa Bay, Weyerhaeuser was felling Western red cedars so big a single tree filled a log truck. The stand had dodged destruction for so long because of its location. "They cut every toothpick on the mainland," Yamaguchi said, "but it was just enough of a hassle to get to the island that they left it alone."

The trees were coming down as part of a timber-for-land swap between the logging company and the federal government, which wanted to turn the island into a wildlife refuge. The stumps would be perfect for Yamaguchi's purposes. Easily more than 600 years old, the trees had weathered the last earthquake—and there was no doubt about the year of their demise. He could see them being felled.

The loggers started work at dawn, toppling the giants and loading them onto a barge for the short trip across the water. Like burglars, Yamaguchi and his assistant waited until the crew knocked off at 2:00 PM, then paddled over in his canoe. "We could have asked for permission," he said, with a laugh, "but maybe they would have said no." On the island, Yamaguchi fired up his chain saw and carved long, thin sections from stumps wide enough to park a car on. He piled the wood in the center of the canoe and paddled back to the mainland. Yamaguchi made surreptitious trips to the island over several days. On some of the return legs, the canoe was so loaded it barely cleared the water.

Yamaguchi sanded the specimens to a high gloss. In November, he loaded them into the back of his old station wagon and drove to Seattle to spend Thanksgiving with his parents. The University of Washington, where he earned his doctorate, had a dendrochronology lab. For a week, he cranked tree sections through a boxy microscope, measuring the width of every ring. It was impossible to match patterns by eye, so he wrote a rudimentary program to tap the power of early microcomputers.

"Pretty quickly, I could see it was going to work."

With growing excitement Yamaguchi zeroed in on dates. There was still uncertainty in the numbers because the outer rings were missing from the ghost forest cedars. But it was clear the trees had lived through the 1680s. Whatever killed them struck after that—and before white settlers arrived.

While Yamaguchi was poring over wood slices, Atwater was pushing radiocarbon methods as hard as he could. High-precision techniques pioneered at the University of Washington narrowed the window for the last Cascadia quake to sometime between 1680 and 1720, at least five decades before European explorers laid eyes on the Washington coast. If those dates were right, the subduction zone had been building up pressure for about three hundred years. Did that mean it might be near the breaking point?

Atwater applied the high-precision dating to all of his buried soil layers, each representing a megaquake. The average interval between them was about five hundred years. The shortest was a scant two hundred.

Before winding up his field trip on the Copalis in May 2011, Atwater submitted to a television interview with the ghost forest as a backdrop. Japan's recent killer quake and tsunami were a mirror image of what the Northwest can expect, and the media had been clamoring for Atwater's expertise. The guy who was turned away from an earthquake workshop a quarter of a century ago was now, at age sixty, a global authority.

Atwater's wife, Frances, said her husband never wanted to be in the public eye or play the role of expert. "He just saw what needed to be done and he did it." Atwater will talk to journalists, community groups, park rangers, engineers—anyone who wants to be better informed and better prepared for what Cascadia has in store. That's why he devoted a spring day to paddling a stretch of the Copalis he's visited more than a hundred times.

By the early 1990s, scientific skepticism had vanished under the weight of the evidence Atwater and other teams of geologists kept piling on. But the scientists still couldn't say whether the most recent quake had been a full-rip 9. The carbon dates from buried soil layers weren't good enough to rule out a series of smaller quakes in quick succession.

A bout with Hodgkin's lymphoma—a kind of cancer that attacks the lymph nodes—gave Atwater a scare but didn't slow his drive. "He would get chemo, be sick for three hours, then go back to work," Frances said. After the 2004 Indian Ocean quake and tsunami, Atwater shifted his attention to developing nations that face the threat of megaquakes. He traveled to Indonesia for months at a time, collaborating with scientists there to learn more about the region's seismic history. His latest focus is Pakistan, where the combination of a subduction zone and bad buildings puts millions of people at risk.

His television interview over, Atwater took a last look at the ghost forest. In hopes of cashing in on a tourist boom that hasn't come, the property owner built a dock that overlooks the site. Several of the trees fell in the past few years, and others are listing. "There are a lot fewer left than when we first came here," Atwater said, a hint of regret in his voice.

He herded the group back into their canoes for the trip downriver. Gauzy clouds muted the sun and the tide lapped up the riverbanks. Relaxed and smiling, Atwater paddled with the ease of a frontiersman. He misses the fieldwork, he admitted, the days governed by tides and capped off by discussions around the table in the old trailer. "It was fun seeing all the new country, all those early, misty mornings."

He hopes to get back to it soon, when his overseas work winds down. Unanswered questions about Cascadia nag at him. "There's still a lot left to do here in the Northwest," he said, dipping his paddle for the final push back to the launch site. Tonight he was headed to Hoquiam for a public meeting on tsunami risks. It would be midnight before he got home.

CHAPTER 3:

PARENT QUAKE, ORPHAN TSUNAMI

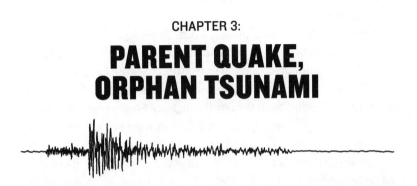

WHEN JAMES GILCHRIST SWAN DIED in 1900, a delegation of Makah Indians paid their respects by making the 120-mile journey from Neah Bay to Port Townsend, a mill town near the mouth of Puget Sound. Arriving just before the casket was closed, they filed past, moaning in grief. "Each affectionately patted the face of the dead man," the local paper reported.

Swan was Massachusetts-born but found his true home when he settled on the Washington coast in 1852. Of all the places he rambled, he loved Neah Bay best. Swan visited the remote village often and lived among the Makah for four years. When he wasn't plumbing a whiskey bottle, he taught school or doctored the sick. His voluminous journals described whale hunts, revenge killings, courtship customs—and a vanishing way of life. The writer Ivan Doig, who spun those journals into a book called *Winter Brothers*, admired Swan's "rare knack of looking at the coastal Indians as flesh and blood, rather than the frontier's tribal rubble."

Swan's Makah friends told him stories never shared with white people before; unlike most whites, Swan listened. That's how his diaries came to hold the first written account of a tsunami on the Northwest coast. The storyteller was Billy Balch, son of a chief and a tribal leader in his own right.

"A long time ago, but not at a very remote period," Balch told Swan, the Pacific Ocean receded for four days, leaving Neah Bay dry. The water surged back, rising for four days without any waves or breakers until everything was submerged but the mountaintops. "Many canoes came down in the trees and were destroyed, and numerous lives were lost."

Swan was skeptical of many Makah legends, but not this one. "There is no doubt in my mind of the truth of this tradition," he wrote more than one hundred years before Atwater scraped at the banks of the Waatch River. "The Waatch prairie shows conclusively that the water of the Pacific once flowed through it," Swan wrote, an observation based on his own spade work. "On cutting through the turf at any place . . . the whole substratum is found to be pure beach sand."

Despite its improbable eight-day timeline, Balch's story also struck Tom Heaton and his USGS colleague Parke Snavely as credible. "The description of water receding from Neah Bay and then returning in a strong current is clearly suggestive of a tsunami," they wrote in the first scientific paper to consider what the region's original inhabitants had to say about its seismic past.

Science and legend don't often intersect. But since Heaton reached across the divide, researchers and tribal leaders have compiled dozens of stories of violent ground shaking, landslides, and ocean surges at sites from the rocky bays of British Columbia to California's redwood forests. The stories leave little doubt that native people bore witness to the repeated geologic cataclysms recorded in Atwater's mud layers. The first Northwesterners invoked the supernatural to explain the upheavals. Lacking written language they passed the knowledge on through story and song.

And they would have been happy to talk about it sooner, if anyone had asked.

"Hello?" said seventy-seven-year-old Viola Riebe of the Hoh Tribe on Washington's Olympic coast. "We've been telling these stories for centuries."

Riebe's uncle taught her about Thunderbird, who lives in the mountains at the headwaters of the Hoh River. The flapping of his mighty wings calls forth lightning and makes the earth move. In native stories from across the region, titanic battles between Thunderbird and his adversary, Whale, roil the sea and make the Earth tremble.

As a young girl, Riebe was playing on the beach with her cousins one morning when the water started to pull away. "We could see all the rocks and boulders on the beach," she said. "We didn't know what was happening." Steeped in tribal traditions, her uncle recognized the warning signs of a tsunami. "He was waving his hat and yelling at us to get off the beach." In retrospect Riebe suspects the cause was a distant earthquake somewhere on the Pacific Rim. At the time she was relieved when a group of fishermen raced up in a truck to rescue the children as fast-rising water pinned them against a tangle of logs.

"We learned a lesson that day," Riebe said. "My uncle told us how a tidal wave like that had happened here a long time ago."

Former University of Washington seismologist Ruth Ludwin has combed through nineteenth-century ethnographies and talked with tribal elders in search of stories that might describe megaquakes and tsunamis. She wondered whether any of the accounts would converge in time with scientists' discoveries of a giant quake about three centuries ago.

Ludwin found the Northwest rich in earthquake legends. The Nuu-Chah-Nulth people of Vancouver Island blamed ground shaking on mountain dwarfs who would entice humans to join their dances. A mortal who stumbled into the wooden drum that kept the beat was cursed as an "earthquake man," whose steps caused the ground to quiver. Ceremonies mirrored similar themes, with dancers shaking scallop-shell rattles or pounding drums filled with rocks to mimic the roar of trees and vibrating ground.

Many stories packed moral lessons. Boys who killed crows or disrespected salmon called earthquakes down on their villages. Mistreated dogs took their revenge by howling up quakes that collapsed their masters' houses. Other stories stressed preparedness: Warriors who braided ropes ahead of time were able to tether their canoes to trees and ride out the floods. Their lazy neighbors were swept away.

Ludwin was particularly interested in stories that spoke of floods, strange tides, or changes in ground level—features that distinguish subduction zone quakes and tsunamis from the run-of-the-mill shakes that strike more frequently.

In a story reminiscent of Atwater's buried marshes, the Yurok people of California's redwood coast tell of Thunder and his rowdy companion Earthquake, who boasted, "I shall tear up the Earth." The rampaging pair caused prairies to sink, allowing the sea to rush in and shellfish to flourish.

The most spot-on account Ludwin found came from Washington's Quileute tribe, now famous as the wolf-men of the *Twilight* vampire franchise. A chill prickled the back of her neck when she first read the legend of Thunderbird plucking Whale from the sea. "'There was a shaking and a jumping up of the Earth beneath and a rolling up of the great waters.' I thought, 'Eureka!'"

But extracting dates from mythic traditions can be harder than pinning a phantom to the wall. It wasn't until the 1860s that anthropologists and settlers like Swan started recording the experiences of Northwest tribes. More than 150 years had passed since the last Cascadia megaquake, and tribal cultures were in tatters. Many groups were forced from their ancestral lands and decimated by disease. Smallpox ravaged the Makah. At the height of the epidemic one witness reported, "The beach at Neah Bay for a distance of eight miles was literally strewn with the dead bodies of these people."

Given the turmoil it's amazing how many oral histories survived and astonishing that Ludwin and her collaborators were able to find nine stories—from the length of Cascadia—with enough detail to yield rough dates. "They're not figurative," she said. "These are stories of somebody who saw the flood or ancestors who experienced the flood."

Robert Dennis, a longtime leader of the Huu-ay-aht First Nation on Vancouver Island's Barkley Sound, learned one of those stories from his great-grandfather. Chief Louis Nookmis, born in 1881, would sit Dennis and his brother down at the kitchen table and regale the boys with tribal history and lore. Some sessions stretched on for hours, an eternity for a twelve-year-old. "You couldn't say, 'I'm going outside to play,'" Dennis recalled.

Despite his fidgeting Dennis was captivated by the old man's tale of a winter's night when the ground shook and a huge wave smashed into the shore at Pachena Bay. More than one hundred people were lost. "There is now no one left alive due to what this land does at times," Nookmis said in a 1964 interview. "They simply had no time to get hold of canoes, no time to get awake." A nearby settlement on high ground escaped damage.

Nookmis explained that the event happened four generations before his grandfather's birth. That placed it sometime between 1640 and 1740—squarely in the time frame for the most recent megathrust quake. Several other stories fell in the same range, including an account collected in the early 1900s from an Oregon coast native. Her grandfather met a woman who broke her back falling from a tree where she took shelter in a great flood. A story recorded in the 1930s told of a village destroyed on Canada's Queen Charlotte Strait. "This is not a myth," the storyteller said. "My tale is seven generations old."

"It was really shocking to discover how closely the dates matched," Ludwin said.

What Dennis had considered a dusty legend came alive for him in 1964. The tsunami from Alaska's magnitude 9.2 megaquake roared up an inlet to Port Alberni, more than fifty miles from the coast. Dennis and his dad rushed to the pier to untie their fishing boat so it wouldn't hang up on the pilings. The boat was spared, but dozens of others were smashed along with more than four dozen homes.

Chief Louis's stories weren't just relics, Dennis realized. After the 1964 tsunami, the elderly leader shared many of his stories with a historian, partly as a warning for white residents who now far outnumber the aboriginal people. He wanted them to know that their homeland has a violent side. "I learned from him how important it is to keep this oral history alive," Dennis said.

That traditional knowledge can save lives was vividly demonstrated in the Indian Ocean tsunami. Two groups escaped the waves: the people of Simeulue Island, where the tsunami hit within fifteen minutes; and the Moken, or sea gypsies, who live on islands off the coast of Myanmar. Stories passed down in both cultures warned of giant surges that rush in on the heels of an earthquake. When they felt the ground shake and saw the water pull away from the shore, villagers ran for high ground.

Native American and First Nation communities didn't take much convincing when Atwater and other scientists began uncovering evidence of giant quakes and tsunamis. "My grandfather said it, and then the geologists were saying it," Dennis said. "These are things we should pay attention to."

At Pachena Bay, where an entire village was wiped out by the most recent Cascadia tsunami, the Huu-ay-aht recently dedicated a new community center on a bluff overlooking the beach. Stocked with food and blankets, the site will give people a place to flee to when the next tsunami comes. Washington's Quileute tribe got congressional approval in 2012 for a land swap that will allow them to relocate a schoolhouse, homes, and offices that sit just five feet above sea level.

Just down the coast, Riebe has earned the nickname "tsunami queen" for her work spreading the message she learned from her uncle so long ago, now validated by modern science. She counts among the highlights of her life a visit to the Copalis ghost forest with Atwater. "It was incredible to know that our Native American stories line up with what the scientists found out there," she said. "Chalk one up for the Native Americans. We do know something after all."

But it was another group of ancient people who would finally nail down the date and size of Cascadia's most recent megaquake with a precision the best technology could never match. The discovery started with a Japanese researcher who reasoned that a Cascadia megaquake might have churned up a tsunami powerful enough to cross the Pacific. If so, one of the most sophisticated societies in the world would have been watching.

What most Americans know about Japanese history they learned from Hollywood. The TV miniseries *Shogun* and films like *The Seven Samurai* depicted a blood-soaked land where bandits raped and plundered and warlords slaughtered one another in a struggle for power. But by the dawn of the 1700s, Japan had been at peace for four generations.

Loosely united under a single ruler, the country was in the midst of a cultural flowering that brought the introduction of haiku and the golden age of Kabuki theater. For the first time, the shogun was a scholar, not a warrior. His government cared for abandoned children and built kennels to house stray dogs. At a time when less than a third of Frenchmen could sign their names, book clubs were the rage in the capital city of Edo, now called Tokyo. Even many peasants could read and write a little.

With no wars to fight, samurai passed their days drinking sake, writing poetry, and patronizing geisha when they could afford it. To earn their keep, many turned to administrative work in a society where bureaucracy had supplanted swordplay.

Regional *daimyos* employed legions of clerks to record crop yields, collect taxes, and catch peasants who skimmed off the top. The shogun's auditors kept a close eye on the daimyos. In every castle and village, registrars recorded the statistics of daily life, from births and deaths to disputes and planting dates. Diaries were a popular medium for self-reflection and observations of the natural world. "The facts must be presented as exhaustively as possible," one teacher advised. "An excess of detail is preferable to brevity."

That conscientiousness extended to natural disasters. Japan's earliest written record of an earthquake dates to 416 AD. Seismic bookkeeping was sporadic during the country's centuries of war, but it became routine with the coming of peace. So a literate and watchful populace took note when strange waves roiled the east coast of Honshu in the twelfth year of the Genroku era under the zodiacal sign of the rabbit—1700 on the Western calendar.

It was a cold night. Villagers in the port of Kuwagasaki were roused shortly after midnight as torrents of seawater swept through their homes. The panicked peasants fled to the hills and watched as fires from overturned lanterns lit the sky and devoured buildings made of wood and rice-paper. In darkness the swells raced up the bay and into a river, swamping a smaller village and pushing more than a mile upstream. Salt water slopped into rice paddies and vegetable plots in the village of Otsuchi, twenty miles to the south. Farther down the coast a barge laden with rice was repulsed by high waves as it tried to thread its way into a river mouth. The headman of another coastal village wondered what to call the pulses that surged and receded like a series of swift tides. It reminded him of a tsunami, but there had been no earthquake.

Accounts trickled in from at least six spots on the coast spanning more than six hundred miles. The authors were mostly samurai and merchants, cogs in the machinery of government and commerce. They logged the emergency rations issued to villagers and petitioned higher-ups to provide "low-grade wood" for temporary shelters. The saga of the rice barge was written up because it ended badly. Unable to enter the river in the face of high water and waves, the vessel was forced to anchor in an open bay where a storm blew it aground. Two crewmen were killed and all thirty tons of cargo lost. Port officials filled out the maritime equivalent of a police report that included eyewitness accounts from villagers and testimony from the unlucky captain.

It's hard to say which is more impressive: the level of detail in the reports or the fact that the reports survived hundreds of years, two world wars, and Japan's transformation into a high-tech mecca. But historical preservation and seismology are twin passions in Japan. In the 1890s scholars began combing through ancient documents for earthquake accounts. By the 1990s the ledger of historical quakes filled twenty-one volumes. Few American geologists had any inkling the record existed or what it might have to say about Cascadia. But Kenji Satake did.

Born in Tokyo, Satake attended college on Japan's northernmost island, Hokkaido. He wasn't interested in earthquakes, but he gravitated toward professors who worked on glaciers and volcanoes because he loved to ski and climb mountains. In 1983 a large earthquake under the Japan Sea kicked up a tsunami that killed more than one hundred people. Satake got swept up in the scientific postmortem on the disaster and was hooked.

He'd never heard of the Cascadia Subduction Zone until he landed a postdoc at Caltech and met Tom Heaton. The USGS researcher told Satake about the possibility of megaquakes on the West Coast and about the Native American stories. Then he posed a question the

Japanese scientist would get tired of hearing: how big was the tsunami triggered by the last Cascadia megaquake?

Satake couldn't say. There were still too many unknowns. But he chipped away at the problem over the next several years, as Atwater and others gathered more and more field data. Satake built a computer model and plugged in everything that could be quantified about Cascadia's most recent rip. Out of curiosity, he let his model run until the hypothetical tsunami crossed the Pacific. Satake was intrigued to see that a magnitude 8 quake would send only piddling waves onto Japan's shores. But a magnitude 9 could create swells of six feet or more.

During his time at Hokkaido University, Satake volunteered for one of the professors compiling that twenty-one-volume opus on historic quakes. He traveled to tiny museums and mountain villages to examine old scrolls and manuscripts. Now Satake wondered, did those records include reports of a mystery tsunami several hundred years ago?

It seemed unlikely he would ever find out. The error bars around the radiocarbon dates were wide enough to span several centuries. "Without a better date, it was just impossible," he recalled. "I didn't really take it seriously."

Then the dates got better. For Satake the turning point came during a paleoseismology conference in California in 1994. He was there to finally answer Heaton's question, with modeling that estimated the height of Cascadia's latest tsunami at thirty feet. But he was most fascinated by the work of Atwater, Yamaguchi and others, whose tree-ring techniques and high-precision carbon 14 analyses had narrowed the window on Cascadia's last quake to about forty years.

"Now that was a much easier period to work with," Satake recalled. "That's when I really got started."

Satake enlisted his PhD adviser in Japan to help search for any records of a tsunami between 1650 and 1750 that arrived without any ground shaking. The older scientist quickly found one.

A Japanese earthquake historian had already laid a lot of the groundwork, singling out several reports about that cold night in 1700 when the sea attacked without apparent provocation from the earth.

A computer simulation shows the tsunami triggered by the 1700 Cascadia quake reaching Japan in about ten hours.

But deciphering dates and times from centuries-old documents isn't a simple job of translation. The language and style used by Edo-period scribes bear so little resemblance to modern Japanese that Satake could make out only a few words. The clock and calendar were even more convoluted, with seasonal variation in the length of an hour, a dozen zodiac signs, leap years, and a five-year master cycle based on elements like fire and water. When the pieces fell into place, Satake could see that the mystery waves first hit the Japanese coast around midnight on January 27, 1700.

The reports covered such a long stretch of coast that Satake ruled out storm surges as the cause. The detail-crazy Japanese also kept meteorological records, of course. None mentioned foul weather. The waves swept down the coast like a tsunami would, hitting northern-most ports first.

But Japan lies in the crosshairs of multiple subduction zones. The tsunami from Chile's 1960 quake caused flooding and damage in several of the same villages hit in 1700. Alaska and Russia's Kamchatka Peninsula were also potential culprits. Satake checked historical and geological records. As best as he could tell from the sketchy data, there was no monster quake anywhere else around the Pacific Rim in early 1700. Satake concluded that the orphan tsunami had a parent, and its name was Cascadia.

What's more, he thought he could date the birth with hospital precision. Racing through the open ocean at the speed of a jet, a tsunami from the Pacific Northwest would take about ten hours to reach northern Honshu. If Satake's story was right, that meant Cascadia's last megaquake hit at about 9:00 PM on January 26, 1700, in keeping with Native American stories of a winter's night when earth and sea convulsed.

"Oh, crap."

In his temporary office at Japan's agriculture ministry in Sapporo, David Yamaguchi stared at the cover of the January 18, 1996, issue of the British journal *Nature*. It was a reproduction of *The Great Wave off Kanagawa*, the well-known woodblock print of a colossal curl dwarfing Mount Fuji in the background. The image has become a tsunami icon, even though tsunamis don't look anything like the wind-whipped wave the artist depicted.

Yamaguchi could guess what was inside the magazine. Preliminary reports were already circulating about Satake's attempt to connect the dots between Cascadia and Japan.

"It just hit me over the forehead," Yamaguchi recalled. "All of a sudden the pressure was on me to somehow wrap things up." Loose ends from his tree ring data on the Copalis ghost forest and other sites on the Washington coast had been bugging him for years. Now Satake had raised the bar.

Until that point no one dreamed it would be possible to establish an exact date for the last Cascadia quake. It didn't even seem important. Ballpark figures were good enough to estimate the intervals between quakes. What difference did it make whether the last monster struck in 1680 or 1720? What planners wanted to know was the monster's size.

But a decade after Atwater's first trip to Neah Bay, geologists were still debating the size question so vigorously that they coined nicknames for the opposing camps. The Apocalypse group believed the subduction zone's last quake was a full-rip 9 that ruptured the entire length of the fault. The Decades of Terror gang insisted the fault ruptured in segments. The quakes would have been smaller—maybe magnitude 8—but they popped off in succession over a period of years or decades. The argument wasn't close to being settled because neither camp had enough ammunition.

Satake's story offered an arsenal. "All of a sudden there was a way to move forward to nail the magnitude," Yamaguchi recalled. According to Satake's computer models, only a magnitude 9 quake could explain the waves that sloshed onto Japanese shores.

Field geologists weren't likely to be swayed by computer modeling, though. They view it the way cops view psychological profiles: suggestive, maybe, but not in the same league as fingerprints on a gun or a layer of buried sand. If someone could dig up hard evidence to back Satake's story, it would prove Cascadia ruptured along its entire length. The Apocalypse camp would carry the day.

But confirmation would require a lot more legwork in Japan and for Yamaguchi an attempt to push tree ring dating to its very limit.

"There was a huge incentive to find out if Satake was right," Yamaguchi recalled. "I was having a great time in Japan, but I knew I had to go home."

Yamaguchi's career hadn't followed the path he had hoped for when he defied his father's wishes and picked science over the family business. He had lugged enough hundred-pound sacks of rice to know he would never be content supplying Seattle's Asian restaurants with groceries and chopsticks. A Hail Mary scholarship to Yale sprung him from the Beacon Hill neighborhood where he grew up. Summers spent working in national forests inspired an interest in trees. When his temporary post at Mount St. Helens ended, he got a job on the University of Colorado faculty and seemed to be launched on an academic trajectory. Then after five years, the university laid him off.

He was crushed for about a week. Yamaguchi is one of those rare people who isn't faking it when he talks about silver linings: losing his job was depressing, but it opened the door to another dream—to live and work in Japan.

He landed a visiting appointment at Japan's equivalent of the U.S. Forest Service. Even though a knee injury spoiled his plans for fieldwork, the third-generation Japanese American delighted in learning his way around the country and language. "I have this Japanese face, but I didn't know anything about Japan," he said.

When Yamaguchi got back to Seattle, he worked days as a number-cruncher for health researchers at the University of Washington. Nights and weekends were spent fine-tuning his tree ring data and huddling with Atwater to figure out their next steps.

Eventually, the scientists would travel to Japan, working with Satake to validate his computer models with on-the-ground observations. Their goal was to extract all the detail possible from the Japanese records and landscape and use it to verify both the size and origin of the tsunami. A tsunami that came from Cascadia would create very different run-up patterns than waves that radiated from earthquakes in Chile, Alaska, or Russia. The extent of flooding would also be key to the size of the parent quake. Like any good detective, Atwater wanted to examine the scene of the crime for himself. Yamaguchi was the perfect Watson to his Sherlock.

The duo visited every site where the eighteenth century Japanese took note of strange waves. Atwater's salary was covered by the USGS and Japan paid his expenses. Yamaguchi had to scrounge. The Japanese government extended one paid invitation. Other times he piggybacked on Atwater's frequent flier miles. "It was all nickel-and-dime stuff."

Yamaguchi's translation skills and ability to navigate the country proved invaluable, particularly in rural areas. He soaked up the history and culture that his Nisei parents had rejected. "We were chasing these scientific facts, but for me it was also an odyssey into my past."

Many of the towns and villages they visited were devastated in the 2011 tsunami. Otsuchi, the fishing settlement where waves flooded gardens in 1700, lost 1,400 people. The images played over and over on television of jet-black water pouring over a seawall were filmed in Miyako, one of the first ports hit by the orphan tsunami of 1700.

But in the late 1990s, the townsfolk were eager to show the visiting Americans the castle logbooks and family journals where the original reports were recorded. Documents older than the Declaration of Independence were stored in government filing cabinets and in private homes. "You go to these little town museums and they just put them in your hands," Yamaguchi said. His favorite was from Miho, a pine-covered peninsula south of Tokyo. A family of innkeepers there preserved the writings of an ancestor, a peasant who has served as the village headman. The floodwaters struck Miho early in the morning, and his was one of the few eyewitness accounts. He described strange currents that flowed back and forth with the force of a river. Like Viola Riebe's finger-wagging uncle, he cautioned future generations to remember that dangerous waves could hit with no ground shaking. "The whole village was puzzled," he wrote.

Unlike the elegant calligraphy of the samurai scribes, the headman's brushwork and language were crude. "I had to laugh," Yamaguchi recalled. "This guy's writing was so bad it looks like things I write in Japanese."

The scientists quizzed residents on geography and any changes to the landscape over the past three centuries. Using historic maps they paced off the run-up described in the old documents. At the spot where water surged up a castle moat in 1700, they found a busy intersection. But on the margins of a wide bay, they could pinpoint the location of a fisherman's shack and salt kilns flooded by the tsunami.

"A lot of what we saw was eerily similar to what the samurai described," Yamaguchi said.

The field studies all pointed to a big wave in Japan—up to sixteen feet high in places—and a full-rip 9 from Cascadia. But the slam-dunk paternity test linking parent quake and tsunami offspring came from the Copalis ghost forest on the Washington coast.

When he first considered the problem, Yamaguchi didn't see any way to wring more precise dates out of the old cedars. The trunks were too battered by time. None had the bark and outer rings he would need to establish an exact year of death.

It was Atwater who stumbled on the answer. Paddling up the Copalis on one of his many excursions there, he noticed that a cedar had

The ghost forest of the Copalis.

succumbed to age and gravity and had toppled into the river. He steered his canoe in for a close look. Protruding from the riverbank were the broken ends of the tree's roots. Grabbing his trenching tool, Atwater grubbed out the mud from around a root stub and saw that the airless muck had preserved its bark in pristine condition.

It was a "D'oh" moment worthy of Homer Simpson.

"In retrospect we should have gone for the cedar roots first," Yamaguchi said. "We just didn't think of it."

Atwater assembled a team of strong backs to wrestle roots from the ground in the summer of 1996. They targeted Yamaguchi's star specimens—the trees with the most distinctive ring patterns—and dug like badgers on steroids. "It was a treasure hunt," recalled Boyd Benson, a UW student at the time. The "nice, juicy roots" were five feet or more underground. Benson excavated pits around the tree bases deep enough to swallow a man. Atwater scrambled into the holes with his chain saw and carved out root chunks. The swampy ground was always wet, and it was a race to extract roots before the incoming tide flooded the pits.

"The hole would be filling up and there would be a rooster tail of wood chips and water flying into the air as Brian cut the roots," Benson recalled.

By the end of each session, the men were so muddy that they jumped in the river to clean off before paddling back. Some of the roots were two feet in diameter. The scientists polished them until they gleamed. "When you're done, they look like pieces of art," Benson said.

To establish the time sequence, Yamaguchi had to match the bar codes in the trunks to the bar codes in the roots, something that hadn't been done in the Northwest. It sounds straightforward, but dendrochronologists can go cross-eyed working with roots. The rings are lopsided and so tiny that the slightest error in measurement can throw the sequence off kilter. Add in the regional curse of abundant rainfall that blurs ring patterns and Yamaguchi was nervous. "This was new territory for tree-ring dating," he said.

Benson packed the sections in cardboard boxes and loaded them and himself onto an Amtrak train headed for Lamont-Doherty Earth Observatory, perched on a bluff overlooking the Hudson River. The tree ring lab there is one of the world's best. Benson worked with lab cofounder Gordon Jacoby to scrutinize the wood slabs with an apparatus that measures rings down to one-millionth of a meter—less than the thickness of a hair. Benson handed off the measurements to Yamaguchi, who fired up his bar code–matching program and held his breath. "We were asking these trees, 'When did you die?'" Yamaguchi said. "They told us."

Seven out of the eight cedars Yamaguchi examined had laid down their last ring in the warm months of 1699. By the start of the next growing season, in May 1700, all were dead. The single outlier limped along until 1708 because one root extended like a snorkel into higher ground, providing a temporary lifeline that delayed the tree's demise.

The results drew a bull's-eye around January 1700. There was no longer any question about the source of Japan's orphan tsunami or about the size of the parent quake.

It was a doozy.

CHAPTER 4

A VIEW FROM THE SEA

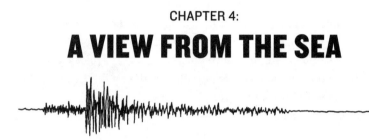

THE BOUNDARIES BETWEEN TECTONIC PLATES make good postcards. Picture the Himalayas lit by a setting sun or Andean spires piercing the sky. The rift valleys in Iceland and Africa, where plates are pulling apart, offer vast panoramas of fissures and volcanic cones.

The Cascadia Subduction Zone has produced calendar-worthy vistas, too—think Olympic Mountains. But the actual boundary where the seafloor and continent collide isn't much to look at, according to Oregon State University researcher Chris Goldfinger, one of the few people who has been there. "All you see is mud and a few fish going by," said Oregon State researcher Chris Goldfinger.

In 1990 Goldfinger dove to the subduction zone aboard the submersible *Alvin*. The descent took nearly three hours with the lights turned off to preserve the vessel's batteries. When *Alvin* settled onto the abyssal plain two miles down, the pilot switched on the high beams. "I expected it to be smooth and flat," Goldfinger recalled. "But it's very lumpy and full of pits." Ghostly white octopuses hunkered in the pits, which were rimmed with the bones of their victims. Albino sharks wove in and out of view.

Goldfinger was just a student, thrilled to visit the submarine world that was the focus of his doctoral research. Crammed into *Alvin*'s 82-inch spherical cockpit, the crew was the first to visit the subduction zone that was causing so much consternation. The pilot asked the young scientist what to expect.

"I don't know," Goldfinger replied. "But if you keep going east, we'll hit North America sooner or later."

Many subduction zones are marked by a deep trench. Cascadia's is filled to the brim with sediment from the Columbia River. There's actually a knoll on the seafloor where mud scraped off the nose of the descending plate piles up. Gliding eastward, *Alvin* bumped into that bank and a cloud of sediment enveloped the craft. The pilot ascended, then motored forward. Another oomph into the mud. "This must be it," Goldfinger told the pilot. "The plate boundary."

He filmed his close encounter with Cascadia and offered the footage to documentary makers. No one wanted it. "It's just so boring," Goldfinger said. Even when *Alvin* finally navigated up and out of the mud foothills and encountered a cliff at the edge of the continental shelf, it didn't make for exciting images. "It's like crawling up to the base of El Capitan in the middle of the night with a flashlight and saying, 'I wonder what that is?' You can't get far enough back to really see what you're seeing."

Goldfinger's underwater adventures since then have been more illuminating. Picking up where Atwater's landlocked history of Cascadia quakes left off, his exploration of marine geology has extended the record of the region's tumultuous past back almost ten thousand years ago. The result is the longest earthquake record for any subduction zone.

Cascadia may look dull through a submarine porthole, but Goldfinger discovered it has probably unleashed quakes even more powerful than magnitude 9. In ocean sediments he found hints that quakes may come in clusters. And he's also unearthed evidence that some parts of the subduction zone snap much more frequently than Atwater found—every 250 years or so. If Goldfinger is right, the odds are higher than one in three that a great quake will hit within the next fifty years.

One of the few things Goldfinger and Atwater have in common is that they both work with mud. Professionally, the two men are often each other's biggest critics, and their approaches could hardly be more different. Atwater drives a beater and paddles a patched canoe. Goldfinger practices a Lamborghini brand of science. A single *Alvin* dive costs $70,000. Those are rare, but he routinely mounts months-long research cruises with price tags of $1.5 million or more. That's the kind of muscle it takes to wrench secrets from the seafloor.

It was almost by accident that Goldfinger discovered the ocean bottom can record earthquakes with as much—or more—sensitivity than Atwater's marshes. The mechanism was so simple he found it laughable at first: big earthquakes can shake loose landslides underwater just as on land. "I thought, no way would that work," he recalled. In fact, he mounted his first oceangoing expedition in 1999 to prove that it wouldn't.

The seafloor is such a messy place that Goldfinger assumed it would be impossible to sort out earthquake-triggered landslides from slides and slumps caused by gravity or the churning of storms. He didn't doubt the power of earthquakes to shake things up underwater. That was established in November 1929, when a magnitude 7.2 earthquake struck near Newfoundland's Grand Banks. Damage from the quake itself was minor. But over the next several hours, a dozen of the trans-Atlantic cables that tethered North America to Europe blinked out one by one. When repair crews fished them up from the seafloor, they found the wire bundles gnawed to bits, as if by giant crabs.

Scientists studied the cable company's records and the underwater topography and concluded the culprit was a turbidity current, a supercharged landslide where sediment and water form a slurry that barrels down the continental slope with more force than an avalanche. At speeds up to 40 mph, the churning mass traveled 450 miles—more than the distance from New York to North Carolina—and tore through every cable in its path.

It took almost seven decades for researchers to make the connection between Cascadia and what happened off Newfoundland, but science wasn't standing still all that time. In the 1960s a small group at Oregon State University (OSU) started pulling up cores from the seafloor, not realizing the haul included the first hard evidence of giant quakes off the Pacific Northwest.

"People ask, 'How could you not have understood?'" said Gary Griggs, who was part of the OSU team. "You've got to transport yourself back to 1965. There was no plate tectonics. There was no Cascadia Subduction Zone. We were just flying by the seat of our pants."

Griggs was twenty-one that year when he landed a graduate slot at OSU. A surfer from Southern California, Griggs figured the fledgling field of marine geology would let him earn a living while hanging out near the beach. His arrival in Corvallis was perfectly timed to catch a wave of exploration fueled by the Cold War obsession with submarines. The Northwest seafloor was still largely unknown, and an OSU ocean-ographer got federal funding for some of the first expeditions. Griggs started out processing mud cores extracted from the ocean bottom during previous trips then collected his own during several cruises.

"It was exciting being out there, bringing up the cores and coming back to the lab to open them up," recalled Griggs, now director of the UC Santa Cruz Institute of Marine Sciences. "It was like going through a history book that nobody had ever seen before." Deep-sea coring was a young science. Pulling up a single thirty-foot tube of mud took more than half a day, and bad luck or poor technique could scramble the contents. In the lab Griggs used a circular saw to slice the cores into ten-foot lengths and a guitar string to split them down the middle. A pattern jumped out almost immediately. Layers of ordinary gray clay were interspersed with jumbled-looking olive green bands that Griggs recognized as the signature of underwater landslides. In some cores he counted as many as twenty-one of these green layers.

With multiple cores he could trace the paths the landslides fol-lowed across the seafloor and estimate their size, which was stag-gering. Some were taller than a thirty-story building as they hurtled down submarine canyons. Griggs calculated that an average turbidity current swept up enough sediment and sand to bury Seattle under a layer seven feet thick. The slurries took two days to roll down the channels and spill out on the seafloor a thousand miles from their source. "That's an enormous event."

The landslide layers, also called turbidites, seemed oddly uniform: they were about the same thickness and evenly spaced. Luckily for

Griggs each of his cores also contained a natural clock that provided a time reference—and posed a puzzle.

About 7,700 years ago, a volcano called Mount Mazama in southern Oregon exploded, creating what is now Crater Lake National Park. Ash flew as far as Nebraska. In almost all of Griggs's cores, those distinctive ash particles first showed up in the thirteenth green layer from the top, which meant the thirteenth landslide must have occurred roughly seven thousand years ago. Griggs couldn't figure out why the layers were so consistent from place to place, but he realized he could use the time window to calculate a rough recurrence interval. Something seemed to be kicking off the massive slides every five hundred years or so. But what? Griggs could think of only two options: storms or earthquakes. The latter seemed almost too outrageous to mention. Griggs noted the possibility in his thesis, then moved on. The report sat on the shelf for nearly twenty years.

It was show-and-tell day on the RV *Melville* in 1999, and Goldfinger was laying out cores in the ship's main lab. It's a tradition on research cruises for the scientists to host a briefing for the crew members who keep the ship running but might not know much about the research itself. The afternoon's presentation would also be the first chance for Goldfinger and fellow cruise leader Hans Nelson to see all their cores side by side.

The scientists had been at sea for several weeks, but they hadn't had time to reflect on their findings. Seagoing research trips are mostly a blur of work orchestrated to wring the maximum amount of data from every moment of vessel time. "It's like being on a factory ship," Goldfinger explained. This factory's mission was to extract and process mud cores.

It had been thirty years since Griggs did his work, but the coring process wasn't much changed. Technicians slowly lowered a steel tube topped with a three-ton lead weight until it hung suspended about sixty feet above the seafloor. With the pull of a lever, the apparatus was allowed to free-fall. The lead weight propelled the tube into the mud like a giant lawn dart. The science team worked around the clock

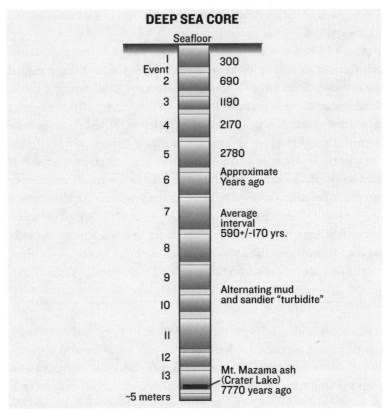

DEEP SEA CORE

Seafloor

Event		Approximate Years ago
1		300
2		690
3		1190
4		2170
5		2780
6		Approximate Years ago
7		Average interval 590+/-170 yrs.
8		
9		
10		Alternating mud and sandier "turbidite"
11		
12		
13		Mt. Mazama ash (Crater Lake) 7770 years ago
~5 meters		

A diagram of a core extracted from the seafloor off the Pacific Northwest shows a history of Cascadia earthquakes recorded in thick, sandy layers formed by quake-triggered landslides, or turbidites, and separated by thin bands of sediment. The thirteenth layer contains ash from the eruption that formed Crater Lake about 7,700 years ago.

in twelve-hour shifts, pulling up two cores a day when nothing went wrong. As soon as a core was fished from the water, scientists and grad students manned their posts on an assembly line. First they ran the four-inch-wide core through a multisensor scanner to measure the density and magnetic properties of the mud. Next, they sliced the core down the middle and chopped it into four-foot sections. The final step was the most time-consuming. Millimeter by millimeter the scientists diagrammed, described, and measured every layer of sand, silt, pebbles, and clay.

"You basically walk off the boat with a complete set of data," Goldfinger said. Today he sails with a crew of forty. But the 1999 cruise was his first time in charge, and he had been able to lure only about a dozen students. Everyone was frazzled. "You'd work sixteen hours, then fall into bed with only a vague idea of what happened that day," Goldfinger recalled.

Still, he couldn't shake his amazement that the National Science Foundation had decided to gamble on a very junior professor. He had swung for the bleachers in his grant application, requesting thirty days of ship time and enough money to bring back fifty cores. The agency said yes. He and Nelson planned to sample sediment from the entire length of Cascadia, a much bigger area than anyone had tackled before. They were confident they could put the lie to claims being made by a geologist named John Adams.

Adams was one of the first researchers to reexamine road surveys and report that the Northwest coast seemed to be tilting ominously. A few years later, the Canadian government scientist had decided to take another look at Griggs's cores in the light of modern plate tectonics. Why, he asked, would cores collected near the California-Oregon border show the same sequence of thirteen landslides as cores collected off the Washington coast? Storms couldn't explain it because they don't churn up such a big area. Adams concluded that giant earthquakes were the only forces capable of shaking lose simultaneous slides along such a long stretch of coast.

Goldfinger didn't buy it. He and Nelson suspected Adams of cherry-picking cores with thirteen layers to support his argument. They were confident samples from a wider area would blow Adams out of the water.

But on show-and-tell day, as the two scientists surveyed the twenty-five cores they'd collected so far on the *Melville*, they started feeling queasy. Most of the cores looked like mirror images of each other, with the same number of layers. "We could see where the Mazama ash was, and we could count to thirteen," Goldfinger recalled. "Our whole hypothesis was going down the tubes."

Goldfinger delivered his presentation to the crew then stumbled off to bed, feeling like an idiot. But his funk didn't last long. There was nothing to do but press on and follow the data where it led. Goldfinger was more experienced at shaking off mistakes than most beginning scientists. It was a lesson he had learned building boats for eight years after college. He would fabricate railings, metal plates for rigging or engine mounts, and inevitably have to do it all over again. Nothing on a boat ever fits the first time, he explained. "It's the same in science. Every idea you think is great—the next day it might turn out to be nonsense."

That willingness to change gears is a hallmark of Goldfinger's personality. He was nine years old when he set out to become the first sailor in his family, inspired by a California teenager's round-the-world voyage. He agreed to paint the family home in Palo Alto if his dad would front him $75 to buy a secondhand Sunfish sailboat.

Goldfinger's father was a radio engineer for the Apollo missions, and the son dreamed of being an astronaut. He reconsidered when he found out fighter pilot training was a prerequisite. The Vietnam War was raging, and Goldfinger couldn't stomach the idea of shooting at people. Geology captured his attention in high school, thanks to a teacher who ran field trips in his spare time. "The biology students were picking apart frogs, but the geology students were loading camping gear into trucks," Goldfinger recalled. "I said, 'I'm going with them.'"

Having a good time ranks high on Goldfinger's list. He wasn't ready to be what he called a "nose-to-the-grindstone working unit" when he graduated from Humboldt State University in Northern California. So he took the boat-building job, the most appealing aspect of which was delivering yachts around the Pacific for rich people. It was only the prospect of even sweeter boondoggles that lured him back to science.

On a run to Fiji Goldfinger met a geologist with the best gig on the planet: surveying island beaches for minerals. "I said, 'That's the kind of job I want.'" The irony of winding up in the soggy Northwest still makes him wince. But with his mediocre grades and long hiatus from school, Goldfinger barely made the cut for Oregon State's graduate program. Bob Yeats, then the chairman of the Geology Department, sensed promise. "There was just something about the guy," Yeats recalled. "He marches to his own drummer." Yeats still considers it one of his luckiest calls. "I've learned so much more from him than he ever learned from me."

Like Yeats, Goldfinger was an early skeptic about Cascadia's threat. His views put him at odds with Atwater, and the two scientists have been sparring for much of their professional careers.

During his dissertation defense, Goldfinger ran down a Letterman-style list of the top ten reasons the subduction zone couldn't produce a magnitude 9 quake. At scientific meetings Goldfinger was the guy who kept questioning Atwater's logic while other researchers rolled their eyes. But Atwater's case kept getting stronger and stronger. "And I didn't have any evidence," Goldfinger recalled cheerfully. "That settled it."

Goldfinger's 1999 cruise turned him into a true believer. After he and Nelson got back to the lab at OSU they reviewed all their cores and agreed that simultaneous landslides were the best explanation for the layers they saw. "Big earthquakes were the only thing that could cause that."

Since 1999 Goldfinger has mounted another four coring cruises. He has also led or participated in thirty-five other seagoing research trips. But the work has landed him at the receiving end of skepticism. Atwater and others argue that he's reading too much into the mud. The debate is more than academic, particularly for the millions of people who live along the coasts of Southern Oregon and Northern California. Goldfinger's evidence suggests that stretch of the subduction zone gets shaken nearly twice as often as the northern stretch.

Rain was sheeting as Goldfinger ducked into his lab on the OSU campus on a fall morning in 2011. When the Northwest weather turns foul, he's always on the lookout for scientific conferences in warm places. One winter he slipped off to Hawaii in his sailboat, answering work e-mails as if he were down the hall. Goldfinger may be a working unit these days, but his nose isn't always to the grindstone.

Shaking the water off his jacket, he popped open the door of a walk-in cooler the size of a classroom. Racks that reached almost to the ceiling cradled hundreds of cores he and other OSU scientists collected over the years. Griggs's originals were there, though too shriveled to be of much use. Nestled in white plastic casings, the cores were about four inches wide and split down the middle like hot dog buns. Goldfinger slid out one of the tubes and carried it into the adjoining lab.

Under the fluorescent lights, the four-foot-long half cylinder of mud was as impressive as, well, mud. "It doesn't really look like much, does it?" Goldfinger said. He pointed to a layer at the top of the core. "That's the 1700 quake." The band of sediment was about eight inches thick and a little darker than the rest of the mud. "From a magnitude 9 quake, you'd expect something as tall as a house with boulders at the bottom, but that's not what you see."

The segment of core held three more dark layers, each representing ancient earthquakes. Goldfinger dates the layers by carbon 14 analysis of the shells of tiny marine creatures. "It's like a telescope looking backward," he said.

It took him a long time to learn how to interpret the messages in the muddy bands. After he did he realized that the turbidite layers revealed something the record on land only hinted at: not all Cascadia's quakes were created equal. "It's not rocket science, but we think a bigger earthquake makes a bigger turbidite," Goldfinger said, fetching another tube from the cold room. He pointed out a layer nearly a foot and a half thick. In cores from the tip of Vancouver Island to Northern California, that layer—number 11 in the sequence—is always huge. "It's our biggest event," Goldfinger said.

What might have been the Godzilla of Cascadia megaquakes struck about 6,000 years ago. Goldfinger estimated its size at magnitude 9.1. That may not sound much bigger than a magnitude 9, but a tenth of a point increase on the logarithmic scale represents more than a 40 percent increase in energy. Goldfinger's cores also hold evidence of some quakes that appear to be smaller than magnitude 9, and at least two others that were clearly bigger. "What we're seeing is that the 1700 event was only average, which is not good news."

Geologists accustomed to working on land were initially skeptical of the seafloor evidence. But it takes only a glance at the underwater topography off the Northwest coast to grasp the basics,

Goldfinger explained, flipping open his laptop and punching up a three-dimensional view.

From the water's edge, the continental shelf extends out in a gently sloping plain wider than the Oklahoma panhandle. About fifty miles offshore, the ground falls off steeply in a rumpled mass of canyons whose feet stand at the edge of the abyssal plain. These are the cliffs, some nearly ten thousand feet high, that Goldfinger surveyed during his *Alvin* dive. Drain the water and the view would be dizzying to a person standing on the ocean floor gazing up at the palisade. "It would make most of the Cascades look puny," Goldfinger said.

Currents continually sweep sediment from the Columbia and other rivers to the edge of the continental shelf. During the quiet centuries between quakes, this mass of terrestrial detritus piles up along the canyon heads like cornices of snow. When the subduction zone rips and the ground convulses, the piles collapse.

The sand and pebbles funnel down canyons with names like Rogue, Trinidad, and Quinault, gathering speed and force until they reach the stage turbidite experts call "ignition." That's when the slides transform into something akin to the pyroclastic flows that sweep down volcanoes and obliterate everything in their paths. "You've got this sandy, silty mass riding on a water cushion, and it can go for hundreds of kilometers," Goldfinger said.

The biggest Cascadia landslides spill out on the abyssal plain. That's where Goldfinger found the best earthquake record, unmuddled by smaller, storm-triggered slides closer to land. By 2012 he and his team had evidence of nineteen quakes that ruptured the entire Cascadia margin in the past 10,000 years. There's not much controversy about those anymore. The layers turn up consistently along the coast, and their dates match up with land-based records.

But Goldfinger also reports another twenty-three thinner layers in cores collected off Southern Oregon and Northern California. Some of the wisps are so faint even he didn't notice them at first. But when he looked closer with CT scans and instruments that measure magnetic properties, the bands jumped out. Goldfinger is convinced they represent smaller quakes—maybe magnitude 8—that rip only the southern half of the subduction zone and strike in between the

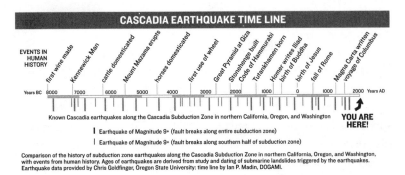

CASCADIA EARTHQUAKE TIME LINE

EVENTS IN HUMAN HISTORY

first wine made, Kennewick Man, cattle domesticated, Mount Mazama erupts, horses domesticated, first use of wheel, Great Pyramid at Giza, Stonehenge built, Code of Hammurabi, Tutankhamen born, Homer writes Iliad, birth of Buddha, birth of Jesus, fall of Rome, Magna Carta written, voyage of Columbus

Years BC 8000 | 7000 | 6000 | 5000 | 4000 | 3000 | 2000 | 1000 | 0 | 1000 | 2000 Years AD

Known Cascadia earthquakes along the Cascadia Subduction Zone in northern California, Oregon, and Washington **YOU ARE HERE!**

I Earthquake of Magnitude 9+ (fault breaks along entire subduction zone)

I Earthquake of Magnitude 9+ (fault breaks along southern half of subduction zone)

Comparison of the history of subduction zone earthquakes along the Cascadia Subduction Zone in northern California, Oregon, and Washington, with events from human history. Ages of earthquakes are derived from study and dating of submarine landslides triggered by the earthquakes. Earthquake data provided by Chris Goldfinger, Oregon State University; time line by Ian P. Madin, DOGAMI.

Seafloor cores show evidence of nineteen full rip 9 Cascadia quakes in the past 10,000 years, and twenty-three smaller quakes on the southern portion of the subduction zone (twenty-two shown in this diagram).

full-rip 9 monsters. That would translate into a major quake every 250 years on average.

It's not unusual for subduction zones to rupture in segments. Indonesia's killer quake and tsunami in 2004 unzipped only the northern end of the Sumatran subduction zone. A quake that followed three months later broke an adjacent segment. But many scientists, including Atwater, question Goldfinger's interpretation. It's possible some of the thin layers were from storm-triggered landslides, or slides that simply sloughed off underwater slopes.

Geologists working in coastal lakes in Oregon found corroborating evidence for some of Goldfinger's smaller quakes in the form of sand layers flung inland by tsunamis at roughly the same time. The search is on for more. In 2011 Goldfinger and his students started pulling cores from lakes in Oregon's Coast Range. They found a record there of landslides that closely mirrors the marine layers.

If the southern part of the subduction zone has been hammered as frequently as Goldfinger believes, it changes the risk equation for the entire region. A magnitude 8 quake anywhere on the coast will have far-reaching effects. Based on the standard view that Cascadia uncorks every five hundred years on average, there's a 10 to 15 percent chance the region will get clobbered in the next five decades. Goldfinger's interpretation raises the odds to 37 percent.

"You say 10 or 15 percent, and to most people that's kind of like the chance of getting hit by an asteroid," Goldfinger said. "But when you say 37 percent, that starts to sound like a real number."

———————————————————~ww/wwwww~———————————————————

The *Pacific Storm* was "mowing the lawn," motoring back and forth off the central Oregon coast while instruments scanned the ocean bottom. It was August 2011, at the tail end of a ten-week cruise. One of the objectives was to refine the seafloor maps that are so crucial to Goldfinger's work.

A geologist without a topo map is like a cell biologist without a microscope. Finding the right place to dig and core, to sample and scan, means the difference between discovery and a pile of dirt. As if underwater geology weren't hard enough, the field was long hampered by military secrecy. Goldfinger's group has devoted almost as much time to mapping as it has to coring. That's why he was onboard the *Pacific Storm*, an eighty-four-foot converted crabber. The federal government had recently lifted some of the last restrictions on the Northwest coast, and Goldfinger was eager to complete as many surveys as possible before the Navy had a change of heart.

But he was in a foul mood that morning after waking to the news that a key instrument was on the fritz. Goldfinger huddled in the deckhouse with two students, trying to troubleshoot the problem. It took four hours of fiddling before the subsurface profiler was back in action, chirping like a demented robin. The high-pitched pulses penetrated the seafloor and bounced back, revealing the layers below. A multibeam sonar simultaneously scanned the bottom, recording every bump and ridge.

Such sophisticated instruments used to be off-limits for civilians, Goldfinger said, settling into a plastic chair on the *Pacific Storm*'s stern. The boat was passing Yaquina Head near the town of Newport. Nuclear submarines still travel the coast regularly, coming and going from a base on Puget Sound and hiding in the same underwater canyons Goldfinger studies. Especially during the Cold War, the Navy didn't want the Soviets to know the detailed topography. "It's all very *Hunt for Red October*," Goldfinger said.

Multibeam sonar, developed in the 1980s, revolutionized underwater mapping with its ability to scan wide swaths of the seafloor. But the Navy kept a tight lid on the technology for years. Goldfinger's graduate school adviser held a security clearance and was allowed to peek at some of the classified maps. But he couldn't share the information. Even after the new sonar was commercialized, the Navy—which owns many university research vessels—leaned on scientists not to publish their results. "They held a kind of government club over everyone's heads."

It was frustrating because sketchy maps hampered the science. The researchers needed to zero in on the best spots to core and know which areas to avoid. Goldfinger pushed the boundaries, winding up in his dean's office once with a furious Navy oceanographer on the phone.

Portions of Washington's underwater landscape stayed secret long after Oregon's was declassified. Over the years, Goldfinger has been working to fill in the remaining gaps in the bathymetry, as he was doing on the *Pacific Storm*. "It's taken us nearly two decades to get the level of detail we have now."

As fog enveloped the boat, Goldfinger ducked back into the cramped laboratory packed with gear and lined with plywood tables. The ship's engineer was cracking jokes with the students, showing off his photo gallery of seasick passengers doubled over the railing. He punched the buttons on his Puke Master key ring to add for a soundtrack of retching sounds.

Goldfinger shrugged and paraphrased the eighteenth-century essayist Samuel Johnson: "Going to sea is like being in prison, with the added possibility of drowning." Bathymetry cruises, with their back-and-forth trajectories, are particularly monotonous. Goldfinger used the downtime to prepare for an upcoming conference.

Among his newest results are hints that Cascadia quakes come in clusters. On his laptop he pulled up a graph of the nineteen full-rip 9 quakes from the last ten thousand years. The quakes appear to clump together in knots of three to five, separated by a few hundred years. In between the clusters, all is quiet for about a thousand years. On the graph, the 1700 quake looks like the latest in a cluster of five.

Some scientists dismiss the patterns as nothing more than a statistical illusion. Goldfinger isn't sure, but thinks there's a possibility the clusters represent a real phenomenon. But the information isn't very useful yet. Does the pattern mean the next magnitude 9 megaquake is a thousand years away? Or could a sequence of five average-sized quakes in a row indicate the fault is overdue for a magnitude 9-plus monster? Even with a ten-thousand-year record, there's no way to tell. "We're still at the blind-man-feeling-the-elephant's-butt stage of plate tectonics," Goldfinger said. "Nobody likes to think of it that way, but it's true."

The groping extends to the question of whether the world experiences periodic flurries of megaquakes—and whether one of those periods started with the 2004 Sumatra disaster. Before Sumatra, seven of the ten biggest quakes on record struck between 1950 and 1965. The lineup included Chile's magnitude 9.5 record-holder and the 1964 Alaska megaquake and tsunami. The next four decades were strangely quiet, without a single quake of magnitude 8.5 or greater. Since 2004, there have been five, including an 8.8 in Chile and Japan's cataclysmic 2011 quake and tsunami. "Everybody has noticed there's something going on," Goldfinger said.

Two USGS scientists analyzed the very biggest quakes and concluded there was only a 2 percent chance the clustering was random. "It's very statistically significant," lead author Charles Bufe said at a 2011 meeting of the Seismological Society of America. "We think we're in an increased hazard situation for these very large earthquakes." Bufe calculated a 63 percent chance another megaquake will strike by 2017, though he can't say where.

But the majority of scientists see no connection between giant quakes. Even coin tosses can produce a string of consecutive heads. Several other statistical analyses attribute the apparent clumps to chance and a short historic record. Another reason most scientists are skeptical is that they can't explain how one megaquake could trigger another on the opposite side of the globe.

It's well-known that earthquakes can beget other earthquakes. That's what explains aftershocks. It makes intuitive sense that those effects are largely localized. When a fault ruptures it's like a cog slipping, and the motion will ricochet through the adjacent geologic machinery. But geologists were caught off guard in 1992, when an earthquake in the Mojave Desert was followed almost immediately by more than a dozen quakes as far away as Wyoming. How could triggering occur over such long distances?

There's still no good answer, even though the list of examples is growing. One of the most dramatic was a 2002 quake in Alaska that set off rumbles more than two thousand miles away in Yellowstone National Park. "The Earth is like a puzzle," Goldfinger said. "Any time one piece moves, it interacts with the other pieces."

Giant earthquakes jolt the Earth so hard its axis shifts slightly. Vibrations sweep over the entire planet and cause it to ring like a bell. The thrusting of plates sends slow waves through the taffylike mantle that underlies the planet's crust. "Just because geologists haven't identified a mechanism that links megaquakes, that doesn't rule it out," Goldfinger said. Geologists ridiculed Alfred Wegner's theory of continental drift because there was no way at the time to explain how continents could move. "Almost everything we discover in nature, we make the observation first and the explanation comes later," Goldfinger said. "It's crazy to say something doesn't exist because we can't explain it."

There was exasperation in his voice. Goldfinger was visiting Japan's Tohoku University on March 11, 2011, and the experience made an activist of him. Watching the world's most prepared nation brought to its knees by a giant earthquake and tsunami, he couldn't help but imagine what's in store for the Pacific Northwest.

Most scientists prefer to lay out their data and let the rest of society decide whether—or how—to act on the information. They couch their public statements in careful terms. Goldfinger doesn't do that anymore: "This is not a good time to be wishy-washy," he said. He's been pushing the USGS to boost the earthquake hazard rating in Oregon and Northern California, where his research suggests more frequent quakes. He's been urging parents to agitate for safer schools.

"Japan really changed my sense of urgency about getting things done here. We need to stop talking about this stuff and take action."

CHAPTER 5:

SEATTLE'S FAULT

REVELATIONS ABOUT THE CASCADIA SUBDUCTION ZONE unnerved North-westerners who grew up believing the worst thing that could happen to them, seismically speaking, was a midsize rattle like the ones that struck in 1949 and 1965. It took some getting used to, this notion that Washington, Oregon, and British Columbia could be slammed by the world's most powerful quakes and tsunamis.

But even before the new reality sank in, geologists were about to ratchet up the region's anxiety level again. A blitz of scientific sleuthing in the early 1990s found that the region is vulnerable to a third type of quake which, for the Northwest's biggest city, could be the most destructive of all.

The story of what is now called the Seattle Fault began in the 1960s with a refugee from behind the Iron Curtain and a bunch of high school students. Decades later, scientists followed a trail of clues from the Olympic Mountains to a sewage plant on Puget Sound and an eerie, underwater forest in Lake Washington. A local business-man who helped with the research wound up in jail. Then in 1995, the once-obscure fault offered a tiny taste of what's to come with a magnitude 5 earthquake that shook the ground from Oregon to the Canadian border.

Through all the saga's twists and turns, Zdenko Frankenburger Daneš watched with a father's interest. The fault was his baby, after all. But being the first to uncover evidence of its existence was for Daneš just the latest chapter in a life filled with adventure. As a young man during World War II he sabotaged telephone lines and derailed trains to foil Nazi occupiers in his native Czechoslovakia. When the Soviets took control of the country, they jailed and executed several of Daneš's professors and fellow students at the University of Prague. He escaped to West Germany on a bicycle, careening down a mountain path with border guards close on his heels. Daneš immigrated to America and worked for the oil industry. By 1964 he was teaching physics at the University of Puget Sound (UPS) in Tacoma.

That summer Daneš volunteered for a program to give promising high school students a taste of scientific research. He had recently convinced university administrators to spend $3,600—enough to buy a new Chevy—on a secondhand instrument called a gravity meter. Daneš was eager to put the costly gadget to work.

Shaped like an oversized thermos, the meter contained a weight suspended at the end of a spring. It was designed to detect minuscule variations in gravity's tug at different locations. Since dense rocks like basalt exert a stronger pull than more porous rocks like sandstone, geologists were quick to seize on the technique to map formations below the surface. Daneš suspected that something interesting lay beneath the spectacular topography of his new home. "The landscape just called out for it," he recalled. So the pipe-smoking professor and nine teenage boys embarked on the first gravity survey of the Puget Sound region.

UPS alumni remember Daneš as a terrific teacher and a terrifying presence in the lecture hall. He always wore suits and never addressed students by their first names. But that summer Daneš let his crew-cut hair down. "He piled us into his old car, and he would drive around with the USGS quadrangle map on the steering wheel," recalled Wayne Gilham. Now a Tacoma yacht broker, Gilham was sixteen that summer and a self-described science nerd.

The group meandered back roads and hiked to hilltops in search of survey markers where they would set up the gravity meter—very carefully. "Dr. Daneš let us know how expensive it was," Gilham said. The teenager hammered together a plywood runabout and used it to motor around Puget Sound with the other boys, taking readings along the shore. Back at the UPS campus, the students crunched the numbers by hand and slide rule.

In 2011, at the age of ninety-one, Daneš amazement over what he and the teenagers found hadn't dimmed. "My God. It was exciting," he said. "We saw it almost immediately."

"It" was an abrupt change in gravity measurements along a line that slices from Hood Canal through south Seattle. North of the line are lighter, sedimentary rocks. To the south, the rocks are dense and heavy. A 150-pound person loses about two-tenths of an ounce traveling north from Sea-Tac Airport to the University of Washington because of the difference in gravity pull.

The gravity gradient is one of the sharpest ever detected in the United States. To Daneš it could mean only one thing: a geologic fault. Motion on the fault—essentially past earthquakes—would explain the dramatic offset in rock layers beneath much of Washington's urban core.

Daneš wrote up the results, crediting all the teens as coauthors. The *Journal of Geophysical Research* published the paper on November 15, 1965. Gilham still keeps the volume in his bookshelf, as does Daneš, who went on to collect more than eleven thousand gravity measurements across the state. But the findings didn't stir up much interest at the time. The loudest reaction came from real estate agents. Any talk of earthquakes was bad for property values, and they gave the professor an earful for scaremongering.

The Realtors were right to be worried. As in the housing market, location is key to earthquake damage. The quakes that hit Puget Sound in 2001, 1965, and 1949 originated more than thirty miles underground, deep inside the subducting Juan de Fuca Plate. The intervening miles of rock act as a buffer to dampen shaking at the surface.

There's no shock absorber when a quake strikes right under your feet. What Daneš was suggesting was a fault that passed a few scant miles below the homes and high-rises of Seattle. A magnitude 6.8 quake on such a shallow fault could rock parts of the city nearly four times as hard as the 2001 Nisqually quake of the same size. California's 1994 Northridge quake, the costliest in U.S. history, came from a shallow fault. So did Haiti's devastating 2010 quake and the one in Kobe that killed nearly six thousand people and leveled one of Japan's busiest ports in 1995.

Daneš's report was tantalizing, but far from conclusive. The fault was probably real, but was it dangerous? Or had it stopped moving long before mammoths roamed the Northwest? Oil companies were intrigued enough to check it out, because faults can create pockets where petroleum collects. Mobil, Chevron, and others sailed Puget Sound in the early 1970s surveying the seafloor. But the companies kept the data to themselves. Over the next decade, USGS mappers noted several features that added to the evidence for the fault's existence. But it wasn't until the late 1980s that Robert Bucknam, of the USGS's Denver office, decided to follow Daneš's footsteps in a serious way.

Even as he flew into Seattle, Bucknam could see it was going to be tough. The landscape wasn't like the Utah desert where he'd been working for the past several years. "There, you could see everything, almost as if the ground was stripped bare," he recalled. In Washington, the glaciers that covered the Puget lowlands as recently as sixteen thousand years ago scoured away most signs of past earthquakes. Lush vegetation hid the rest. Working in an urban area that was home to nearly three million people would also be a challenge.

Like Atwater on the Pacific coast, Bucknam focused on shorelines to see if they had dropped or had been shoved up in the past. One of his best leads was on Bainbridge Island, the low-slung land mass Seattleites see when they look west. The USGS mappers had found clam beds there sitting more than a dozen feet above the modern water level. Bucknam decided to explore the island for other signs that it had been jolted in the past.

He soon found what he was looking for at the island's southeastern tip. British Navy Captain George Vancouver dropped anchor there during his 1792 explorations, intrigued by the treeless bench that wrapped around the point and was so unlike the steep bluffs and closed-in forests that dominated most of Puget Sound's shores. He named the spot Restoration Point, in honor of England's return to monarchy after a fit of republicanism. A golf course now occupies much of the point, and some of the priciest homes north of Beverly Hills gaze out on Puget Sound from a gated community. But what Bucknam saw in the serene landscape made him suspect a history of violence.

The bench that caught Vancouver's eye is what geologists call a marine terrace: an ancient waterfront that rose out of the sea. On its surface Bucknam found beach gravel and fossil clams burrowed into the rock. The broad bench is backed by a cliff that once sat at the water's edge and still shows the marks of lapping waves. "It was quite clear it had been uplifted," Bucknam recalled. But landforms can rise for many reasons. He couldn't rule out the possibility that the point had simply rebounded when the immense weight of Ice Age glaciers melted away.

Tall and quiet, Bucknam worked methodically. He paced every square meter of the bench, looking for the type of erosion that would have eaten away at the sandstone if it had risen slowly over a period of centuries. He found none. The bench must have popped out of the water in a matter of moments. Bucknam measured the uplift at twenty-three feet.

The USGS scientist had found the first physical evidence that Daneš's fault was not only real but active. It had produced at least one quake, and a big one at that. A similar upheaval today would devastate the cities and suburbs that had sprung up across the region since Vancouver dropped anchor two centuries ago. But how widespread were the quake's effects? And when did it hit?

From where Bucknam was working on the tip of Restoration Point, he could look across Puget Sound to Alki Point in the West Seattle neighborhood. It was on Alki that the city's first white settlers established their foothold. Bucknam saw that Alki was also ringed by a broad, flat bench. For centuries native people found a dry perch there above the tides, a feature that must have been attractive to the white pioneers, too.

Bucknam shifted his focus from Bainbridge Island to the mainland. His assistant for much of the work was Brian Sherrod, a stocky graduate student from Virginia who would eventually land a job with the

USGS and delve even more deeply into the Seattle Fault's past than his mentor. More than a decade after he and Bucknam first studied the area, Alki remains Sherrod's favorite place to bring visitors and students who want to see what the Seattle Fault is capable of. "To me, Alki really brings it home," Sherrod said. "It's right in the middle of the city."

On a spring morning in 2012, after a line of squalls blew through, Sherrod drove past Tully's, Pegasus Pizza, and the condo complexes on Alki Beach that boast the city's best views of the Seattle skyline. He rounded the point, with its century-old lighthouse, and turned onto Beach Drive Southwest.

The road skirts the beach for miles. It's such an urban scene—sidewalks, streetlights, houses, and apartments—that it's hard to read anything menacing into the fact that the pavement rests atop a bench several feet higher than the beach. The bench is crowded with homes and apartment buildings, stacked four deep at its widest spots. Sherrod pulled his truck to the side of the road and got out. "We're basically standing on the old beach," he explained. Just as at Restoration Point, he and Bucknam found that Alki Point had been lifted abruptly in the past.

Well back from the road, Sherrod pointed out a steep cliff cloaked in blackberry and ivy and topped with houses. On a rainy Saturday nearly ten years before, he and Bucknam hopped the fence of an adjacent city pump station and dug holes at the bottom of the cliff. What they found a full city block from the waterline was beach gravel— proof that the cliff once stood at the water's edge. The earthquake lifted the land here more than twenty feet. "Just picture it," Sherrod said, looking around at the densely-packed neighborhood.

When Sherrod and Bucknam cast a wider net for the earthquake's footprint, they found evidence of uplift twenty miles east on Hood Canal and nearly fifty miles south near Olympia. The fault geometry really clicked for Bucknam when he poked around in a small marsh back where he started, on Bainbridge Island. The bog was only three miles from Restoration Point, but it lay on the other side of the gravity line Daneš and his students had mapped across Puget Sound.

Bucknam discovered that the marsh hadn't been lifted at all. In fact, it had dropped slightly.

The pieces fell into place. When the Seattle Fault slipped, shorelines to the south, including Restoration Point and Alki, were raised. Shorelines and marshes to the north either stayed put or dropped. Based on the size of the uplift he measured around Puget Sound, Bucknam figured the Seattle Fault quake was at least magnitude 7, and quite possibly bigger.

He was less successful pinning down a date. A botanist and diatom expert carbon-dated marine fossils and organic material from the sunken bog on Bainbridge Island. But the best they could say was that the quake struck sometime between 500 and 1,700 years ago.

News of Bucknam's early findings spread quickly in the late 1980s through a community of scientists already energized by the Cascadia discoveries. Through coincidence, serendipity, and design, more than a dozen researchers joined forces in a kind of scientific SWAT team to figure out when the quake hit and flesh out its impact. Their findings showed that the most recent spasm on the Seattle Fault did a lot more than lift beaches. It also sent old-growth forests plunging into a lake, set off avalanches of rock that plugged valley bottoms, and hurled a tsunami across the shores of Puget Sound. Collectively, the threads of evidence added up to one of the most comprehensive cases ever made to prove an ancient earthquake.

Brian Atwater got drawn onto the SWAT team in 1991. He was mostly working on the Pacific Coast, but heard about a billion-dollar construction project under way on Puget Sound. New federal rules were forcing Seattle to upgrade its aging sewage-treatment plant at West Point, near the city's Magnolia neighborhood. Engineers were installing a new outfall pipe big enough to drive a Humvee through. The trench they dug would open a once-in-a-lifetime window into the geologic past.

Atwater convinced project managers to call him when crews finished excavating each new section of trench. He would then rush down to examine the soil layers before pipe was laid and the hole filled in.

The angled walls of the trench loomed three stories above Atwater's head, and held thousands of years of history. The site's long occupation by Native Americans was recorded in a purple midden of mussel shells, animal bone, and fire-blackened rock. Layers of mud marked ancient landslides that had sloughed off the surrounding cliffs and spread across the salt marsh. The wetlands were trampled during World War II, when the army used the area to practice amphibious landings. In the 1960s the marsh was buried under ten feet of sand for construction of the original treatment plant.

Between the peak of the native occupation and the modern era, Atwater discovered a layer unlike all the others. It was a sheet of sand several inches thick, like those he found in the banks of the Niawiakum River. A huge wave had washed over West Point at the same time the land dropped by several feet. Entombed in the sand were bulrush stems, still standing upright. He unearthed barnacle-encrusted sticks so well preserved they snapped in two with an audible *crack*. "It was just spectacular," Atwater recalled. A graduate student working with him found a similar buried sand sheet in a pasture at the tip of Whidbey Island, twenty miles north of Seattle.

Radiocarbon analysis at both sites yielded a date between 900 and 1,300 years ago. That was close enough to Bucknam's time frame to suggest more than coincidence. It also made sense that big waves would have rushed up the Sound. If a quake thrust beaches twenty feet in the air, it would have done the same to a big swath of Puget Sound's bottom. Just as in the ocean, displaced water can create a tsunami in inland waterways.

A team of geologists working in the Olympic Mountains reeled in radiocarbon dates in the same ballpark when they sampled snags in lakes likely formed when the earthquake shook loose avalanches of rock and dammed streams. The rising water killed the trees.

Another group extracted mud cores from the bottom of Lake Washington that showed a succession of underwater landslides. The biggest corresponded in time with the Puget Sound tsunami and the Olympic Mountain avalanches. In fact, so many radiocarbon dates were falling into the same time window that scientists joked they didn't even need to bother with the tests.

But the window was still too wide. As with Cascadia's most recent quake, drowned trees would prove to be the most precise chronometers.

People who live around Lake Washington have long known about the mysterious forests that rise from the lake bottom. The long-dead trunks don't poke up above the water, but they extend close enough to the surface to have snagged miles of fishing line and eaten countless anchors. When construction of the Ballard Locks lowered the lake level in 1916, several boats ran afoul of the trees. The U.S. Army Corps of Engineers used steel draglines to wrench nearly two hundred Douglas firs out of the navigation lanes. The largest was 9 feet in diameter. The longest measured 121.5 feet. Many were impossible to budge, so the engineers used dynamite to blast off their tops.

A diver who explored one of the forests in 1957 found himself "engulfed in a densely forested bottom" 90 feet down. Many trees were standing upright, apparently having ridden a landslide into the water. Using a crane, workers pulled up one intact fir for scientists to sample. Radiocarbon dating was in its infancy, but the results suggested the tree died between 800 and 1,400 years ago.

Growing up on Mercer Island, Pat Williams was fascinated by the submerged forests. They were marked on the charts he navigated by as he explored the lake in his skiff. Neighbors swapped stories about lost gear and theorized over what might lurk among the waterlogged trunks. "They were mythic," Williams said.

Even after he became a geologist, Williams never stopped wondering about those trees. Landslides big enough to sweep such huge tracts of forest into the lake would have dwarfed any slides that occurred since white settlers arrived. The charts from Williams's boyhood mapped out three submerged stands in Lake Washington. There's at least one in Lake Sammamish, to the east. He suspected they all got there because of earthquakes.

Williams decided to collect samples from the underwater forest off the southeastern tip of Mercer Island where he fished and swam as a boy. A giant divot in the shoreline marks the slide's origins. If the trees weren't rotten, Williams thought he might be able to date the slide and the earthquake that caused it.

Williams worked with Gordon Jacoby, a pioneer of dendrochronology and founder of the tree ring lab at Lamont-Doherty Earth Observatory, where samples from the Copalis ghost forest were analyzed. Jacoby was accustomed to extracting wood samples from tricky terrain, but neither man had worked under conditions so difficult and dangerous.

"It was a really creepy place," recalled Brendan Buckley, Jacoby's lab assistant in the summer of 1991. "The whole thing was quite the debacle." Buckley, Williams, and the team's other SCUBA divers had to descend nearly thirty feet just to reach the tops of the trees. The trunks vanished into the inky depths, their roots embedded in the mud one hundred feet down.

With only headlamps to penetrate the murk, the divers encountered a labyrinth of logs. Strands of algae wafted from the branches like the hair of drowned maidens. Snarls of fishing line threatened to entangle the divers. "It was pretty hard not to get snagged," Williams recalled. "We always carried a sharp knife to cut ourselves out of the mess."

Buckley tried using a hydraulic chain saw to carve up the trunks, but the billowing sawdust hampered visibility so much he feared he might slice into his own limbs or someone else's. "That spinning blade scared the hell out of us." The best method proved to be the simplest: a two-man bow saw, like the crosscut saws loggers called misery whips. The divers positioned themselves on either side of a tree trunk, hammered stakes into the wood to brace their feet, and slowly pulled the blade back and forth.

The work was so demanding they couldn't stay down more than twenty minutes at a time. Under pressure to finish in two weeks, they pushed the limits until they were loopy from nitrogen narcosis—or ran out of air. Yet for all their efforts, they got no decent samples.

The divers weren't equipped to work much deeper than sixty feet. But at that level, the bark and outer layers of the trees were rotted away. Such crummy wood would never yield a useful date. The scientists knew the root ends of the trees were intact, preserved in the airless muck on the lake floor. But the prize was out of their reach.

As they later testified in King County Superior Court, it seemed like a godsend when John Tortorelli turned up. A log salvager, Tortorelli was on the prowl for sunken trees he could sell to timber mills. He parked his barge nearby, and the scientists salivated at the sight of the crane and claw he used to pluck snags from the lake floor.

Williams jumped in his skiff and hailed the barge. He proposed a deal: The divers could help Tortorelli locate logs, if the salvager would let them cut slices off the bottoms. Friendly and charming, Tortorelli agreed.

The project was saved.

"We would have left with nothing if he hadn't been there," Buckley said. It never occurred to the researchers that Tortorelli was breaking the law. "Who would have the balls to do it right in the open like that if he wasn't legitimate?"

Long after the scientists were gone, state regulators raided Tortorelli's home and charged him with stealing $165,000 worth of trees. The researchers weren't implicated in the crime, though some were subpoenaed by the prosecution. Tortorelli, who maintained his operation was legal, was convicted of theft, profiteering, and trafficking in stolen property. He was sentenced to eight concurrent terms ranging from twelve to forty-three months.

But Tortorelli's tree sections allowed the scientists to say with confidence that the forests had slid into Lake Washington about 1,100 years ago—a time when Mayan culture was reaching its apex and the Byzantine Empire was battling for control of eastern Europe. The link between the underwater forests and the earthquake was cemented after backhoes at the West Point sewer plant unearthed a Douglas fir trunk carried ashore by the tsunami.

The scientists compared ring sequence bar codes and found that the tree from the sewer plant and the trees from Lake Washington all died in the same season of the same year, fellow victims of the Seattle Fault. The exact year remains unknown, but radiocarbon tests of the sewer plant log narrowed the window to three decades. The quake struck sometime between 900 and 930 AD.

The tsunami waves that raced through Puget Sound 1,100 years ago also drowned native settlements, including one at West Point. The layers exposed in Atwater's trench showed that many decades passed before the beach was inhabited again.

Ancient Native American stories from around Puget Sound warned of *a'yahos*, shape-shifting spirits that appeared sometimes as double-headed snakes, sometimes as monsters with the head of a deer and the hindquarters of a snake. The places where the spirits dwelled were perilous, the land torn and the trees twisted. Shamans described rushes of turbid water and ground shaking when the *a'yahos* stirred.

Ruth Ludwin, the UW seismologist who had studied earthquake and tsunami stories from Pacific coast tribes, joined with experts from Seattle-area tribes to compile several of the accounts. They found the spirit sites fell roughly along the route of the Seattle Fault. A'yahos lurked near Lake Washington's underwater forests. Their malevolent power was in evidence on Alki Point. Nearby, at what is now a ferry terminal, a large "spirit boulder" still marks the spot where native stories reported havoc caused by the shape-shifters. Geologic mapping revealed a good reason for those stories: That site and several others linked to a'yahos were buried by giant landslides in the past.

Five of the studies validating the Seattle Fault's menace were published simultaneously in the December 4, 1992, issue of *Science* magazine. A commentary dryly noted, "There has not yet been time to assess the hazard implications." But there was no question that a similar quake would be devastating today. The problem was, scientists had no idea how often the fault might rip or how big future quakes might be.

The urgency to learn more about the fault increased in 1995, with the Robinson Point earthquake. The magnitude 5 temblor struck just before 11:30 PM on January 28. Centered on Vashon Island, about midway between Seattle and Tacoma, it didn't do much damage. But when geologists analyzed its source, they realized it occurred on, or very close to, the Seattle Fault.

The USGS embarked on a series of field investigations that stretched over several years to uncover all they could about the fault's structure and scope. Research vessels cruised the length and width of Puget Sound towing twenty-ton arrays of air guns that fired off earsplitting blasts. The sound waves penetrated the seafloor and bounced back. Based on the same principle as prenatal ultrasound, the technology is able to look below the surface. On land, scientists dug two-hundred-foot shafts, poured in explosives, and set off charges along a transect from the Olympics to the Cascades. More than one thousand sensors tracked the way the shock waves ricocheted through the ground. The USGS even ponied up $50,000 to buy the data from oil company surveys in the 1970s.

Combined with old-fashioned observations of the type that inspired Professor Daneš's original surveys, the results revealed the Seattle Fault as a major force in sculpting the surrounding landscape. It's not too much of an exaggeration to say that the city owes its existence to the fault.

Unlike the strike-slip San Andreas Fault, where blocks of rock move sideways past each other, Seattle's Fault is of the thrust variety. In an earthquake, rocks on the south side of the fault thrust up and over the north side. That's what caused the uplift on Bainbridge Island and Alki Point. It's also what formed a line of hills east of Seattle called the Issaquah Alps. On the tops of those peaks, geologists found bedrock that had been lifted nearly five miles. All that movement occurred during earthquakes, which means the Seattle Fault has been grinding away for millions of years.

Some of the features that lured settlers are the fault's handiwork. The 900 AD earthquake raised the broad valley of the Duwamish River enough to turn sandy tide flats into fertile soil. The depth of Elliott Bay, which the city's founding fathers first measured with horseshoes attached to a clothesline, may be due to the uneven terrain created by the Seattle Fault. Some scientists suspect the steep gradients could have funneled glacial meltwater, gouging out an exceptionally deep hole on Seattle's waterfront.

As the south side of the fault jerked upward over the eons, the north side sank. The result is a depression five miles deep, filled with

sediment and topped with the hard-packed till left behind by glaciers. Most of Seattle sits on this basin, as do Bremerton, Bellevue,
and everything else across a huge expanse of the urban corridor. But
the USGS team quickly realized that living on top of a basin is not the
best place to be in an earthquake. Seismic waves can get trapped and
reverberate in the same way water sloshes around in a bathtub.

The USGS team tested the effect in March 2000, when Seattle's old
baseball stadium, the Kingdome, was imploded. The blast created the
equivalent of a magnitude 2.3 earthquake. More than two hundred
temporary seismometers recorded the ground shaking. Just as they
had suspected, the scientists found that the ground shook two to
three times harder inside the basin than out. "The whole Seattle basin
is going to have such an extra kick it's going to shake like a bowl of
Jell-O in an earthquake," said Craig Weaver, chief of the USGS earthquake contingent in Seattle.

But what locals really want to know about the Seattle Fault is, where
is it? You'd think there would be an answer by now, but the exact route
has proved elusive. Unlike the San Andreas and other faults whose
presence is announced by scars on the ground, Seattle's fault is what
scientists call blind: It doesn't split the surface during earthquakes
(though some of its offshoots do). The grainy images pieced together
from seismic and ultrasound surveys revealed that the fault isn't a single crack but a five-mile-wide swath of fault strands. Between downtown Seattle and Vashon Island, as many as eight separate strands
extend east and west. "You can pretty much figure that if you're in
that zone, you're on top of a fault or near a fault," Sherrod said.

But ask three geologists to point out the strands on a map, and
you'll get five different answers. The images are ambiguous enough to
leave room for interpretation and argument.

Most geologists think the major strands bisect the city just south
of the stadiums where the Seahawks, Mariners, and Sounders play.
The fault takes a jog around the base of Beacon Hill, then tracks Inter-
state 90 across Lake Washington and continues to North Bend in the
Cascade foothills. But some scientists think the fault zone extends
further north, with strands that run right under Seattle's downtown
waterfront and beneath the city's center.

Proximity matters in earthquakes. Damage is always worst closest to the fault. But no matter the strands' exact path, a powerful quake anywhere on the Seattle Fault zone will be more damaging and deadly to the city and its environs than a megaquake on the coast. When the subduction zone rips, the ground will shake much longer, but the motion in Seattle will be muted by distance. "With the Seattle Fault, the strongest shaking will be right in the middle of where we live and work," Weaver said.

A detailed scenario for a magnitude 6.7 quake on the Seattle Fault put the death toll at 1,600. The violent lurching would knock pedestrians off their feet and collapse bridges, roads, and power lines, the report warned. It would take months or longer to repair the shattered transportation system. The waterfront seawall would collapse into Puget Sound, pulling the supports out from under docks and ferry terminals. The nation's sixth busiest seaport would slide into Elliott Bay—cranes, container terminals, and all. Sloshing waves in Puget Sound, Lake Washington, and Lake Sammamish would swamp waterfront property.

The numbers are numbing:

- $33 billion in property damage, on a par with the Northridge quake
- 24,000 people injured
- Nearly 10,000 buildings destroyed and more than 180,000 unsafe or restricted due to change
- A third of homes closest to the fault unfit for habitation

When this scenario was released in 2005, an emergency planner summed it up in five words: "It's going to be ugly."

But the realization was a long time coming, Weaver said. For more than a decade after Bucknam and the other scientists laid out the evidence of a massive quake on the Seattle Fault, the local community didn't take the threat seriously. The response ranged from puzzlement to hostility. Builders were especially dubious. In their view, a fault that had last slipped in 900 AD wasn't worth fretting over. Who knew when, or if, the thing might quake again? The USGS didn't.

Weaver recalled several tense meetings with local engineers and architects. "They were really skeptical," he said. "We were basically told to prove it." If the Seattle Fault was really dangerous, it would have slipped repeatedly over the past thousands of years, not just once. The builders told Weaver and his team to come back to the table when they had evidence of more earthquakes.

Thanks to a new technique that revolutionized earthquake science in the Pacific Northwest, that wouldn't be long.

CHAPTER 6:

SEEING THE FAULTS FOR THE TREES

ASK GEOLOGISTS ABOUT LIDAR, and here's what they say:

"It knocked our socks off."
"I look at it first thing in the morning."
"Every new batch of data is like unwrapping a Christmas present."
"Crack cocaine for geologists."

But the best way to grasp the power of the airborne laser imaging technique is to visit a spot like the northwest slope of Mount Hood, a Cascade volcano in Oregon where Ian Madin led a small expedition on a September morning in 2011. Shouldering through a tangle of subalpine fir, hemlock, and bear grass wet with dew, he followed fluorescent flagging and backhoe tracks to a freshly dug trench. Madin, chief scientist for the Oregon Department of Geology and Mineral Industries, pointed to the low ridge bisected by the ditch. "That was really tough to find," he said. A team of USGS volcanologists who mapped the area years ago didn't notice it, even though the road is just a stone's throw away.

On a lidar (lie-dar) map it took only a glance to see the innocuous-looking ridge for what it is: the scar created when an earthquake ruptured the ground from the volcano's flank all the way to the

Columbia River. "It just jumps out at you," Madin said. "It looks like somebody drew it in with a Sharpie."

Before lidar, geologists knew of a single earthquake scar west of the Cascade Mountains and north of California. They stumbled across that one only because it showed up on aerial photos of a clear-cut. Everywhere else the region's dense forests concealed features like the eight-foot-high ridge slicing across Mount Hood National Forest. But lidar can distinguish wrinkles on the ground as small as six inches high.

Thanks to the technique's near-magical ability to "see" through trees, geologists now count more than a dozen faults, all with big quakes in their pasts, knifing across the region from northern Oregon to the Canadian border. The list is growing so fast there's a backlog of scarps waiting to be trenched—the best way to tell how often a fault has snapped. "Everywhere we look these days, we find more faults," said Madin. Lidar revealed the fault on Mount Hood in 2008. It took him three years to scrape together the money to dig into it.

Beyond their astonishment at the sheer number of faults, geologists were surprised to learn that Seattle's is by no means the biggest, nor was the 900 AD quake a solo event. Several other faults snapped around the same time, as did the Cascadia Subduction Zone. The sequence of the concatenation is blurry, but a similar barrage in the future is a real possibility.

Lidar is also revealing a network of faults running through the sagebrush flats near the Hanford Nuclear Reservation, home to the region's only nuclear power plant and North America's biggest radioactive waste dump. Insights gained from lidar are helping geologists piece together a unified theory of the region's seismic hazards and quantify the forces that are loading the faults for the next earthquakes. "We're finally starting to see the big picture," Madin said.

Lidar's first contribution to seismic science in the Northwest came as geologists were struggling to get a better handle on the Seattle Fault. They knew it had ripped in spectacular fashion at least once—but that was more than a thousand years ago. Maybe what happened around 900 AD was a fluke. The people and builders of Puget Sound were anxious to know how often the urban corridor might be jolted.

The USGS team hit a wall in their search for answers. Scientists spread out across the region looking for beaches, bluffs, and wetlands uplifted by earlier quakes. They didn't have much luck. Brian Sherrod, who got his start assisting Robert Bucknam with the early Seattle Fault studies, pulled cores and hacked into stream banks at more than one hundred marsh sites across the region.

It was frustrating, because geologists knew that a fault that snapped as recently as a thousand years ago couldn't possibly be dead. Sediment cores from the bottom of Lake Washington pointed to repeated landslides, probably triggered by earthquakes. But the overall record was too paltry to draw conclusions. Then a tiny, public utility went bargain hunting and came back with a treasure.

In 1996 Bainbridge Island wanted a high-resolution topo map for land-use planning. The arrangements fell to the Kitsap Public Utility District. The PUD operated a handful of water systems and had a geographer on staff who knew his way around the latest digital mapping technology. Greg Berghoff estimated it would cost more than a quarter of a million dollars to make a map the old-fashioned way, with a team of surveyors.

He decided to check out a local start-up that was pioneering a system called Light Detection and Ranging (lidar). The company offered to do the job for less than $70,000. Developed by NASA and originally used to measure things like cloud height and ice caps, lidar was new to the commercial world. The company's plan was to fly grids across the island, shooting thousands of laser pulses at the ground every second and calculating elevations based on how quickly the pulses bounced back.

Most of the signals bounce off treetops or roofs, but about one in ten strikes the ground. The magic is performed by computer programs that weed out ricochets and save the true surface data. In a lucky coincidence, the Bainbridge company flew its survey just after a snowstorm knocked off the last of the leaves, which made for even crisper images.

The finished map was so sharp it was as if a giant hand had peeled back the island's skin of vegetation. North-south scorings chiseled by glaciers popped out in stark relief. Watershed boundaries jumped off

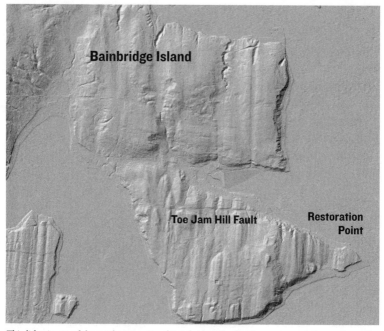

This lidar image of the southeastern tip of Bainbridge Island strips away vegetation and reveals the Toe Jam Hill Fault, which is closely associated with the Seattle Fault. Also visible is the bench around Restoration Point, uplifted in the Seattle Fault quake about 1,100 years ago.

the page. Berghoff also noticed an odd east-west line cutting across a hill not far from Restoration Point. At first he figured it must be a road cut. But the lidar data were fine-grained enough to show that one side was higher than the other. "I saw that offset, and I thought, 'Uh oh. If that thing isn't a data error, it might be a fault,'" he recalled.

Berghoff pinned up the map in the PUD lobby where a local geology buff did a double take when he saw it. The next thing Berghoff knew, he was shaking hands with Craig Weaver, leader of the USGS earthquake team in Seattle.

Weaver and his colleagues were so jazzed by their first look at the Bainbridge lidar that they hopped a ferry as soon as they could and bushwhacked through devil's club and blackberry vines to the exact GPS coordinates on a promontory called Toe Jam Hill. What they found looked very much like the scarp on Mount Hood—which is to say that it didn't look like much at all.

"You can't see the forest for the trees, and you can't see the fault when you're standing out in the brush," Madin, of Oregon's geology department, explained at his trench site in 2011. Fault scarps in Washington and Oregon are also hard to spot because they're usually not very striking. On the San Andreas Fault, millions of years of motion and erosion have etched out a gash that's visible from the space station. Northwest faults may be just as ancient, but glaciers wiped the slate clean less than twenty thousand years ago, then dumped a thick layer of sand and gravel on top.

Geologists get excited by scarps for several reasons, Madin said. They reveal the presence of faults. They prove that at least one earthquake broke the surface. The length of the scarp and the amount of offset are rough yardsticks for quake size. But most important, scarps provide a portal into the geologic past.

"That's where digging comes in," Madin said, watching as a backhoe struggled to dislodge a rock the size of a dishwasher. "The scarp tells us the fault is here and that it moved sometime in the recent past. What we want to nail down now is, 'When were the earthquakes? How big, and how often?'"

Those are the same questions the USGS team posed in 1996 about the newly-discovered fault on Toe Jam Hill.

With the lidar image for leverage, the USGS pried loose enough funding to mount a major assault on the Northwest's first urban scarp. "It was a big deal," recalled Sherrod, who had recently landed a full-time job with the USGS. "There was a lot of interest and we wanted to document it well." A team of two dozen scientists converged on Bainbridge Island, working on and off for two years. They excavated five trenches.

For his project on Mount Hood, Madin had two weeks and one full-time helper. The backhoe was a loaner, normally used to dig up broken water mains, and seriously overmatched by some of the boulders it bit into. "I work for a state agency," he said with a shrug. "We always have to bootleg it."

Despite the shoestring, the approach is the same. When one side of a fault pops up or down during an earthquake, the result is a kind of stair-step on the ground surface. Dirt, sticks, and leaves tumble off the high side of the step and accumulate at the base. Over time, the scarp is buried under a fresh layer of soil. Then a new quake splits the surface and the cycle starts over.

When geologists dig into a fault, they scrutinize the walls of the trench for soil layers broken or offset by past quakes. They also look for buried pockets of sticks, leaves, and other organic material, hoping for something well-preserved enough for radiocarbon dating.

What sounds straightforward in theory is usually a muddle in the field, Madin said. He scrambled into the ten-foot-deep trench where the dusty walls proved his point. A uniform tan, they revealed no obvious layers, no clear lines of displacement. Madin's crew whisked the sides of the trench with push brooms to remove loose dirt. He fired up a smoke-belching leaf blower and followed behind for a final polish. After several hours of labor, a few faint features emerged.

Embedded near the middle of the trench wall was a patch of volcanic rocks. Instead of lying flat, as they were formed, the rocks were tipped on edge. "That's evidence of some kind of violent shoving in the past," Madin said. He poked his finger into air pockets in the soil, which he explained also indicated a time when the ground churned. "It would be nice to have distinct layers where one side is three feet higher than the other, but that's only in textbooks. In the real world, there's a lot of scratching your head and trying to make out subtle differences."

Compared to sunken marshes and drowned forests, fault trenches are often blurrier windows into the past. In the Northwest, it's unusual to find evidence of more than two or three quakes and harder to interpret radiocarbon results. "About the best you can get is a general sense of the rate of recurrence," Madin said, settling down in the dust to probe the trench wall for bits of charcoal or wood.

On Bainbridge Island, the USGS team discovered that the Toe Jam Hill Fault is an offshoot of the Seattle Fault, so closely linked that both fired off together 1,100 years ago. The trenches revealed that the fault has been rocked by three or four quakes in the past 2,500 years, some of which shoved the ground up by as much as fifteen feet. It was the first evidence that shallow quakes strike the Puget Sound area on a regular basis, and the first proof that some of those quakes actually rupture the ground.

"It was a really important find," Sherrod said. The Bainbridge trenches also marked the beginning of an era of breakneck discovery that is still going strong more than a decade later.

After its first trenching success, the USGS was eager to collect wall-to-wall lidar coverage of the Seattle Fault and the Puget Sound basin. Some of the early funding came from NASA, which was equally eager to see its technology commercialized. By the late 1990s, the USGS's fault-finding mission was launched.

There were already hints that the Seattle Fault wasn't the only player in the region. Seismic data collected by oil companies in the 1960s and newer magnetic and gravity surveys all suggested the shadowy outlines of several possible faults. Lidar confirmed past earthquake on one candidate after another.

There's a fault that slices through Tacoma. Another passes near the state capital and is sometimes called the Legislature's Fault. The Saddle Mountain Fault skirts the eastern edge of the Olympics. The Devil's Mountain Fault cuts a path from the tip of Vancouver Island to the foothills of the Cascades. A broad avenue of subterranean cracks passes south of Everett. Two of the newest additions to the list lurk along the Canadian border, near Bellingham. Interspersed between the faults are basins like the one that underlies Seattle—many of which will experience an extra boost of shaking in future quakes.

As the faults kept coming and trenching proved most of them dangerous, the USGS hosted briefings for communities across the region. "Each time it was a big deal," Weaver recalled. "We would have these workshops, three hundred people would show up, and we would explain what we'd found on the newest fault. At some point the engineers got it."

A modern fault map shows that it's hard to find a place where an earthquake-phobe could feel cozy. The few blank spots are mostly areas where geologists haven't looked yet, like southwestern Washington. Sherrod has probably spent more time in the earthquake

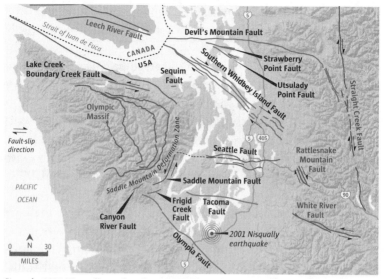

Since the 2001 Nisqually earthquake, scientists have discovered nearly a dozen shallow faults that split the Puget Sound area. Not shown in this map are two recently discovered faults near Bellingham.

trenches than anyone else in the Northwest, and he has come to view the hazard regionally rather than fault-by-fault.

"Draw a box from the Canadian border to Olympia, and from the Olympic Mountains to the foot of the Cascades," he said. "Anywhere in that box, we need to be thinking we could have a pretty big, shallow earthquake." And no matter which specific fault breaks the next time, everybody in that box is going to feel it.

Toe Jam Hill was Sherrod's first scarp excavation, but it wasn't his first experience rooting around in the ground. As a college student in his home state of Virginia, he worked on dozens of archaeological digs. The most memorable was at the site of a Civil War field hospital, where his team unearthed surgical instruments and pits filled with amputated arms and legs.

But Sherrod's professional career started out on a much finer scale. He earned a master's degree in micropaleontology, the study of fossil diatoms, dinoflagellates, and other creatures invisible to the naked eye. When consulting on construction projects proved unsatisfying, Sherrod applied for the doctoral program at the University of Washington, but got turned down. By the time he decided to take another run at admission, the Seattle Fault studies were under way. Robert Bucknam and his UW collaborators needed someone to analyze marine fossils from uplifted beach terraces. Sherrod was in.

He took to trenching like a beaver takes to dam building. Plain-spoken, with a shaved head and a wrestler's build, Sherrod loves the logistical challenge of cobbling together projects and reconstructing history. He's wired to think in three dimensions—four, if you factor in a geologic time scale so vast it leaves most people woozy. "I can't explain it," he said. "It's one of those things that you've either got, or you don't." Sherrod's other passions include riding his Harley and catching big fish.

As the lidar surveys started turning up one fault after another, Sherrod and two of his USGS colleagues developed an assembly-line approach to identify and prioritize the most promising ones. Lidar remained the cornerstone, and Ralph Haugerud was its virtuoso. A former hard-rock geologist, Haugerud carved out a new niche when the market for geologic maps dried up along with the American mining industry. He wrote one of the earliest computer programs to sort through millions of lidar points and discard all but the true ground hits.

As a boy Haugerud decorated his room with topo maps. As a man he spent decades traversing the West on foot, by horseback, and behind the wheel of pickup trucks, honing an eye for landforms that he applies to lidar images. Rivers, gullies, and landslides can all masquerade as fault scarps, and Haugerud is expert at identifying the impostors and zeroing in on the real thing.

Not every scarp is worth paying attention to, either. "There are lots of faults out there, but if they stopped moving twenty million or fifty million years ago, who cares?" Haugerud asked. The bar is set by the Nuclear Regulatory Commission, which considers a fault active if it has ruptured within the last ten thousand years. By that criteria most scarps west of the Cascades are automatically suspect because of the recent passage of the glaciers.

Haugerud hands off the likely candidates to Rick Blakely, a geophysicist out of the USGS Menlo Park office. Blakely's forté is airborne magnetic surveys. Different types of rock have different magnetic properties, so the measurements can reveal places where layers broke and shifted in the past. The aeromag validates the existence of a fault and is often able to pick out segments that don't show up on the lidar.

But the technique is temperamental. The airplane that carries the instruments has to be covered in coils to snuff out its own magnetic field. It also needs to fly as low as possible. In remote areas pilots skim along two hundred feet above the ground. When the terrain allows, Blakely fine-tunes his data by getting even closer, strapping a magnetometer and antenna on his back and walking the length of a scarp.

The newest aeromag technology is so good at finding faults that Weaver decided to test it near his home east of Seattle. Overlaying the magnetic data on a street map, he drove to the spot where the aeromag indicated the road crossed a fault. Sure enough, the pavement took a dip. "The trees are maybe six feet higher on one side than the other," Weaver said. "I was stunned."

Trenching is the last step in the assembly line. Only when the lidar and aeromag agree that a fault is real and probably ruptured in the not-too-distant past will Sherrod call in the earth-moving equipment. In nearly fifty excavations, he's fine-tuned the routine. He and his crew can be in and out in two weeks. Still, trenching is expensive, and he can't afford to waste money on a dry hole.

Even before Sherrod lines up excavators, he has to convince landowners to let him tear up their property. The owners of an environmental education center on Bainbridge Island welcomed the geologists and used the trench as a teaching tool. But not surprisingly, some folks aren't delighted to find out there's a fault running through their backyard. One couple okayed digging as long as Sherrod promised not to tell the press. Others turn their backs the instant they hear the word *government*. "I've had folks who would love to take a gun to us," Sherrod said, chuckling.

Along the Seattle Fault and its offshoots, Sherrod and his team excavated ten trenches, including several on Bainbridge Island and one near a submerged forest in Lake Sammamish, east of Seattle.

What the geologists found was a mix of good and bad news. Best was the discovery that the 900 AD quake seems to be one of a kind—so far. Nothing else in the record wrenched the ground so hard or had such far-reaching effects. But the Seattle Fault is no geologic slacker: Sherrod and his USGS colleagues uncovered evidence of three to four significant quakes in the past 2,500 years.

The numbers are uncertain enough that geologists still don't agree on how frequently Seattle might get slammed by shallow earthquakes. A consensus conference in 2004 came to the unhelpful conclusion that the Seattle Fault could snap every five hundred years—or every five thousand. "That's the range from 'oh shit' to 'who cares,'" said Haugerud. "It's frustrating that repeat time on the Seattle Fault remains so ambiguous."

That's one of the reasons Sherrod prefers to pool the data from all the Puget Sound faults and trenches. Although individual faults may go several thousand years between quakes, collectively Western Washington seems to get hit with a large, shallow quake every thousand years or so. The really big quakes, like the one that hit in 900 AD, are much rarer, striking perhaps every 3,000 years or more.

With the last Seattle Fault quake 1,100 years ago, the thousand year recurrence interval isn't comforting. The Seattle Fault scenario that estimated more than 1,600 fatalities wasn't based on the magnitude 7-plus quake that shoved up Restoration and Alki points. It was a more modest magnitude 6.7, the variety that averages suggest could be due any time in Western Washington.

Geologists still don't know what to make of the fact that almost every fault in the region seems to have popped off roughly in concert with the massive 900 AD upheaval on the Seattle Fault. The Tacoma Fault ripped around then. So did Toe Jam Hill, Olympia, Devil's Mountain, and the Little River Fault, which skirts the northern edge of the Olympic Peninsula.

Radiocarbon dates are so imprecise there's no way to tell whether the quakes hit all at once, over a period of decades, or over more than a century. But the syncopation is unnerving. Add in a possible quake on the Cascadia Subduction Zone that occurred at roughly the same time, along with an eruption of Mount Rainier, and you've got what geologists call "Puget mayhem." It's something they talk about when they're shooting the breeze in a bar. After the second round, some even speculate that the next subduction zone quake could set off a similar domino effect.

"It sounds like a horrible period," Haugerud said. "I think most of us are a little bit hesitant to say there's a cause-and-effect relationship." He paused, then raised his eyebrows. "But, my. That's quite a coincidence."

The seismic domino effect could even extend beyond the Northwest. Chris Goldfinger's seafloor cores show that some Cascadia megaquakes were so closely followed by quakes on the San Andreas Fault that he suspects triggering. Several volcanoes around the world have erupted so hot on the heels of major earthquakes that scientists don't doubt cause and effect. In 1975 Kilauea began spewing lava half an hour after a magnitude 7.5 quake under the volcano's south flank. Cordon Caulle in central Chile sent a column of ash soaring nearly five miles into the sky two days after the record-breaking 1960 subduction zone quake.

The link between Rainier's eruption about a thousand years ago and the 900 AD quake is less clear. Massive debris flows that roared off the volcano and ran all the way to Puget Sound suggest Rainier may have let loose before the earth shook, though by how much is hard to tell. David Hill, a USGS researcher based in Menlo Park, wonders if a spike in eruptive activity throughout the Cascades in the 1800s might have been set in motion by the 1700 Cascadia quake. He wouldn't be surprised to see volcanic rumblings the next time the subduction zone rips. "The Earth does amazing things," he said. "My own feeling is that there are lots of things going on that are related that we don't quite appreciate."

There's certainly plenty of precedent for big quakes setting off seismic cascades. The monster subduction zone quake that triggered the 2004 Indian Ocean tsunami lit up the region like a pinball machine. Hundreds of aftershocks rattled the area, some as big as magnitude 8. Aftershocks from Japan's killer quake in 2011 were still jolting the islands more than a year later. Most were on the subduction zone itself, but aftershocks also radiated on land, breaking shallow faults.

It's easy to imagine the same fallout in the Pacific Northwest from the next Cascadia megaquake. Seismologists have an equation that predicts how many major aftershocks a given quake will produce. For a magnitude 9 on Cascadia, the best answer is eleven: one bigger than magnitude 8 and ten between magnitude 7 and 8. Most would hit within days or weeks of the original shock, but smaller rumbles can continue for decades as the crust adjusts. But as far as anyone can tell, the most recent full-rip 9 on the coast did not set the dominos tumbling. Only one of the faults Sherrod and the USGS group trenched showed evidence of a quake in 1700: Devil's Mountain Fault, which cuts across Northern Puget Sound.

A fault that appears not to have quaked 1,100 years ago is the one geologists now view as the most dangerous player among the region's surface faults: the South Whidbey Island Fault, called SWIF for short. It was named for the biggest island in Puget Sound, home to a naval air station and the nation's premier mussel farm. The fault's existence was suspected for years, but it wasn't nailed down until the mid-1990s when the USGS got its hands on the old oil company surveys. When geologists walked the island's shorelines, they found lots of evidence that the ground shook violently in the past. Waterfront cliffs reveal striking swirls and blob-like patterns that form only in soil that's been rattled hard enough to liquefy.

At first, the SWIF seemed like just another fault in the growing pack. The earliest reports estimated its length at about forty miles, cutting diagonally from the old mill town of Port Townsend through Whidbey Island's southern tip. The terminus appeared to be on the mainland between Seattle and Everett. But the SWIF kept growing. Scientists tracked it northwest to Victoria on Vancouver Island. At the other end, the SWIF struck out for the Cascade foothills, where it appeared to link up with several other faults.

Sherrod trenched several scarps on the SWIF, including one that ran through the site of a new sewage treatment plant. He found signs of four major quakes in the past sixteen thousand years, with many more smaller quakes likely. The most recent was about 2,700 years ago. It was while excavating a strand near the wineries northeast of Seattle that Sherrod started to puzzle over a possible link with the Seattle Fault.

The Seattle Fault appeared to terminate in the Cascade foothills. But faults don't just end abruptly. As they examined the aeromag data and the scarps, Sherrod and Blakely came to a surprising conclusion: the fault that Seattleites most dread is just a branch of the SWIF.

Eventually, the scientists tracked the SWIF across the Cascade Mountains as far as the town of Richland on the Columbia River—home of Hanford. It's not a single break in the crust, but a band of fractures up to fifty miles wide. At nearly 200 miles long, the fault zone dwarfs every other shallow fault in the region. Only Cascadia is bigger.

The longer the fault, the bigger the quake. But nobody expects a full rip on the SWIF. A rupture on one segment could trigger a quake on the adjoining segment—say the Seattle Fault—but the SWIF is unlikely to slip along its entire length at once, Sherrod said. "What we're dealing with is a system of faults that we think are linked. But if you have a fault system that's three hundred kilometers long and you rupture half or a third of it, that's a big earthquake. That's 7.5."

The SWIF forms a bridge that joins Western and Eastern Washington in a common seismic framework. For those who live east of the Cascades, it's not a welcome alliance. The dry sides of Washington and Oregon have long been considered more like the nation's heartland than Puget Sound when it comes to earthquakes.

But red flags were there all along. In 1936 a quake estimated at magnitude 5.8 broke windows, collapsed chimneys, and opened two-hundred-foot-long cracks in the ground near the Washington-Oregon border. The towns of Milton-Freewater and Walla Walla bore the brunt. One of the most powerful quakes in Washington history struck east of the Cascades in 1872, setting off massive landslides along the Columbia River.

Following the SWIF's trajectory, Sherrod and his colleagues shifted their assembly line eastward in the mid-2000s. Their focus has been a series of east-west folds in the Earth's crust that show up on lidar maps like wrinkles in a tablecloth. Viewed up close, some of the long, grassy ridges sprout windmills; others are green with a patchwork of vineyards. They have names like Horse Heaven Hills, Rattlesnake Ridge, and Saddle Mountain. Geologists passed through this country many times over the past century, and most concluded that any faults that underlay the ridges would be too shallow to pose much of an earthquake threat.

It was a convenient interpretation during an era of nuclear proliferation. Throughout the Cold War, the Hanford reactors that fueled the first atomic bombs continued to churn out plutonium for the nation's growing stockpile. Then came WPPSS, with plans for three nuclear power plants on the Hanford reservation. Consultants analyzed the seismic risks but tended to err on the sunny side. As one geologist put it, "Nobody wanted to suggest that Hanford was a bad place to build large, sensitive structures."

Once Sherrod started trenching the area, it didn't take him long to find signs of at least seven quakes of roughly magnitude 7. In a region that was never covered with glaciers, the trenches reach back in time fifty thousand years. That suggests Central and Eastern Washington enjoy thousands of years of quiet between big quakes. But there's a rule of thumb for active faults, Sherrod explained. For every magnitude 7 or bigger quake that splits the ground and leaves behind evidence in a trench, smaller quakes of magnitude 6 to 6.5 or so strike much more frequently.

Data from recent oil and gas surveys confirmed that the faults under Central Washington's ridges aren't shallow. They originate more than twelve miles below ground and cut through massive layers of basalt. In other words, the faults that formed the ridges are much more dangerous than anyone realized. "It's a fundamental rethinking of the seismic risk over there," Sherrod said.

What it will mean for the Hanford Nuclear Reservation and the vast accumulation of radioactive and toxic waste stored in underground tanks isn't clear yet. In 2012 the Department of Energy, which is responsible for cleaning up the mess, ordered new studies of earthquake risk. Hanford is also home to the Columbia Generating Station, WPPSS's only atomic success story and the Pacific Northwest's sole nuclear power plant. The reactor generates about 6 percent of Washington's electricity.

After the Fukushima meltdowns spawned by Japan's 2011 tsunami, the NRC ordered several safety upgrades at the plant but decided there was no need to bolster its seismic safety. The agency also extended the plant's license another twenty years, allowing it to operate through 2043.

The 1970s-era reactor wasn't designed for a specific earthquake, but rather for a specific level of ground shaking. The shaking is expressed in g's, a measure of gravity that also describes the g-forces pilots experience. At 1g, earthquake shaking is fierce enough to overcome gravity and objects and people fly into the air. Based on what they knew at the time, engineers designed the reactor to stand up to .25 g.

So it was disconcerting in 2009 when a swarm of more than a thousand quakes shook the eastern edge of the Hanford site. None of the quakes was bigger than magnitude 3. But because they occurred so close to the surface, the peak motion force was .15 g, which isn't far below the nuclear plant's design level. Blakely and Sherrod traced the swarm back to one of the ridges they've been studying—and the fault that lies beneath it.

Geology can feel like an avalanche of numbers—every fault a recurrence interval, every quake a magnitude, every seismic wave an amplitude and frequency. But at its core, earth science is about telling stories. What happened to create the landscape we see today? What is the future likely to bring? There's no better storytelling tool than a picture, which is why Ray Wells travels with a three-foot-wide briefcase like artists use to carry their portfolios.

Wells's masterpiece is a laminated map of the Pacific Northwest with movable sections. Northern California is purple. Western Oregon is pink, Western Washington green. The map represents the culmination of more than two decades of research by dozens of earth scientists—and the key to calculating an earthquake budget for the region.

Wells assembled the map to show why it's hard to turn a corner in Washington without running into a fault. By sliding the pieces, he can animate the tectonic forces squeezing the region. "Looking at it as an integrated system helps explain what we see," he said. Though it took a long time to tease apart the details, the story turned out to be fairly simple. It's a train wreck on a geologic scale.

On a visit to Seattle in 2012, Wells held the map in his lap like a ventriloquist's dummy. The main driver behind the train wreck is the giant Pacific Plate, he explained. Moving northward at the geologically brisk pace of two inches a year, the Pacific Plate pulls California in its wake. Wells slid the purple California piece north, setting the wreck in motion.

California rammed into Oregon. But Oregon is also being shoved from the side by the Juan de Fuca Plate, which is subducting under North America. The pink Western Oregon block on Wells's map accordingly slid north and pivoted clockwise.

Then came the crunch.

Washington is caught between Oregon pushing from the south and the unyielding bedrock of inland British Columbia to the north, Wells explained. The Evergreen State crumples like a line of box cars slamming into a mountain. "That's why you have the Seattle Fault, you have the Tacoma Fault, you have the Whidbey Island Fault. They're all driven by this north-south compression." Ditto for the rumpled ridges and faults in Central and Eastern Washington.

Much of the groundwork for Wells's map was laid in the 1970s by geologists who laboriously drilled samples from ancient lava flows across the Northwest. Iron-bearing minerals in the rocks act like tiny compass needles to reveal how the rocks have shifted since they formed. Today, scientists track ground motions in real-time thanks to a network of more than five hundred GPS stations.

The measurements show the Puget lowlands are being compressed by about a quarter of an inch a year. That adds up to more than twenty feet of crunch since the last time the Seattle Fault fired off. Central and Eastern Washington are being squeezed at a slightly lower rate. Inexorably, the pressure is accumulating, loading the Seattle Fault and its associates like springs.

"The plates are moving, but the faults are stuck," Wells said. "You build up strain on the fault, and then the fault slips." Around the world, the rate of tectonic-driven strain buildup is a rough yardstick of seismic activity.

The Juan de Fuca Plate is bearing down on North America at about 1.5 inches a year, which makes the Cascadia Subduction Zone one of the continent's most active faults. Strain buildup on the San Andreas and its offshoots adds up to about 2 inches a year, which explains why California gets more frequent earthquakes than Washington. Japan, where noticeable earthquakes pop off several times a day, is being squeezed more than 3 inches a year.

Wells used strain rates to calculate a rough earthquake budget for the Pacific Northwest. The squeeze on the Puget Sound region is enough to produce a magnitude 7 quake every five hundred years. That's about twice as often as Sherrod's trenches indicated, but trenches are spotty recorders.

It's possible the last quake was so big it left a budget deficit that still hasn't been filled, Wells said. But it's also possible that the region's earthquake account has accumulated a dangerous surplus that will be expended in more powerful quakes in the future.

Back at Madin's fault on Mount Hood in 2011, a week had passed since the trench was opened. The volcano sported a fresh coating of snow, and huckleberry bushes were tinged red by frost. Madin and his assistant were rushing to finish their work before the backhoe returned in a few days to fill in the hole.

Multicolored pins and bits of flagging dotted the walls of the trench, outlining the different types of rock and dirt—geologists call them units—exposed in its walls. Wearing two jackets, rubber boots, and fishermen's gloves, Madin was plucking bits of charcoal from a crevice and tucking them into Ziploc bags.

"Ohhoho, that's a nice one," he said, displaying a fat morsel ripe for carbon dating.

Oregonians have plenty to worry about seismically, with the possibility of megaquakes off their coast every 250 years or so. But the state isn't rattled nearly as often as Washington is by other types of quakes, which has been a bit of a puzzle. Madin spent much of his career studying the Portland Hills Fault, which runs through the center of the city and across the Willamette River. But he still hasn't found any signs of recent earthquakes.

The train wreck model helps explain Oregon's relative quiet—though Madin prefers to visualize a car. "If you've seen those slow-motion crash-test-dummy movies, you know that the damage is always worst at the bumper," he said. "Washington is the bumper and Oregon is the backseat of the car that's going along for the ride."

Oregon isn't free of damaging quakes. In 1993 the small town of Klamath Falls, east of Ashland, was hit by back-to-back magnitude 6 quakes that damaged more than a thousand homes and businesses. One man was killed when a boulder dislodged by the quake smashed his truck. But so far, lidar surveys have revealed only a handful of scarps in Oregon. Of those, the few that have been studied don't seem to crank out quakes very often.

In the midst of his excavation, Madin theorized that the fault on Mount Hood might be a more significant player in the region's geology. "It's probably no coincidence that it appears to run directly under the volcano," he pointed out. "It's quite possible that the mountain is here because the fault is here." Fractured rock can create zones of weakness, making it easier for magma to percolate up from the depths.

But when the fieldwork was done and the results from the carbon-dating were in six months later, the trench yielded evidence for only a single quake in the past twelve thousand years. "That's kind of sleepy," Madin conceded.

He presented the findings in March 2012 at a Seattle workshop to reevaluate seismic hazards in the Northwest. At the same time, he also reported that the most recent lidar surveys found no hint of surface fractures from the Portland Hills Fault. Maybe, Madin suggested, it was time to downgrade the hazard rating there.

"Lidar gives," he said, "and lidar takes away."

CHAPTER 7:

THE EARTHQUAKE THAT WOULDN'T STAY PUT

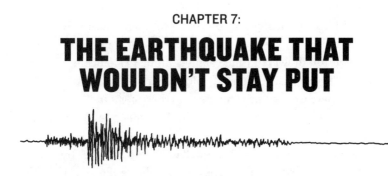

LIKE MOST OUTLAWS John McBride knew how to wiggle out of jams. When a handyman fingered him for selling liquor to Indians, McBride and his partner slipped $150 worth of gold dust in the pocket of the prosecutor, a man with a taste for whiskey and a sizable saloon bill. Not only were the charges dropped, but the court branded the handyman a liar and ordered him out of town.

McBride wasn't able to buy off the jury the next time a deputy served him with a warrant for the same offense. But he spent only a couple of weeks of his six-month sentence behind bars. On a June night in 1873, McBride pried loose a piece of sheet iron and shimmied through a hole in the ceiling of his cell in Walla Walla. "The pursuit has been made quite lively," reported the local newspaper. The writer speculated that a popular purveyor of spirits like McBride would no doubt find friends to assist his flight. "He is now probably half way to the British line, and will soon shake the dust of Washington Territory from his feet." Indeed, McBride was reported to be selling horses in British Columbia by the time the snow fell.

A rancher with a spread near Wenatchee described McBride and his sidekick, Jack Ingram, as "scoundrels who, for pure cussedness, could not be excelled anywhere on the border." So it's a toss-up as to who would laugh louder—those who knew McBride or the rascal himself—to learn that more than a century after he skedaddled to Canada his credibility would lay at the heart of a high-stakes duel over nuclear energy and one of the most powerful earthquakes in the Pacific Northwest.

It struck in 1872, the year Ulysses S. Grant won his second term as president. Margaret Hopper, a USGS geophysicist, has studied dozens of historic earthquakes but none so memorable. Newspaper clippings, tattered maps, and reports about what transpired in 1872 occupy two full drawers in the cabinets lining her office in Golden, Colorado. "It was easily the most colorful quake I ever looked into," she said. "There were some characters up there, for sure."

The shaking started on the evening of December 14. A steamboat captain in Olympia named James S. Lawson used his chronometer to time the initial jolt at forty and one-half minutes past nine. The quake was felt in such far-flung places as Jasper, Alberta; Eugene, Oregon; and Victoria, British Columbia, where windows shattered and glassware tumbled to the floor. "Not since Washington has been known to white man has there been so great an earthquake within its confines," one newspaper declared.

Printing presses hadn't arrived yet in the Central Washington foothills where McBride and Ingram plied their trade. According to an early head count, the pair comprised two-fifths of the white population in the Wenatchee area. Most of the initial newspaper reports on the quake came from the bustling towns west of the Cascades. In Olympia chimneys cracked, doors swung on their hinges, and chickens were rattled off their roosts. A group of gamblers fled the saloon "in such haste they forgot to carry off the stakes." Trees toppled along the Puyallup River valley. Dishes broke and water slopped from tanks in Seattle. Fissures split the marshy ground south of town.

A dispatch from Dungeness Spit, a five-mile-long arm reaching into the Strait of Juan de Fuca, reported that the lighthouse "rocked to and fro most alarmingly" and was badly damaged. Vibrations were severe enough at Snoqualmie Pass to knock people off their feet. Proving that human nature hasn't changed but newspaper writing has, one scribe described the panic: "Nimble old ladies were seen to rush out of doors and into the street looking like human comets with linen tails. One young lady who always wears a profusion of beautiful curls, which she claims were curled on nature's tongs, was seen to rush into the street, ... her head bristling with curl papers."

Several correspondents expressed surprise that the quake didn't seem to have emanated from California. The *Puget Sound Express* blamed it on Washington's immediate neighbor to the south: "If it was a genuine ague our mother earth had, she must have caught it in Oregon, as our Territory is comparatively free from bowel diseases." Lacking seismometers, the citizenry could only speculate about the quake's size and source.

Aftershocks continued for more than a year, some so strong that merchants hammered railings onto their shelves to prevent breakage. The owner of a trading post on the Columbia said some of the shocks opened cracks in the ground up to three feet wide. "The inhabitants of the entire region were in a state of considerable fright from the numerous repetitions and the violence," the *Oregonian* reported in 1873.

The earliest earthquake catalogs for the region assumed that the epicenter must have been somewhere in the Puget Sound basin. It wasn't until the 1950s that a Canadian geologist named W. G. Milne made the first detailed study of the quake. He looked for historical accounts and, finding many in his own British Columbia backyard, concluded the quake must have been centered there. A newspaper in Chilliwack reported a landslide that lopped one thousand feet off the summit of a local peak. Other stories described the ground oscillating like the sea. Acknowledging it was a guess, Milne pegged the quake's magnitude at 7.5 and drew a bull's-eye just outside the town of Hope, British Columbia, nearly 130 miles north of Seattle.

There the quake stayed until the atomic gold rush of the early 1970s. With seven nuclear reactors on the drawing board and predictions that the region would need at least a dozen more to quench its thirst for power, what had been a seismological footnote in the region's history was now a potential threat to multiple multimillion-dollar projects. For a few years, getting to the bottom of the 1872 quake was geology's equivalent of the Apollo project. Consultants cranked out so many reports and proposed so many rival epicenters that Bob

Royer, Seattle's deputy mayor during part of the debate, dubbed it "the earthquake that wouldn't stay put."

In order to design a nuclear power plant, utilities must identify the "maximum credible earthquake" the facility could face. If the 1872 quake was really centered in British Columbia, then it wouldn't be much of a problem for WPPSS. All five reactors the utility consortium intended to build—two at Satsop near the Washington coast and three on the Hanford Nuclear Reservation—seemed safely removed. But what happened in 1872 was a more pressing question for Puget Sound Power & Light. The utility planned to build twin reactors on the Skagit River north of Seattle, uncomfortably close to British Columbia.

Puget Power dispatched consultants to dig more deeply into the historic record. They visited libraries and museums across the Northwest and pored over old diaries and manuscripts. Among the new sources they uncovered were dramatic stories from east of the Cascades, where the mountains meet the Columbia Plateau and where McBride was well-known. Unfortunately, the reports weren't timely. Most were recorded decades after the quake when newspapers finally sprang up in the area. But despite the time lag, witnesses were unanimous in recalling massive upheaval near the hamlet of Entiat.

A man called Wapato John lived in a log house with his family. His son Peter told an interviewer that a ferocious quake struck in darkness with a booming sound like thunder. The force wrenched the cabin apart, and rocks rained down from above. The terrified family huddled in a field until dawn when they could see the extent of the devastation. A geyser spouted nearby and would continue to gush for months. One band of Indians lost its winter food cache when sulfurous water surged from the ground. But most astounding was the Columbia River. A steep hillside had collapsed, damming the territory's mightiest waterway.

Trading post owner Sam Miller went to the Columbia to fetch water and was spooked to find it nearly dry. "I would have given every gray hair on my head to have been out of the country," he told a historian. According to other accounts, Native American women who saw the same strange sight sounded the alarm. People rushed down to see for themselves just as the river broke through the dirt dam. "They saw in the distance coming for them a rush of water," *The Wenatchee World* reported. "They ran for their lives and escaped."

The gash in the hillside remains unmistakable today. Called Ribbon Cliff for its multicolored bands of rock, it's more than one thousand feet tall and extends for at least half a mile. Highway 97, which parallels the Columbia, sits on the toe of the slide. Remnants of the slide form small islands in the river.

Proponents of the Skagit nuclear plants argued that the 1872 quake must have been centered very close to Entiat to wreak so much havoc there. Accordingly, they leapfrogged the epicenter over the Cascades, conveniently distant from their site. WPPSS was not pleased. A quake that had been nearly 250 miles and a mountain range away was now practically in Hanford's backyard.

WPPSS and its consultants countered with their own analysis. They dismissed the significance of the Ribbon Cliff landslide, pointing out that it wouldn't take much of a shake to knock down a slope already undercut by the river. One WPPSS study—later refuted—claimed the slide predated the quake by several years.

WPPSS also picked at discrepancies in the newspaper reports and questioned the reliability of stories told so long after the fact. "As is common with such legends, memories are distorted and individual accounts are elaborated," the consultants cautioned. Throwing out all the stories they considered dubious, WPPSS drew its own map and lobbed the quake's epicenter back where it started: west of the Cascades and north of the Canadian border.

"It was like a tennis game," recalled University of Washington geologist Eric Cheney, who represented the citizen's coalition battling the Skagit nukes. "It would have been comical if it wasn't so serious."

As the ultimate referee, the NRC decided it was time to end the game of seismic hot-potato. Even the utilities agreed. Around the same time the NRC recruited Margaret Hopper and her USGS colleagues to conduct an independent review, the utilities jointly commissioned their own "blue-ribbon panel" to settle on a final resting place for the troublesome quake. The man in charge was Howard A. Coombs, professor emeritus and former chairman of the University of Washington Geology Department.

An influential figure, Coombs had a hand in every dam construction project across the Northwest. He served as a geological adviser to the Allied Supreme Commander after World War II, helping Japan establish a network of hydroelectric plants. When a dam on Idaho's Teton River blew out in 1976, killing eleven people and sweeping away thousands of cattle, Coombs was one of the experts called in to investigate. He was also a paid consultant to most of the Northwest nuclear power projects.

Coombs, Hopper, and their respective teams set off down parallel paths. Each team member independently reviewed the historic reports, gauging their credibility. The scientists ranked the force of the quake at various locations using a measurement scale much older than Richter's. The Modified Mercalli Intensity (MMI) scale was invented in the late 1800s by Giuseppe Mercalli, an Italian scientist and priest who was also renowned for his studies of Mount Vesuvius. The scale has been tweaked multiple times and still comes in handy. The USGS "Did you feel it?" network uses an online questionnaire to quiz people about their experiences in a quake and the damage they witnessed, the same factors Mercalli focused on.

A quake with an MMI rating of Roman numeral I is barely a tickle. A IV feels like a convoy of trucks passing by. At VII, everyone runs outside, windows break, and chimneys fall. Only a few quakes in history have attained a rating of XII, succinctly defined as "total destruction."

But as Coombs and his team sorted through the accounts from the 1872 quake, one of the things they found most striking was something that didn't happen: the Omak Rock didn't fall. Located about thirty miles from the Canadian border in Eastern Washington's Okanagan Valley, the rock is a forty-ton chunk of granite perched atop a narrow stone base like a golf ball on a tee. The utilities hired yet another consultant to estimate how much force it would take to topple the boulder and what that suggested about the ground shaking in 1872. His conclusions later proved wildly off the mark. But at the time, Coombs and his team found it hard to believe that a powerful quake centered near Entiat, a scant fifty miles away, would have left the Omak Rock upright.

Hopper was less impressed with the rock. Mercalli's scale doesn't mention boulders, so she focused on the effects people reported across the region. "The kind of proof you want is a good report from a reliable person who says, 'The furniture was knocked over, things fell off shelves, windows broke,'" Hopper said. "That's the kind of thing I can work with."

And that's exactly what the outlaw John McBride seemed to offer.

From the moment researchers came across it in the archives of a long-defunct newspaper, there was no doubt McBride's description was vivid and compelling. But was it reliable? "When you're working with historical data, you take what you get," Hopper said. Every other account from Central Washington—the tales of Ribbon Cliff and the day the Columbia ran dry, the yarns about geysers, and even the destruction of Wapato John's cabin—were committed to paper years later. But McBride was chatting with a big-city journalist almost before the dust had settled.

In his interview with the *Portland Press Herald*, McBride didn't explain why he had traveled to Oregon's biggest settlement a couple of weeks after the quake. But the experience was fresh in his mind. When the shaking started, he told the reporter, he and Ingram were asleep at their ranch on the Wenatchee River, just a few miles from its confluence with the Columbia. The commotion was so loud they thought the stove had tipped over. "They immediately sprang from their couch, and were about donning their clothes, when they were thrown to the floor in a rather sudden manner," the article said. McBride had weathered two quakes in California, and he quickly realized what was happening. He and Ingram jumped on their horses in the moonlight and headed for the trading post, "the ground undulating in a disorderly manner as they rode along."

The trading post owners were in a tizzy, McBride told the reporter. When the quake shook them from their beds, they figured the store was being attacked by Indians. Armed with shotguns and pistols, they found a mess instead of would-be thieves. Flour sacks were strewn on the floor. The roof of the cabin was knocked askew and the kitchen had ripped away from the main building.

"The effect outside, Mr. McBride says, was terrible," the article continued. The peaks of several hills were "hurled over and broken" and trees crushed to bits. "Great masses of earth, as if from a tremendous landslide, rushed down the mountainside, mixed with stone and wood, and the gulches lost their identity by being filled with debris." Some of the shocks were preceded by explosions like "the discharge of several pieces of artillery simultaneously." Panicked tribal members gathered at the trading post, adding to the chaos. "The entire country was still alarmed and unsettled when (Mr. McBride) left there, fifteen days ago," the report concluded.

McBride's flamboyant narrative implied that the quake's fury was focused east of the Cascades, which wasn't good news for WPPSS. But it wasn't hard to find evidence that impugned the witness's credibility. There were ledgers from the trading post where McBride and Ingram were frequent purchasers of whiskey. Records also revealed the pair had originally owned the store but were forced to sell as a result of their legal entanglements. When the quake struck, McBride was out on bail, awaiting the trial that would send him to Walla Walla.

Coombs was inclined to trust the Omak Rock more than this ne'er-do-well. "Some of his observations are open to question," the blue-ribbon report noted. In the end Coombs split the difference. His blue-ribbon panel put the quake's epicenter east of the Cascades, which pleased the Skagit proponents, and close to the Canadian border, which pleased WPPSS. "He found a place to park it where it wouldn't be a problem, and everyone was happy," Cheney said.

But if the utilities expected that to be the final word, they should have known better.

Hopper and her colleagues gave McBride's account more weight. "It was reasonable enough," she said. "I didn't see why he would have lied about it." Nor did she see any reason to downplay stories from multiple sources about the Ribbon Cliff landslide. The USGS team ranked the ground shaking around Wenatchee and Entiat at level VIII—higher than either WPPSS or the blue-ribbon panel had. That difference, along with a few others, was enough to land the epicenter just north of Entiat, near the south end of Lake Chelan.

As the 1970s drew to a close, the nuclear plant files were bulging with geologic reports and maps suggesting at least four possible locations for the 1872 quake. In 1979 a University of Washington seismologist weighed in with a different interpretation that put the magnitude at 7.4 and the epicenter in the North Cascades, back in Skagit's court.

It didn't really matter. Public opposition in Skagit County was boiling over, and the project's budget was out of control. As the Skagit plants foundered, WPPSS was nearing its own precipice. The NRC approved the seismic analysis for the Columbia Generating Station, the only WPPSS plant to go into operation. The study concluded that the biggest historic quake in Hanford's vicinity was not 1872, but a magnitude 5.8 that struck near the Oregon border in 1936.

By 1980 McBride and his quake were fading back into obscurity. Two decades would pass before another USGS researcher decided to whack the tennis ball again. Bill Bakun, who worked in the agency's Menlo Park office, was armed with the latest science, including a method he developed to statistically weigh and cross-reference eyewitness accounts of historic quakes and factor in data about the way seismic waves reverberate in different areas.

Colleagues warned him off 1872. One described it as a can of worms that Bakun didn't want to get tangled up in. That only intrigued him more. A Seattle native, Bakun was keen to work in the Northwest. "For me, it was like going home," he recalled. With the nuclear controversy defused, there was none of the hyperventilating that surrounded the early studies. "No one really cared anymore, so we could look into these things without anybody getting upset."

Sorting through the old records again with Hopper, Bakun agreed that McBride made a credible witness. "It's really important, because if you believe his account, there was a lot of strong shaking there." But equally important was Bakun's new approach, which is now used around the world. It did away with the old method of mapping out intensity levels, then drawing concentric circles. Instead, computers crunch the data and come up with a more accurate estimate of where a quake was centered and how big it was. The approach also helped solve the mystery of whether the 1872 quake originated deep underground or on a shallow fault.

The picture Bakun and his colleagues assembled was unambiguous in concluding that the quake struck on a shallow fault near the southern end of Lake Chelan, just north of Entiat. He pegged the magnitude at 6.8, though with enough uncertainty that it could have fallen anywhere between 6.5 and 7.

Bakun's study may or may not be the final word. The Entiat area continues to rumble, with hundreds of small quakes in recent years. Most are tiny, but a few are as big as magnitude 4. It's enough to make the utilities that operate several Columbia River dams nervous. They're reevaluating seismic risk and contemplating ways to shore up the structures if necessary.

Depending on which magnitude estimate you believe, 1872 was the biggest or second-biggest quake in Washington's written history. The fact that it struck Central Washington makes sense in light of the tectonic squeezing that continues to crumple the area like a throw rug. "It's all riddled by faults," Bakun said. "It wouldn't surprise me to have a magnitude 6.8 quake anywhere in that region, including near Hanford."

During the nuclear rush, geologists scoured the surrounding hills for signs that the 1872 quake broke the surface. They found nothing. But the newest lidar surveys show a suspicious scarp not far from Entiat that Brian Sherrod and his team can't wait to dig into. If McBride were around, he'd no doubt be happy to wet their whistles while they work—for a price.

The Northwest's first seismometer was installed in Victoria, British Columbia, in 1899, nearly thirty years after McBride's earthshaking experience. The second was set up in 1909 by the Jesuits at Gonzaga University in Spokane. The Catholic order, which has always emphasized the teaching of science, began installing the newly developed instruments at missions and universities around the world in the late 1800s. The Jesuit Seismological Service was once the world's most extensive. Most of the stations were closed in the 1960s, when an explosion of seismic monitoring rendered them superfluous. By 2012 the Pacific Northwest was wired with more than four hundred seismometers that capture every twitch and automatically spit out epicenter information within seconds.

But pinning a size on an earthquake remains such a convoluted process that seismologists break out in a sweat trying to explain it to a layperson. The Pacific Northwest Seismic Network, based at the University of Washington, uses three scales, each measuring different properties. One yardstick works only for tiny shakes. Another covers the middle range. The biggest quakes demand a scale of their own.

No wonder, then, that *magnitude* is a term almost everyone knows but few understand. "It's even hard for the specialists to keep it all straight," admits John Vidale, the network's director. In some ways Charles Richter set an impossible goal in attempting to develop a single scale to measure and compare earthquakes. How can one number sum up something so complex? It's like trying to measure a hurricane. Should you focus on the storm's dimensions or on its vortex dynamics? What about wind speed, which varies widely from place to place, just like earthquake shaking?

Richter picked the simplest yardstick he could think of for earthquakes: how much they move the needle on the recording drum of a seismograph. Big quakes will trace out taller wiggles than small quakes, he reasoned. By comparing the height of the tallest wiggles from different quakes, it should be possible to rank them by size. Richter picked a specific type of seismometer for his measurements and developed equations to correct for the epicenter's distance from the recorder.

What he mainly wanted was a simple answer for the reporters and citizens who bombarded Caltech's seismology lab with questions after every quake. "We felt a certain responsibility to keep the public informed," Richter said in a 1982 interview, "particularly as misinformation was often seized upon and twisted in a way that was contrary to the public interest."

In the early 1930s, when Richter was testing his scale, the Southern California seismic network consisted of seven instruments. A true understanding of tectonic forces was decades away. But it was immediately clear that earthquakes came in such a staggering range of sizes that there was no way to squeeze them all onto the same scale without using numbers so big they would cause more confusion than clarity. "If there was anything you could call an actual discovery that came out of that scale, it was that the biggest earthquakes were enormously bigger than the little ones," Richter recalled.

At the suggestion of his boss, Beno Gutenberg, Richter resorted to what he called "a device of the devil." To keep the numbers on the scale manageable, he made it logarithmic instead of linear. The result was the deceptively straightforward numbering system seismologists still use today. And just as in Richter's time, a system that was meant to inform the public still leaves many people scratching their heads and wondering how earthquakes that are so close to one another in number can be so different on the ground.

An earthquake that measures 4 on the Richter scale isn't just slightly bigger than a 3. It's ten times bigger—if by bigger you mean the height of the tallest wiggle on a seismograph. (The instruments are all digital these days. The UW keeps a drum recorder in the basement so television crews have something to film after a quake.) A magnitude 5 is one hundred times bigger than a 3. Jump up to 6 and you've got a quake that's one thousand times bigger than a 3, and so forth, stepping up the scale by factors of ten.

But if you're more concerned with the amount of energy unleashed by earthquakes—a truer mark of destructive force—then you have to pull out your calculator and multiply by 31.6 for each step up the scale. That makes a magnitude 6 more than thirty thousand times stronger, or more energetic, than a magnitude 3.

Over the years a few lonely voices have pleaded for a more user-friendly scale. In his book *The Sizesaurus*, Canadian science writer Stephen Strauss pitched a fit. "Why is something that looks as simple as 1-2-3-4-5-6-7-8-9 so bloody confusing?" he asked. An op-ed in the *San Francisco Chronicle* titled "It's Time to Dump the Richter Scale" pointed out that computer owners don't blanch at big numbers, like gigabytes. Why can't a public that's well acquainted with trillion-dollar deficits digest an earthquake scale that ranges from 1 all the way up to 20 trillion, asked the author. "We know that a 20 mph wind is twice the velocity of a 10 mph wind. Two inches of rain is twice as wet as one inch of rain," he wrote. "Our new scale should reflect the actual energy or shaking a person would feel." Then, as if to underscore his point, the writer was forced to append a lengthy correction because he screwed up describing the current scale. A few scientists have even called for a linear scale. But they might as well insist the United States go metric or dump "The Star-Spangled Banner" because no one can hit the high notes. Maybe it ought to happen, but it's not going to.

Seismologists don't have any problem with logarithms, but they were quick to find other faults in Richter's scale. Designed for the shallow quakes typical in California, it didn't do a good job of sizing up deep quakes that shake the ground in a different way. Nor was it good at measuring quakes from far away. In fact, as seismologists studied earthquakes in more detail, they realized that "shaking" encapsulates a wide range of motions, from back-and-forth and side-ways to up-and-down and everything in between. Some waves hit fast and hard. Others are slow and undulating. Just as the human ear can't detect all the sounds a dog's ear can, no single type of seismometer can capture all the different ground motions. And the very biggest quakes simply blow most instruments off the scale.

Richter's system was tweaked many times, and entirely new scales and instruments were developed to better capture the diversity of shaking. By the 1990s, more than twenty different scales were in use, and scientists were arguing that Richter's original was obsolete. "The many different magnitude scales are generally all included together in the maddeningly vague term 'Richter scale,' which is popular with the press but meaningless to a seismologist," wrote Tom Heaton, who had joined the faculty at Caltech by then.

The favored replacement, the moment magnitude scale, is a more complete measure of a quake's fury. Unlike Richter's it's based on actual measurements, calculated from seismograms, of the size of the fault rupture that generates a quake. It was only after developing the moment magnitude scale that seismologists were able to fully appreciate just how powerful some past quakes were, including Chile's

THE MOMENT MAGNITUDE SCALE

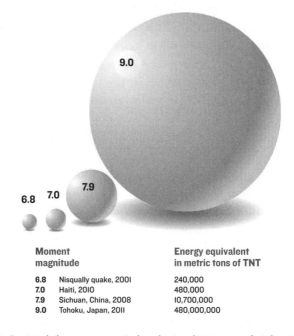

Moment magnitude		Energy equivalent in metric tons of TNT
6.8	Nisqually quake, 2001	240,000
7.0	Haiti, 2010	480,000
7.9	Sichuan, China, 2008	10,700,000
9.0	Tohoku, Japan, 2011	480,000,000

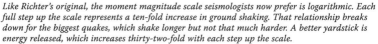

Like Richter's original, the moment magnitude scale seismologists now prefer is logarithmic. Each full step up the scale represents a ten-fold increase in ground shaking. That relationship breaks down for the biggest quakes, which shake longer but not that much harder. A better yardstick is energy released, which increases thirty-two-fold with each step up the scale.

world record 9.5 in 1960. But moment magnitude is useless for very small quakes. The signals they create are too weak.

So seismologists engage in a juggling act with every quake. The smallest are sized up on something called a "coda magnitude scale," which measures how long it takes for ground shaking to die out. Middling quakes of magnitudes 2 to 4 are measured using what is essentially Richter's scale, though seismologists call it "local magnitude." (Richter wouldn't mind. He was never comfortable with his name being attached to the scale.) For quakes bigger than that, the moment magnitude scale prevails.

When the Nisqually quake struck the Puget Sound area in 2001, the regional seismic network was tuned to the coda scale. As a result the first size estimate the system spit out was a paltry magnitude 4.8. Seismologists knew that was way too low, but the network wasn't set up yet to automatically calculate the magnitude of bigger quakes. They had to do the math by hand. The answer they got was magnitude 6.7, but they still weren't sure it was right. It was possible the quake was even bigger and had simply saturated the local instruments. Like students comparing answers on a math quiz, local seismologists got on the phone with the USGS National Earthquake Information Center in Colorado, which ultimately put the quake's official size at magnitude 6.8.

It's not unusual for different groups of scientists to come up with different magnitudes for the same quake. Numbers for the 2004 Indian Ocean quake range from 9.0 to 9.3. But like Richter, seismologists still want that single number for public consumption. "We just try to give the press a number we're not going to have to change," Vidale said. "We don't want to adjust it later and have to explain why, because it's almost impossible to explain these magnitude scales."

CHAPTER 8:

IT CAME FROM THE DEEP

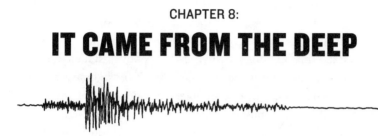

NO ONE IN THE PAST THREE HUNDRED YEARS has witnessed a Cascadia megaquake. Not a single soul in the past millennium has weathered a rupture on the Seattle Fault. But hundreds of thousands of people across the Northwest have stories to tell about the third type of earthquake that stalks the region: deep quakes, like the one that struck between Olympia and Seattle in 2001. Some old-timers have lived through three of them, including the biggest quake in Washington's recorded history.

Brian Schimpf was in the control tower at Sea-Tac Airport when the Nisqually quake of 2001 started rattling the glass just before 11:00 AM on February 28. It was a rare sunny winter's day. With two planes ready to land and another half-dozen taxiing for takeoff, Schimpf quickly sized up the situation.

"All right, we've got an earthquake," he announced over the radio. As the shaking intensified, ceiling tiles and insulation rained down on the controllers. *The Seattle Times* reported that Schimpf sounded "almost calm" as he continued broadcasting. "Attention all aircraft in Seattle. We have a huge earthquake going on. The tower is collapsing. I say again: The tower is falling apart." With a Boeing 767 on final approach, the three-quarter-inch-thick windows began to shatter. "For the first time in my life," Schimpf told the newspaper, "I thought I was probably going to die."

On the West Seattle Bridge, streetlights popped and smoked and cars skidded to a stop. Some drivers feared the bridge was falling. Nearly two thousand people were at work in Starbucks' headquarters, a brick behemoth south of downtown built in 1912. One employee said it felt like the building was slammed with a battering ram. "People were screaming. Things were falling off the walls, flying off desks, and filing cabinets were falling over," he told a reporter. Chunks of facade and parapet tumbled nine stories to the ground, and water pipes burst. The building's owner had recently installed massive X-beams to make it more earthquake safe. "If those braces weren't there, we'd be looking at a pile of rubble," said one worker. Repairs and upgrades still cost $50 million.

Paula Vandorssen's home was a total loss. She was lucky to escape with her life when a river of mud sloughed off the slope in her backyard south of Seattle. "It was two seconds I had, and by the third my house was gone," Vandorssen said. The slide cracked her white frame house in two and filled it with four feet of muck. Her Volkswagen was buried, her cat killed. "If my kids had been home, we would have been dead," she told a reporter.

The churning mass of mud and logs poured across Vandorssen's lawn into the Cedar River, damming its flow and threatening to flood neighboring homes. A quick-thinking streets supervisor dashed to a construction site and commandeered backhoes to scoop up the mud and return the river to its banks.

In Olympia state workers dove under tables as two-hundred-pound light fixtures came crashing down. The dome on the capitol building shifted and twisted on its base while sandstone columns pulled away from the edifice. One of the hardest-hit areas was Seattle's historic Pioneer Square. Merchants were still cleaning up from an ugly brawl during Mardi Gras celebrations the previous night. Like a scene from a slapstick movie, a worker who had just finished replacing broken windows at The Elliott Bay Book Company watched his handiwork shatter. Around the corner bricks rained from an old hotel, crushing cars parked on the street.

"I'm just stunned that there hasn't been a greater loss of life," FEMA director Joe Allbaugh said when he toured the state. The only person to die during the quake suffered a heart attack. More than four hundred people were injured, though, and about forty thousand applied for federal assistance, the most from any natural disaster in state history. Official estimates put the total damages at $2 billion. The quake clocked in at magnitude 6.8.

As she cleaned up broken knickknacks after the shaking stopped in 2001, Seattle-area resident Carol Davis recalled riding out similar quakes in 1949 and 1965, and how much she hated feeling the ground shift under her feet. She started to throw out the fragments of ceramic angels and crystal doves, then changed her mind. "I put them back where they were to remind me to be alert and think about how I can help others when things like this happen," she told a reporter.

It's entirely possible seismic veterans like Davis will be around for the next Nisqually-style shakeup. The USGS estimates that damaging deep quakes strike the Puget Sound region every thirty years, on average. But that's just a guess. Some scientists suspect as many as seven or eight have hit the region over the past century, which pencils out to a quake every dozen years or so. Two of them struck a scant three years apart. The odds are the region's next destructive quake will be of this type. Yet even though deep quakes are the Northwest's most common big ones—with a small b—they are also the least understood.

Deep quakes emanate from dozens of miles underground, where the laws of geophysics say rocks shouldn't fracture at all. They leave so few clues on the surface that they're almost impossible to study. Except for a short historic record, scientists are largely flying blind as they try to estimate how often deep quakes strike and how destructive they can be. One of the only things known for sure is that deep quakes in the Northwest originate inside the oceanic plate being shoved under the continent. But exactly what transpires down there to make the ground shake over hundreds of thousands of square miles remains an enigma.

The depth of the quakes is a blessing, because it moderates their destructiveness. The shallow Northridge quake in 1994 was smaller than the Nisqually quake but did ten times more damage, killing seventy-two people and snapping freeways apart in Southern California. The curse of the Northwest's deep quakes is that they seem to cluster under the population centers of Puget Sound, though scientists warn that Oregon and British Columbia aren't immune. Nor was the Nisqually quake the worst case. Despite its multibillion-dollar price tag, the 2001 quake was a feeble example of what the deep Earth can serve up. The 1949 quake Carol Davis experienced as a girl measured magnitude 7.1, the most powerful in the state since record keeping started. Nisqually was about a third as strong.

"Some of the worst damage in the Western Hemisphere has come from these kinds of earthquakes," said University of Washington geophysicist Ken Creager. A deep quake under central Chile in 1939 killed almost thirty thousand people, far more than died in that country's world-record magnitude 9.5 megathrust in 1960. One of the most catastrophic quakes in modern history struck deep under the Peruvian coast in 1970, killing seventy thousand people. Most of the victims were buried under a debris avalanche that sloughed off the country's tallest peak—very much like past lahars from Mount Rainier that roared down valleys where tens of thousands of people live today.

Conventional wisdom in the Northwest holds that deep quakes here can't get much bigger than magnitude 7.2. But the Peruvian disaster measured 7.9. A similar quake in Japan hit magnitude 8. Could the Pacific Northwest see something that size, more than sixty times as powerful as Nisqually? "It wouldn't surprise me," Creager said. "To me, that's one of the big questions from a hazards perspective: What's the biggest deep earthquake we should be prepared for?"

Carol Davis was ten years old on April 13, 1949. She remembers playing at a friend's house and drinking lemonade before lunchtime. School was out for spring break. Davis was just about to head home when the porch started rolling so violently she could barely stand. More than sixty years later, she could clearly summon the feeling of choking on an ice cube as the railings danced in one direction and the steps gyrated in another. "It was horrible." When her father got home from work, he described racing out of his downtown office building, only to encounter a hail of bricks on the street.

Almost every building in Seattle's Pioneer Square was battered. The damage was equally extensive at the state capital complex in

Olympia. Twenty-five miles south in Chehalis, the shaking left four out of every ten homes and businesses in need of structural repairs. One golfer watched the fairways around him "roll like a shaken rug."

Bridges jammed, blocking ship traffic on the Duwamish River. In Puyallup, backyards erupted with mud geysers and so much water shot out of the ground that streets flooded. Eleven-year-old crossing-guard Martin Klegman was on patrol duty at his Tacoma school when the quake hit. He dashed back into the building to pull another boy to safety and was crushed to death as he shielded the youngster from falling debris.

Seven other people died across the Puget Sound region. Workers rebuilding the Tacoma Narrows Bridge, which had been ripped apart in a windstorm nine years before, clung to safety lines as bolts sheared and the five-hundred-foot towers whipped back and forth. A twenty-three-ton saddle designed to hold the suspension cables in place plunged into the water, crashing through a scow and injuring both men on board.

From his seismology lab at Caltech, Charles Richter classified the quake's intensity as "near major." The needle of the University of Washington's sole seismometer was jolted off the drum by the shaking. Scientists conferred and ciphered for more than two weeks before mistakenly pinning the epicenter on the Olympic Peninsula when it was really near Olympia. Monitoring wasn't a whole lot better on April 29, 1965, when a magnitude 6.5 quake rumbled up from somewhere between Seattle and Tacoma. Once again the UW instrument, one of only three seismometers in the Pacific Northwest at the time, was knocked offline. As data came in from more distant stations, local scientists realized they were dealing with a deep source, even if they couldn't quite figure out what it was.

"For decades, really, in the history of seismology these were difficult earthquakes to explain," said USGS scientist emeritus Steve Kirby. Kirby spent much of his early career in rock labs, subjecting chunks of quartz to bone-crushing pressures and temperatures hot enough to wilt steel beams. That's how geologists try to simulate what goes on in the depths of Earth, far below the reach of any drill rig. One of the things Kirby was curious about was why deep quakes happen when they aren't supposed to.

Most earthquakes pop in the Earth's uppermost layer, the crust, where rocks are cold and brittle. Quakes like Nisqually originate thirty to sixty miles down, where temperatures are approaching two thousand degrees Fahrenheit and rock is becoming more like Silly Putty than porcelain. At the same time, the weight of those miles of crust and mantle presses down so hard that any cracks in the rock are sealed shut. How could a fault possibly slip and generate an earthquake under those conditions?

"It was a big controversy," Kirby said. "One of the most famous geophysicists in Great Britain declared that deep earthquakes were not possible."

As seismometers improved, the data became harder to dismiss. By the late 1930s, Japanese seismologist Kiyoo Wadati had documented the locations of more than a dozen deep earthquakes in Japan. Some originated four hundred miles or more below decks. Victor Hugo Benioff, a Caltech colleague of Charles Richter's, took a similar inventory of deep earthquakes around the world. The dots on Benioff's map clustered along the edges of continents, many positioned under volcanic arcs like the Cascades. The bands of deep seismicity were angled like ramps descending from the coastline into the planet's bowels. Scientists named them Wadati-Benioff zones.

It remained for plate tectonics to make sense of the pattern. An understanding of what happens when oceanic and continental plates collide was one of the last pieces of the tectonic puzzle to fall into place. Scientists had already figured out ocean rifts and seafloor spreading by the time they hit on subduction. The realization that the seafloor sank under the continents and melted down in the Earth's interior furnace set mental lightbulbs flashing among the handful of scientists who were curious about deep earthquakes. Kirby's thesis adviser was one of them, and he urged his protégé to help unravel the mystery.

As seismologists looked closer, they saw that all deep quakes occur within subducting slabs. The reason is temperature. As a slab of ocean floor like the Juan de Fuca Plate dives into the Earth, it keeps

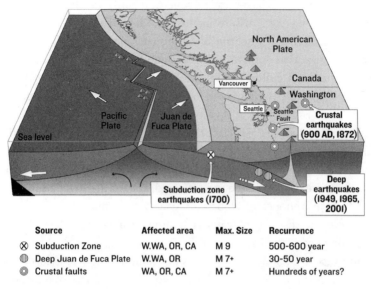

CASCADIA EARTHQUAKE SOURCES

	Source	Affected area	Max. Size	Recurrence
⊗	Subduction Zone	W.WA, OR, CA	M 9	500-600 year
⬭	Deep Juan de Fuca Plate	W.WA, OR	M 7+	30-50 year
◎	Crustal faults	WA, OR, CA	M 7+	Hundreds of years?

The process of subduction is responsible for all three types of earthquakes that occur in the Pacific Northwest: deep quakes, shallow crustal quakes, and megaquakes.

its cool on a geologic temperature scale. Even one hundred miles or more below the surface, the rocks remain stiff enough to snap. Down where Nisqually-type quakes are born, the subducting Juan de Fuca Plate is about a thousand degrees Fahrenheit, half as hot as the surrounding rock. The still-rigid slab is under enormous strain as it's shoved, bent, stretched, and crunched beneath North America. Imagine trying to bend and twist a marble countertop. No wonder the rocks might crack.

But the fact that the subducting slab is cool enough to crack isn't enough to explain deep earthquakes. Even if the rocks in the Juan de Fuca Plate were riddled with cracks, thirty miles of the Earth's mass pressing down from above would pinch those cracks—or faults—tightly shut. There's no way the faults should be able to slip and generate earthquakes under pressures that intense. And yet they do. Something must be greasing the skids, and Kirby and other scientists think it's probably water.

Kirby knew from the types of lab experiments he conducted early in his career that if you heat rock and squeeze it hard enough, it can morph into something else. Pressure and heat can also wring water from crystals in the rock, like squeezing a wet sponge. Consider basalt, the black volcanic rock that dominates the seafloor. When shoved down a subduction zone, it pulls a Cinderella act. The result is a drop-dead gorgeous stone called eclogite (ek-lo-jite), laced with green and studded with blood-red garnets. A very lucky rockhound might find a chunk of eclogite that shot to the surface through the kind of volcanic pipes that also transport diamonds. During basalt's high-pressure metamorphosis into eclogite, water is ejected. If that liquid accumulates in existing cracks or weak spots in the rock, it could serve as a wedge to pry open the fault, and enough of a lubricant to allow the fault to slip.

There's no shortage of water-rich minerals in oceanic slabs like the Juan de Fuca Plate. Kirby saw it for himself on an expedition off the southwest coast of Africa. Using a ship-mounted rig, scientists drilled nearly a third of a mile into the seafloor. The cylinders of dark rock they pulled up were shot through with cracks. Lining the cracks was a type of emerald-colored mineral called greenschist that's loaded with water. "You could see it from across the room," Kirby recalled. "That really rang a bell with me."

The mineral-laden cracks struck him as triggers, cocked to set off future earthquakes. As the plate subducts deeper into the earth, the water would be squeezed out of the minerals. "So the water is right where you need it to reactivate these faults," Kirby said. The observation inspired him to return to the lab, where he conducted experiments using ice as a stand-in for oceanic crust to show the types of fractures that might result. Later, a team of British scientists went even further, subjecting rock cores the size of a pencil lead to searing temperatures and some of the highest pressures ever generated in a lab. Water rushed out of the crystals and the rock fractured with a pop. "You can hear it," Kirby said. "It's like creating a mini-earthquake."

The water idea is the best anyone has come up with to explain what makes the Northwest's deep quakes tick, but there's no way to prove it. The study of seismic goings-on deep underground is a classic example of what's sometimes called black-box geology. Another word for it is geophysics. Author John McPhee captured the tension in the early 1980s between the old-school field geologists whose numbers were dwindling and the new breed who spent most of their time sitting in front of computers. In *Annals of the Former World* one geologist groused, "The name of the game now is 'modeling.' A lot of it, I can't see for sour owl shit."

A hint of that sentiment remains, though it mostly takes the form of good-natured banter between the few field geologists left and the geophysicists who far outnumber them on university faculties. The debate over the Cascadia Subduction Zone's ability to generate big quakes pitted field geologists like Brian Atwater and others against geophysicists whose models and calculations suggested the fault was dead. There was a saying going around back then that could have come from McPhee's hard-rock man: "When geology and geophysics clash, throw geophysics in the trash." In other words, believe the evidence in front of your eyes. Most geoscientists would agree on that point, Kirby included. "My own view is that there's no substitute for being able to actually lay your hands on the fault and look at the rocks," he said, wistfully.

But until someone invents a machine to descend into the Earth à la Jules Verne, Kirby and his colleagues aren't going to get their hands on the rocks involved in deep quakes. Instead they pore over fuzzy gravity images, break rocks in the lab, and build mathematical models to extrapolate those results to what goes on in a Nisqually-style quake. Seismology is a type of geophysics that uses seismic waves, both natural and man-made (as in the Kingdome implosion), to probe the Earth. The seismic signals from deep earthquakes proved to be a particularly powerful tool. Much of what scientists know about the planet's inner layers—the mantle and the core—came from analyzing the ways waves from deep quakes reverberate and ricochet through the Earth.

Kirby coined the term *intraslab* to describe the deep quakes common in the Pacific Northwest. The name caught on, but there hasn't been a stampede of scientists eager to study them. In addition to being out of reach, the quakes don't leave geologic fingerprints that researchers can follow. Intraslab quakes don't rupture the ground like quakes on shallow faults, so there aren't any scarps to show up on lidar. Nor do deep quakes uplift beaches or drown forests, like subduction zone quakes. The Nisqually quake was the region's first since GPS and satellite sensors came on the scene, and the instruments detected just a half-inch slump at the epicenter. With no way to burrow into the distant past, scientists have little more than a hundred years of history to rely on as an indicator of what the future holds.

Since the start of the twentieth century, the Northwest has been rattled by eighteen quakes known or suspected to have deep roots. Quakes from the pre-seismogram era were included on the list if newspaper accounts didn't mention aftershocks. The lack of significant aftershocks is another mystery about deep quakes, but it's a feature they seem to share around the world.

Eight of the suspects on the list had estimated magnitudes of 5.5 or more. A quake in 1909 severed underwater telegraph cables and cracked concrete walls near the Canadian border. Mr. Ed. R. Novak, a rubber salesman whose residence was Seattle's Lincoln Hotel, was moved to compose a poem about his experience. Published in the *Seattle Daily Times*, it read, in part:

"Just then, Ha! Ha! I felt a feeling. Was I drunk or sober?

And gazing on my eggs I found that they had been turned over."

In 1939 a tremor estimated at magnitude 6.2 shook the ground so hard that water mains broke in Seattle and cornices toppled from buildings. "I was never so scared in my life," Washington Governor Clarence D. Martin admitted. When a more powerful quake struck in 1946, UW Professor G. E. Goodspeed assured a rattled citizenry that "no more strong shocks will occur for five or six years." The biggest quake in the state's history arrived three years later, in 1949.

The following sixteen years were a period of relative seismic peace. By the time Carol Davis experienced her second major earthquake, in 1965, she was married and working as a schoolteacher. On the morning of April 29, Davis was in her home economics class at Renton Junior High School south of Seattle when she felt the familiar, sickening motion. "It scared the living daylights out of the students," she recalled. Bricks fell at the school, but no one was injured.

Elsewhere across the region, six people died. A fifty-thousand-gallon wooden water tank toppled seven stories from a flour mill on Seattle's Harbor Island, killing one man and injuring another. A huge landslide ripped down Mount Si, east of Seattle. The shaking toppled power lines near Everett and knocked out circuits at Grand Coulee Dam, nearly two hundred miles from the epicenter. *The Seattle Times* published a picture of a worker up to his knees in suds at the Rainier Brewery, where fifteen thousand gallons of beer spilled from tanks and broken pipes.

It's no more than an interesting coincidence that the last three major quakes all struck in late February or April. But their geographical proximity is probably no accident. The 2001 and 1949 quakes seem to have originated from almost the same spot under the Nisqually delta. The 1965 quake was centered a bit farther north. Every significant deep quake in the past century had its epicenter somewhere under the Puget Sound basin or Georgia Strait.

"Why do they occur there?" Kirby asked. "That's a very good question and we don't have many clues."

Creager, the UW professor, thinks the answer lies in simple geometry. Along most of its length, the Northwest coastline is as straight as a ruler. The exception is the seaward jog that begins at the central Washington coast and continues along the southern end of Vancouver Island. The subduction zone, which parallels the coast, seems to have a hard time negotiating that curve.

Like a tablecloth draped over a corner, it bunches up. But a basalt slab doesn't pleat as easily as linen. "It creates a huge strain, geologically speaking," Creager said. That stretch of seafloor is also slightly older and colder than segments to the north and south, which could make the plate there even less pliable. "That may be why we get more earthquakes in this corner."

The absence of deep quakes elsewhere in the Northwest in recent times doesn't mean those places get a free pass. The quakes might strike more frequently where the subduction zone is squeezed into a corner, but there's no obvious reason why they couldn't strike in Oregon and southern Washington as well. "I think we're just in a quiet period," Creager said. Come back in another hundred years and the record will probably include deep quakes throughout the region.

Time alone will answer the size question, as well. Theory suggests deep quakes bigger than about 7.2 aren't likely in the Northwest. It's a matter of space, Creager explained. Most of the region's deep earthquakes seem to originate in the brittle crust of the subducting Juan de Fuca Plate. That crust is only about five miles thick, which isn't big enough to contain a rupture of the size it would take to generate a giant quake. In places like Japan and Bolivia, where the biggest intraslab quakes occur, the subducting plates are older and thicker.

But Creager isn't convinced that deep quakes as big as magnitude 8 couldn't happen in the Northwest. There's a lot scientists don't know about the phenomenon, including whether the deep quakes under Puget Sound are strictly confined to the subducting crust. Maybe ruptures can propagate through both the crust and mantle of the subducting plate—which would allow for bigger quakes. Creager agrees that it's highly speculative, but he thinks it's worth considering.

Even if Creager's theory isn't right, the region could still be in for some very nasty deep quakes in the future, said Craig Weaver, the regional USGS seismology chief. A magnitude 7.2 would be four times more powerful than anything the Northwest has experienced in more than fifty years. Not only would the ground shake harder—it would shake longer. The Nisqually quake lasted about forty seconds. Another five to ten seconds of shaking, and many of Seattle's old brick buildings probably would have collapsed, along with the rickety Alaskan Way viaduct along the city's waterfront.

Nisqually was Carol Davis's most serene seismic experience. From the chairlift at Crystal Mountain ski area, she noticed something odd about the treetops. "They were dancing, waving back and forth," she recalled. The chair stopped for about ten minutes. "I said to my friend, 'I'll bet that was an earthquake.'" At the top of the hill, a message board confirmed Davis's hunch. The road down the mountain was blocked for hours by boulders and fallen trees. Back at home Davis's broken bric-a-brac were the only casualties.

USGS seismologist Bob Norris's day got off to a more explosive start. He was bumping along a gravel road on Seattle's Harbor Island, a sprawling industrial complex that sits on what used to be the Duwamish River Delta. Fill shakes harder than any other type of ground, so the USGS had installed a strong-motion seismometer near a tank farm in the former tide flat. Norris was there to download data from the instrument.

When the earthquake hit, he thought he had run over something. Norris stopped the truck. "I went through several seconds of confusion because the truck was still rocking sharply," he recalled. In most parts of town, the strongest motion lasted about twenty seconds. But the ground under Norris's truck kept pounding like a jackhammer. All he could do was hold on and hope his head didn't smash into the windshield. As the motion eased, he watched two-hundred-foot cargo cranes flexing "like huge steel giraffes trying to dance."

What happened next was something even the seasoned earthquake scientist had never seen. Almost ten minutes after the shaking stopped, water started pouring from the ground, then coalesced into a muddy geyser. Norris at first thought the quake had broken a water pipe. But what he was witnessing was liquefaction. When sandy soils take a seismic pounding, they turn to a watery slop. Some of that water is ejected from the ground under pressure. By the time Norris left, the swirling pool was fifty feet across and growing by the second.

Liquefaction in built-up tide flats, waterfronts, and along river valleys is a serious cause of damage in major quakes, undermining structures and heaving up buried utility lines. In the days and weeks that followed the Nisqually quake, scientists fanned out across the region to catalog liquefaction effects. They found sinkholes, buildings with lopsided foundations, and cracks in airport runways.

Scientifically, the quake was a bonanza. One group of researchers examined stream gauges and discovered that water levels spiked in many areas, presumably because the quake compacted the soil and squeezed out groundwater. Another team followed the trail of broken chimneys to identify neighborhoods that shook harder than others.

Spectacular sand volcanoes, like the one Norris saw, erupted around Lake Sammamish east of Seattle, as buried sand liquified by the shaking burst to the surface like toothpaste shot from a tube. Worms surfaced, too—as many as one per square foot in the most jostled areas. Every evening scientists and building engineers gathered at the University of Washington to drink beer and talk about what they'd seen. "It was a pretty intense ten days that followed the quake," said UW seismologist Bill Steele.

The most sobering insights emerged later, when seismologists analyzed patterns of shaking and seismic waves. The UW had just installed more than two dozen sturdy new instruments that wouldn't be knocked off scale by strong ground motions. Nisqually was the first big quake in the Northwest to be so thoroughly documented. The payoff was unequivocal proof that the five-mile-deep basin underlying Seattle and its environs is bad news.

During the Nisqually quake, the basin trapped and amplified seismic waves even more than scientists had expected. The ground in the basin shook longer, and it shook up to three times harder than elsewhere. The effect will come into play in every type of future quake, whether deep, shallow, or from the subduction zone. "There's always going to be that extra kick from the basin," Weaver said.

The USGS calculates 80 percent odds that another deep quake will strike the Puget Sound region in the next fifty years. That's as close to a sure bet as seismology can offer. What scientists have no way of estimating is whether the next one will be a relative lamb, like Nisqually, or whether it might set a state record. "People have a tendency to think, I made it through 1965 and 2001 so my building must be ready for the next one," Weaver said. "They don't appreciate the fact that there's a lot of variability in these things."

CHAPTER 9:
RUN FOR YOUR LIFE

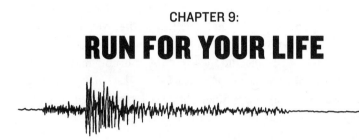

THE PARENTS STILL COME to Okawa Elementary. Alone or in groups, they leave toys on the makeshift altar or stand silently in front of a stone carving of a mother cradling her child. When the weather is cold, they dress the statue warmly in a cap and scarf. Snow blanketed the ground on the day their children died, and it's as if the grieving mothers and fathers can't shake the chill.

Like shell-shocked Americans after the twin towers fell, the Japanese gave a name to the most devastating trauma of their generation. They call it 3/11.

When the ground jolted on the afternoon of March 11, 2011, the youngsters in Okawa knew what to do. They dived under their desks and held on. But this quake was different than the ones they'd experienced before. The shaking seemed to go on forever. "Wow, it's a big one," one boy said to another, eyes wide with alarm. "Are you OK?"

Everyone was. The school northeast of Sendai was built to ride out quakes. In a well-rehearsed routine, the students grabbed helmets to protect themselves from aftershocks and falling debris and followed their teachers onto the playground. They assembled by grade, first through sixth.

Tsunami evacuation wasn't part of the school's regular drills. The concrete complex was nearly two miles from the sea, near the banks of a meandering river. It seemed impossible any wave could reach that far. When the tsunami alarm sounded, people who lived nearby evacuated to the school, confident the two-story building would be safe.

While the students shivered, teachers debated whether to stay put or head for higher ground. One teacher argued they should lead the children up a steep hill behind the school. But it was brushy and slick with snow. Precious minutes ticked by before the teachers decided to shepherd their flock to an elevated roadway by the river. The children marched in orderly ranks, oldest in front, youngest in back. Only as they approached the bridge did they spot the churning mass of water spilling over banks and pouring across fields. The smallest children couldn't see what was happening. They were bewildered when the fifth- and sixth-graders wheeled around and raced past them. Then the water swallowed them all.

"It felt like a huge gravitational pull," one twelve-year-old survivor told the BBC weeks later. "I was struggling for breath." The wave slammed him against the hillside, burying him up to his waist in mud. Another boy used his helmet as a flotation device, then scrambled onto a refrigerator bobbing in the water. The fast-moving flood overtopped the two-story building and crashed through the classrooms.

Cut off from the school by the floodwaters, the children's families waited anxiously through the night. Rumors circulated that the students were safe, that all of them had made it to the top of the hill. The next day, volunteer firefighters reached the site by boat. The building was a battered shell. Small bodies floated in the filthy water. Of the school's 108 students, 74 had been swept away. Only 1 teacher out of 11 survived.

When the water finally receded, family members picked through the wreckage and mud, desperate to find their children's remains. The search dragged on through the spring and early summer. After official efforts ended, one mother learned to operate a backhoe and kept dredging for any sign of her twelve-year-old daughter. "I just wanted to find her with my own hands," she told a reporter. "To do whatever I could." In August the girl's torso washed up in a cove down the coast.

Standing in front of Cannon Beach Elementary, it's hard not to think about the children of Okawa. The school on Oregon's northern coast sits a scant half mile from the Pacific Ocean, its playground nestled in the crook of Ecola Creek. The next time the Cascadia Subduction Zone ruptures, the first tsunami waves are expected to hit Cannon Beach in about fifteen minutes.

"This is eight feet above sea level," said Patrick Corcoran, pulling his truck to a stop outside the 1950s-era school building in September 2012. A row of pine trees and cedar-shingled homes is all that stands between the school's eighty-some students and the beach. "The water will come from that way like a huge surge," Corcoran said. "When it does it will pulverize the houses and carry away the school and everyone in it."

It's Corcoran's job to be the bearer of bad news. As a coastal hazards specialist for Oregon Sea Grant, he works to instill in Northwesterners the visceral acceptance that what happened in Japan will happen here. It's not a message people welcome. "Nobody wants to hear that we're on top of a subduction zone that rips magnitude 9 earthquakes and generates huge tsunamis. But dude, it's been 312 years since the last one. We're overdue on the southern half."

Corcoran can riff nonstop on the theme of preparedness and the Northwest's lack thereof, but he has a harder time finding words to describe his visit to Japan a year after the tsunami. Towns just like Cannon Beach, Seaside, Newport, and other Oregon costal communities were scraped bare. All that was left were neatly sorted piles of debris. Corcoran couldn't keep from crying as his Japanese hosts described the way fishermen lashed themselves to their vessels when they saw the wave approaching. The men didn't want their bodies to be lost, compounding their loved ones' grief.

To the Japanese, the loss of nearly twenty thousand lives represented a shocking failure of the country's disaster preparedness. But only about 10 percent of the people in the tsunami zone perished. Ninety percent evacuated to safety. To Corcoran, it was clear the numbers won't be as good in the Pacific Northwest. "We'd be lucky if 9 percent would intentionally do the right thing."

No place in Oregon is better prepared for a tsunami than Cannon Beach, and even the community's biggest boosters admit they have a long way to go. The upscale tourist town has been holding tsunami drills for more than a decade. For a small fee, residents can stash emergency supplies in one of two shipping containers tucked in the hills above Highway 101.

The youngsters at Cannon Beach Elementary walk the 1.2-mile evacuation route to high ground several times a year. On a clear day, with no buckled pavement and fallen power lines in their way, it takes them twenty-five minutes.

There's a shorter route, but it leads over Ecola Creek. In 1964 the tsunami from Alaska's megaquake ripped out the bridge there and deposited it in a horse pasture. Its replacement will likely be shaken to smithereens in a Cascadia megaquake.

Corcoran walked onto the narrow span and pointed out the high ground, just a few blocks from the school playground. "This is the missing link, guaranteed to fail."

The school complex itself is so wobbly the kids might never make it out the door. Engineers warn that the wooden gymnasium, shaped like a Quonset hut, stands a good chance of collapsing when the ground heaves for several minutes. Classrooms could cave in when the wall of windows on one side shatters. The flimsy covered walkway will tumble down, blocking exit doors.

Local folks know this. They realize that every day students file into the school is a roll of the dice. The long-term plan is to relocate Cannon Beach Elementary and several other schools to a joint campus on high ground. But first the small communities have to buy the land. Then they have to scrape up enough money to construct the buildings. Nobody even ventures a guess as to how much it will cost and when the students will finally be out of harm's way.

In the meantime Cannon Beach set a more modest goal of building a footbridge over Ecola Creek sturdy enough to survive the earthquake. There's no need to bother making the bridge tsunami proof, Corcoran said. "If you're not over it by the time the tsunami gets here you're going to die."

If Corcoran speaks more bluntly than most emergency managers, it's because he isn't one. Oregon Sea Grant is a kind of maritime extension service affiliated with Oregon State University. It gives Corcoran the freedom to be a pain in the butt. At public meetings he's the one who keeps steering the discussion away from science to the practical tips people need to survive. It irks him that after spending millions on research to identify the threat, society invests pennies in public education. "This isn't a geological problem anymore," he said, driving north from Cannon Beach toward the neighboring community of Seaside. "What we have now is a learning problem."

Japan hammered home the point that tsunamis can kill many more people than the earthquakes that spawn them. At least 95 percent of those who died on 3/11 were drowned or battered by the tsunami and its deadly load of debris. In a Cascadia megaquake, the toll from the ground-shaking itself will almost certainly be higher than in Japan, simply because the roads and buildings aren't up to Japan's standards. But just as in Japan, the tsunami is likely to be the biggest killer. "In my mind, there's no doubt about it," said Eddie Bernard, a tsunami expert and former director of the National Oceanic and Atmospheric Administration's Pacific Marine Environmental Laboratory in Seattle.

Just how bad it will be depends on so many factors that it's almost impossible to predict. More than 125,000 people live and work in tsunami-vulnerable areas of the outer coast, from Esperanza, British Columbia, to Eureka, California. On a sunny day in August, with festivals, 5K races, and antique car shows in full swing, the population can more than double. Even if people in the Northwest were as conscientious as the Japanese about heading for high ground, ten thousand or more could die in the next Cascadia tsunami.

Hurricane Katrina claimed 1,800 lives. The 9/11 terrorist attacks killed 3,000. "How would our nation respond to 10,000 or 20,000 dead?" Bernard asked. "This is not something we're psychologically prepared for."

Japan's response to its tsunami threat was a multibillion-dollar program to buttress the coastline with gargantuan gates and breakwaters. The biggest seawall in the world was constructed across Kamaishi harbor, at a cost of $1.6 billion. On 3/11, the tsunami blew past the barrier like a locomotive over a speed bump. Even if Japan's fortifications had held, the United States would no more armor its coastline than it would outlaw construction on waterfront property. Over the coming decades, coastal communities like Cannon Beach may succeed in gradually shifting schools, fire stations, and other critical facilities to high ground—if the subduction zone holds off that long. But when it rips, people caught in the danger zone still won't have any better option than to follow the tsunami evacuation plan spelled out on the back of the sweatshirt Corcoran was wearing: Grab beer. Run like hell.

Minus the beer, that's the message he preaches over and over. "When you feel the earthquake, get as high as you can, as fast as you can, probably on foot," he said, as if reciting a mantra. "You've got fifteen to twenty minutes." Only when people grasp that reality do they really begin to prepare themselves and pay more attention to their surroundings. A true believer, Corcoran always carries a backpack stuffed with rain gear, fire starter, and food in his truck. Whether he's shopping for groceries or hiking on the beach, he always knows where high ground is. It's not a fearful mind-set, just matter-of-fact.

Pulling into Seaside, Corcoran snagged a rare parking spot on Broadway. The boulevard leads from the waterfront promenade through the downtown strip where shops sell seagull art, pizza, and tee shirts. "We're in the inundation zone right now," he said. With a convention center, aquarium, and some of the most inviting beaches on the coast, this town of four thousand can swell to ten times that size in peak season.

No community on the Oregon coast is more vulnerable. Almost every hotel and restaurant is directly in the tsunami's path, as are more than three-quarters of the homes. Researchers at Oregon State University built a scale model of Seaside in a giant wave tank and slammed it with the equivalent of a thirty-five-foot surge, moderate by Cascadia standards. Community and business leaders watched in silence as the water rushed up Broadway and poured over the tops of buildings. The quake will also permanently lower the ground by several feet in Seaside and other coastal towns, turning waterfront property into tideflats.

High ground is a little more than a mile inland, Corcoran explained. But evacuees will have to pick their way through shattered glass and fallen bricks and cross two creeks on bridges that may not be there anymore. Corcoran once ran the route in seven minutes and thirty-three seconds with a documentary cameraman filming from a helicopter. "Everybody thought I was Brad Pitt. At least that's what I told them."

Corcoran's salt-and-pepper goatee is neater than Pitt's and he's a little too tall to body double for the movie star. He makes his rounds of Oregon's seaports and surfing coves with a yellow paddle board strapped to the roof of his Toyota Tacoma. Everywhere he goes he encounters obstacles and policies that could cost people their lives when the big one hits. You can almost see steam coming out of his ears as he ticks off some of his top peeves.

Take those Tsunami Evacuation Route signs on the roads. "Have you ever seen a sign that said, 'Stop. You're in a safe place'?" he asked. High ground isn't always obvious, and if people don't learn where it is in advance, they may never get there in time. In many Northwest towns, the closest upland is a knoll choked with blackberries. "We need to identify high ground and make it accessible."

The tsunami sirens that tower over the beach like something out of the Jetsons drive him crazy. Sure, a few might remain upright and functional after the quake. But don't count on it. "Don't be waiting for a siren or an emergency manager to come and take you by the hand," Corcoran said. "Be your own Jesus."

And don't get him started on the fact that it's legal to sell a beachfront home to a family of six from Iowa and never mention tsunami risk. Nursing homes that sit a few blocks from the beach accept patients without disclosing that their tsunami evacuation plan may be nothing more than moving patients to the top floor of a two-story building.

Gated communities? Imagine trying to pry open that tangle of wrought iron after the ground bucks and heaves for four minutes. Businesses that tout tsunami burgers and sell sweatshirts like the one Corcoran is wearing? No problem. But their employees shouldn't respond with a blank stare when customers ask them what to do in an earthquake. Corcoran will never forget the motel clerk in Florence, Oregon, who assured him that a jetty would protect the building from a tsunami. When Seaside's volunteer tsunami advisory group suggested asking overnight visitors to chip in to help replace bridges and improve evacuation routes, hotel owners balked. No one wants to remind customers that a beach vacation could be harmful to their health.

In Japan tsunami awareness is woven into the fabric of life. "When your grandma has gone through a tsunami and earthquake, you'd better believe you get drilled," Corcoran said, watching tourists stroll Seaside's sand at low tide. How many of them would know what to do if the ground shook violently? Many would jump in their cars, only to be caught in gridlock or trapped on impassable roads. Others would bolt for the five-story Shilo Hotel, not realizing it could be overtopped or gutted by the water. For those who aren't able-bodied enough to hike a mile, the eight-story Wyndham resort on the beach is a better bet, Corcoran said. But anyone who can hoof it to high ground should.

Corcoran's challenge is finding ways to pound those lessons into people's heads. One-on-one discussions work best, he's found. At meetings he'll stay until every question is answered, then chat with folks in the halls. But there's only one of him. Local emergency managers are stretched equally thin. So Corcoran is always hatching schemes, always brainstorming ways to integrate tsunami awareness into popular culture. If he were a comedian, his motto would be I've Got a Million of 'Em.

Why not design a slot machine that reflects the odds of a megaquake? Better yet, build casinos on high ground and host a tsunami day when the slots are free. Those hang-outs in the hills where teenagers go to drink beer and make out? Designate them as assembly areas. When Seaside hosted the annual Hood-to-Coast relay to raise money for cancer research, Corcoran suggested a Run for Your Life 2K, from the promenade to high ground. Some of his ideas are wacky, and people find plenty of reasons to turn him down.

"Oh, that's impossible," he mimicked the naysayers in a voice dripping sarcasm. "It can't be done. It's too *hard.*

"You know what's hard?" Corcoran leaned in for emphasis. "Outrunning a freaking tsunami is hard."

One thing former NOAA administrator Eddie Bernard used to know for sure is that tsunamis top out at about thirty feet. That's why he takes expert opinion with a grain of salt now. "I'm from that community that says, 'Oh, we know this stuff,'" Bernard said. "My experience is that everything I thought I knew, I underestimated."

The 2004 Indian Ocean tsunami, with hundred-foot surges, upended prevailing theories. Japan rewrote the book with waves that reached 130 feet in some places. Japanese seismologists were wrong, too. They assured the public that quakes off the northeast coast couldn't get much bigger than magnitude 8. The country's costly tsunami defenses were overwhelmed when a quake thirty times more powerful than expected unleashed a tsunami four times bigger than what Bernard's professors taught him was possible.

So he hesitates to predict how big the next Cascadia tsunami will be. After watching nature slap other parts of the world, Bernard warns it would be foolish not to brace for a similar blow here. But the Pacific Northwest is actually better prepared than Japan in one important way: American scientists haven't lowballed the earthquake risk. Tsunami simulations and evacuation maps have always been based on a full-rip 9. After Sumatra and Japan, scientists in the Northwest upped the ante even more, factoring in the possibility of quakes up to magnitude 9.2 and larger amounts of slip on the fault. Under those scenarios the models predict waves of one hundred feet in many areas. Under an "ordinary" magnitude 9 megaquake, the models suggest wave heights of up to sixty feet.

That doesn't mean towering curls sixty feet high will slam the coast. As videos from Japan and Sumatra showed, tsunamis come ashore as massive surges. When scientists measure their size, what they're talking about is run-up: how high the water reaches relative to sea level. A sixty-foot tsunami will flood coastal areas up to an elevation of sixty feet.

"In my mind Japan is a good proxy for what could happen here," said Bernard, who almost single-handedly kept tsunami research alive in the United States at a time when few people took the threat seriously. When the tall Texan started graduate school in oceanography in 1969, tsunamis were of interest only because they occasionally snuck up on places like Hawaii, triggered by earthquakes far away. When he first heard Brian Atwater describe sand layers deposited on the Washington coast by ancient tsunamis, Bernard, by then the leader of NOAA's Seattle lab, didn't believe it. "I was one of Brian's severest critics," he recalled.

How could Atwater be sure the sand wasn't washed in by storms, Bernard wanted to know. Maybe the shape of the coastline was different hundreds of years ago, making it more vulnerable to floods. At the time, NOAA's small tsunami program was focused mainly on preventing false alarms. A needless evacuation after a 1986 Alaska quake cost the state of Hawaii $40 million, and it wasn't the first. Officials there were fed up with rousting locals and tourists for piddling waves a foot or two high.

But a tsunami on the West Coast's doorstep would be a much deadlier threat. Following in Atwater's footsteps, geologists started digging in bays and marshes all along the coast. Almost everywhere they looked, including Seaside and Cannon Beach, they found similar layers of sand. Some of the ancient waves that roared up Ecola Creek left their tracks nearly a mile and a half inland. Other tsunamis seem to have been less ferocious. The surge kicked up by the 1700 megaquake—the one that flooded villages in Japan—left a sand layer so much smaller than some of the others that scientists called it "the wimp." Muddy cores from one coastal lake in Oregon revealed a period when quake-triggered tsunamis were slapping the coast every three hundred years or so, lending credence to the argument that the southern portion of the subduction may rip more frequently.

What really launched tsunami science in the United States, though, was a 1992 earthquake in Northern California that might have been a dress rehearsal for a Cascadia megaquake. The main shock struck on April 25, when the artist colony of Ferndale was hosting a Wild West festival. The ground shook so hard that participants, many dressed in cowboy costumes, staggered and fell to the pavement. Elegantly restored Victorian homes collapsed.

In nearby Petrolia the post office, gas station, and general store caught fire and burned to the ground. Fissures a hundred feet long ripped through pastures where horses had been grazing minutes before. The ground motions were some of the strongest ever recorded, but the Church of Scientology's underground vault in rural Humboldt County was reportedly unscathed. As the extent of the damage became clear, President George H. W. Bush issued a disaster declaration.

In the redwoods north of Eureka, Humboldt State University geology professor Lori Dengler and her family were getting ready for a picnic on the beach when their two-story house began to rock. After she caught her breath, Dengler started counting. When she ticked off seventy-five seconds, she knew it wasn't a typical California temblor. "I could tell it was big," she recalled. Her outing cancelled, Dengler sped to the office.

During the hubbub that followed, Dengler was pressed for one media interview after another. *Good Morning America* sent a prom limo to her doorstep to fetch her for a 3:00 AM spot. It was a few days before she and her colleagues were able to sort through the curious accounts trickling in from the coast. Some beachcombers described being chased out of the surf by violent churning. Others reported shellfish-covered rocks rising from the water.

When Dengler finally got down to the shore, she was floored. More than fifteen miles of coastline had been shoved up three feet or more. Mussels, periwinkles, and seaweed clung to the new shelf, rotting in the sun. "The stench was amazing." Abalone beds normally too deep to reach were lifted so high that people were able to snag the prized shellfish by wading out up to their knees. The churning water on the day of the quake turned out to have been a tsunami, triggered when the seafloor jerked upward. Luckily for those on the beach, the three- to five-foot surge arrived at low tide.

Seismologists traced the magnitude 7.2 quake back to the southernmost tip of the Cascadia Subduction Zone. The stub of the Juan de Fuca Plate that lies off Northern California is sometimes called the Gorda Plate. It sits in the knotty, tectonic conflux where the San Andreas Fault ends and Cascadia begins. Riddled with cracks and under pressure from every direction, the area is a seismic hot spot, so it wasn't immediately clear which fault was to blame. It was only after sorting through the data that scientists realized the region had just experienced a very close call. In a miniversion of a Cascadia megathrust, the very tip of the subduction zone had ripped. Blocks of seafloor and continent jerked past each other. Why the fault didn't keep unzipping along its seven-hundred-mile length remains a mystery. "Mother Nature was kind to us," Dengler said. "It could have easily been a 9."

For the handful of experts and officials on the West Coast who paid attention to such things, the 1992 Cape Mendocino quake and tsunami was a shocker. If a tiny Cascadia rupture could trigger a five-foot tsunami, the prospect of scaling that up along the entire coast was hair-raising.

Tsunamis have always ranked among the most terrifying of natural disasters. They lure the curious by drawing back the sea, then rush in with deadly speed and a force that's impossible to resist. The waves can travel halfway across the globe and still strike hard enough to kill. Although an earthquake lasts a few minutes at most, tsunami surges often pummel coastlines for twelve hours or more.

Underwater landslides and volcanic eruptions can trigger tsunamis, but most of the giant waves are born in subduction zone quakes. As tectonic forces overcome the friction that locks oceanic and continental crust in a tight embrace, masses of rock lurch violently. The continental margin, which is dragged downward by the subducting seafloor, breaks free and springs up. Parts of the seafloor also drop. It's the combination of that upward flick and downward drop that initiates the tsunami by displacing tons of seawater. Strike-slip earthquakes, caused when blocks of rock jerk past each other side by side, don't usually trigger tsunamis because they don't raise or lower the ocean floor.

Japan's 2011 tsunami was so enormous because the underwater upheaval was beyond what anyone had considered possible. In some places plates slid past each other by a staggering 160 feet—more than half the length of a football field. Expanses of rock thrust up 35 feet—taller than a three-story building. A robot submarine filmed

MAKING A TSUNAMI

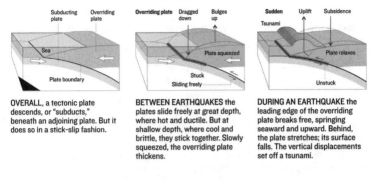

OVERALL, a tectonic plate descends, or "subducts," beneath an adjoining plate. But it does so in a stick-slip fashion.

BETWEEN EARTHQUAKES the plates slide freely at great depth, where hot and ductile. But at shallow depth, where cool and brittle, they stick together. Slowly squeezed, the overriding plate thickens.

DURING AN EARTHQUAKE the leading edge of the overriding plate breaks free, springing seaward and upward. Behind, the plate stretches; its surface falls. The vertical displacements set off a tsunami.

the seafloor soon after the quake and found towering new cliffs and fissures so deep they appeared bottomless.

At its origin a tsunami seems innocuous. The sea surface might bob a few feet as water bulges upward then ripples out in concentric rings. But unlike ordinary waves, which merely ruffle the surface, tsunamis shift a water column that can be two miles deep. Multiply that across the thousands of square miles of seafloor warped by a giant quake and it starts to explain the unstoppable momentum behind the waves that ripped through Japan and Indonesia.

Tsunamis traverse the open ocean as fast as a jetliner flies. As they speed out in either direction, underwater ridges and canyons can steer the waves. Crescent City, on the Northern California coast, is a tsunami magnet largely because it sits in the crosshairs of a 1,200-mile-long submarine hogback called the Mendocino Escarpment. The ridge steers tsunamis toward the small harbor, which is also the perfect size and shape to amplify the sloshing.

Until a tsunami nears shore, it's barely noticeable among the surface waves that roil the sea. The surge starts to build only when its leading edge scrapes across the shallow continental shelf. As the water at the front of the wave slows, the steamroller behind it keeps coming. The sea piles up, building into a churning mass that grows like an out-of-control tide. Many victims venture back to the water's edge after the initial surge retreats, only to be caught up by subsequent waves.

A year after California's 1992 warning shot, an earthquake and tsunami wreaked havoc on a small island off Japan's west coast, killing nearly two hundred people. Eddie Bernard was part of the scientific team that documented the devastation. He came home more convinced than ever that this was something the United States needed to pay attention to. Propelled by Bernard's enthusiasm and backed by powerful senators from the Northwest, Alaska, and Hawaii, the National Tsunami Hazard Mitigation Program was launched. "It was a hard sell," Bernard recalled. Congressional earmarks were the only thing that kept the program alive in its early days. Then the Indian Ocean tsunami hit and everything soared off the scale.

In 2004 Vasily Titov, the lead tsunami modeler at Bernard's lab, was spending a lonely Christmas in Seattle. He'd planned to join his wife and her family in Chicago, but his flight was cancelled. When he got an automated phone message on Christmas Day alerting him to an earthquake near Sumatra, Titov figured he might as well check it out. The initial magnitude report wasn't very big. Titov tracked aftershocks on his home computer. Following major quakes, the fault segment that just ruptured keeps twitching and slipping and popping. The pattern of aftershocks offers a rough measure of the rupture length. Titov could barely believe what he was seeing on his screen. Aftershocks were flaring up over an area nearly seven hundred miles long. "I knew then that this was a much bigger event and that it was going to be a sizable tsunami."

Titov dashed to his car and sped to the NOAA complex on Lake Washington. It was around 7:00 PM. The building was dark and deserted as Titov switched on his office lights and fired up his computer. He started setting up a numerical grid and feeding in bathymetric data from the Indian Ocean. The tsunami model he'd been working on for nearly a decade was one of the most advanced in the world, but it was still experimental. It had never been tested against an actual tsunami, unfolding in real time.

But that had always been Titov's goal. He wanted a model that was useful, not theoretical. Ideally, he would someday be able to predict within minutes of an earthquake when the tsunami surges would hit shore and how big they would be.

Titov, a Russian native, started studying the giant waves in the world's most unlikely spot: Novosibirsk, a Siberian science city at the geographical center of the Asian continent. "If you want to get as far as possible from the sea, that's where you go," Titov said.

In the 1980s tsunami research was exotic. Except for grainy black-and-white pictures, few of those working in the field had ever seen one of the giant waves. Titov expected to spend a few years tinkering with the model, then move on to something with better career prospects. But when Bernard offered him a job in Seattle with top-notch computing facilities and an opportunity to help figure out a way to forecast tsunami flooding, Titov couldn't resist.

On that Christmas in 2004, he worked through the night. Procedures that now take minutes ate up hours. Titov switched on CNN, but news reports were sparse. It was nearing 3:00 AM when he was finally ready to start running his model. The tsunami had already spread death and destruction along the coasts of Indonesia, Thailand, and India, and was racing toward the coast of Africa where more than three hundred people would be swept away. But there was nothing Titov could do to warn those in the tsunami's path. His model wasn't fast enough yet to get in front of the speeding waves. During the days that followed, however, Titov's map of the tsunami's intensity became the go-to source for search-and-rescue crews and relief operations targeting the hardest-hit areas.

The Indian Ocean disaster prompted the United States to triple its funding for tsunami research, modeling, and preparedness. Bernard's six-person team expanded to more than two dozen scientists and technicians. Much of the new money went to bolster the country's fledgling network of tsunami detection buoys, which Bernard and his colleagues had spent more than a decade developing. In 2004 there were six buoys anchored in deep water off Alaska, the Pacific Northwest, and Hawaii. By 2012 a network of forty U.S. instruments and fifteen from other nations stood watch over the world's ocean basins, lowering the odds that another giant tsunami would take people on distant shores by surprise.

The heart of the instruments is a sensitive pressure sensor that sits on the seafloor. As a tsunami passes by, the sensor detects the shift in water pressure and calculates the wave's height. Even a centimeter-high tsunami can't sneak past unnoticed. The buoy beams the data direct to labs and government agencies around the globe.

Before the network existed, determining whether a tsunami would be destructive was a tough call. Two out of every three warnings were false alarms. The only thing forecasters had to go on were seismograms, which provided a quick estimate of the earthquake's size and location. But size alone isn't enough to tell whether a tsunami will be generated or how big it may be. By directly measuring the wave, the buoys eliminate most of that uncertainty. Japanese forecasters realized they had vastly underestimated the size of the 2011 tsunami when the wave reached the closest buoy. The measurement was a whopping 5.5 feet, the largest ever detected in the open ocean. "When we saw that, we could see that it was going to be huge," Titov said.

As Japan's 2011 calamity unfolded, Titov was finally able to show that his model could get ahead of the curve. Using data from the buoys, he accurately forecast the arrival times and heights of the modest waves that came ashore along the U.S. West Coast and Hawaii. One town on the island of Maui experienced damaging floods, which the model predicted six hours in advance. Titov's model is also helping communities map out areas that are likely to flood in a Cascadia tsunami and plan evacuation routes.

But on the day the megaquake strikes, neither the high-tech model nor the state-of-the-art tsunami detection buoys will be of much help to people in Seaside, Cannon Beach, Ocean Shores, and other communities close to ground zero. The buoys are stellar sentinels for tsunamis that arrive from far away, affording the luxury of hours to evacuate. For a tsunami that will slam into shore in less than half an hour, the data they provide arrive too late to help with the initial warning.

It will take about fifteen minutes for Cascadia's tsunami to reach the closest buoy off the Northwest coast. If everything works perfectly, Titov might be able to feed that initial wave height into his model and produce a flooding forecast within thirty minutes. That will be welcome information for communities along the Strait of Juan de Fuca and northern Puget Sound, where the tsunami won't arrive for one to two hours. But communities on the coast will have already been hit by the time the forecast is finished.

The first formal alert will come from the West Coast and Alaska Tsunami Warning Center near Anchorage. Based on initial seismic readings, which often underestimate quake size, the center should be able to push out a warning within five minutes. Data coming in from the buoys will help update and refine subsequent alerts and track the multiple tsunami surges. But in the chaos and blackouts following one of the world's most powerful earthquakes, it's a crapshoot whether those messages will get through to the people in harm's way.

In the final analysis, the best advice Titov, Bernard, Dengler, and every other tsunami expert can offer is the same mantra Corcoran preaches: Don't count on sirens or other technology. Don't wait for official confirmation. If you feel the earth quake, head for high ground.

"If you want to sit around and argue about it, go right ahead," Corcoran added. "I just hope you haven't bred yet and you're out of the gene pool."

The videos of 3/11 that hit Stephanie Fritts hardest were from Sendai. Cars were creeping like ants across an expanse of rice paddies, their drivers trying hopelessly to outpace the water. "That wave was going so much faster than the cars," Fritts said, shaking her head as if to block out the image. "That big, black, dirty wave."

As emergency management director for Pacific County, Fritts's territory includes a section of the Washington coast that looks a lot like the Sendai Plain. With twenty-eight miles of beach that gleam like mother-of-pearl, the Long Beach Peninsula isn't nearly as developed as Sendai is. But it's just as flat.

The spit owes its existence to the Columbia River. As the waterway merges with the Pacific, the freshwater current swings north, dumping sediment as it goes. The peninsula measures about two miles across at its widest point. Some five thousand souls live there year-round in homes that open onto the sea or sit tucked behind grassy dunes. As many as twenty-five thousand people crowd hotels and campgrounds during the annual kite festival in August. An abundance of bogs makes this prime country for growing cranberries. Oysters love it, too. Some of the highest spots around are the mountains of shells piled outside local seafood plants.

At the county building in the town of Long Beach, Fritts unfolded the tsunami hazard maps for the peninsula on a fall day in 2012. Except for green patches at each end designating high ground, the entire spit is colored various shades of yellow. The only reason it's not red is because the maps are designed with the color-blind in mind. Yellow is as bad as it gets. A Cascadia tsunami half the size of Japan's biggest waves would completely submerge most of this narrow tongue of land, just as the black water engulfed the flat fields around Sendai. The outlook is equally grim on the Ocean Shores Peninsula to the north, Washington's most popular beach resort. Even by car there wouldn't be enough time to evacuate, and the roads are likely to be jumbled blocks of pavement anyway.

With nowhere to run, folks in these vulnerable spots are considering a very Japanese option: engineering their own high ground. The town of Long Beach, where a cheerful arch welcomes visitors to "The World's Longest Beach," is applying for federal grants to build the country's first tsunami evacuation structure. Working with architects and engineers from the University of Washington, residents decided on a high, grassy berm that could be incorporated in the elementary school's athletic fields. With gently sloping access ramps and a broad top, the artificial hill could provide refuge to one thousand people.

"It's a last-gasp solution," said Dengler, who toured post-tsunami Japan and reported on the spotty performance of the so-called vertical evacuation structures common there. "On a place like the peninsula, it's absolutely appropriate—but you had better be damn sure it's tall enough." Dengler counted more than a hundred buildings, elevated platforms, and towers designated for tsunami evacuation that were overtopped by Japan's 2011 tsunami. In the town of Minamisanriku, once famed for its seawall, 120 people died in the emergency management building. The 10 people who survived clung to railings and antennas on the roof as the torrent swept over them.

Horror stories like those leave Fritts and the people of the Long Beach Peninsula paralyzed. Do they need to supersize their berm?

How tall is tall enough? Fritts keeps asking those questions, even though she knows the answers will never be as rock solid as she wants. "We're relying on the scientists," she said. "But tsunami science is in its infancy."

Fritts's introduction to the subject of giant waves came soon after she and her husband quit their corporate jobs in Portland and moved to the fishing port of Ilwaco to manage her father's hardware store. They were living on the main drag in 1986 when the Alaska earthquake that caused Hawaii's costly false alarm spurred a similar, pointless panic in the Northwest. Fritts was in the front yard washing her car that day. She couldn't figure out why a line of vehicles was speeding out of town at seventy-five miles per hour. When she clicked on the radio and heard the warning, she bundled her kids into the car and joined the exodus.

Fritts's first assignment when the county hired her a couple of years later was to fix the tsunami mess. Her bosses were mostly concerned about botched evacuations because of distant tsunamis, but Fritts soon realized that the real danger lay right off shore. The first tsunami layers Brian Atwater unearthed were from Willapa Bay, the aquatic hub of Fritts's county. She was so alarmed by the discovery she wanted to take action immediately. The only thing she could think of was to post tsunami-warning signs, but there weren't any in Washington yet. So Fritts started calling other states, shopping around. When Washington emergency managers got wind of her plan, they didn't know what to make of the crazy lady from Pacific County. Eventually, they followed her lead.

Since then Fritts has watched the worst-case tsunami for the Northwest coast inflate like a balloon. At first thirty feet seemed almost too outrageous to imagine. After Sumatra many communities began to consider the possibility of fifty-foot waves. Corcoran now advises people to keep running until they reach an elevation of one hundred feet. The original plan for Long Beach's tsunami "safe haven" called for a berm about thirty feet high, which could be built for $1 million. After watching the videos from Japan, residents now fear it's ridiculously puny.

Fritts takes comfort in the fact that tsunamis can be capricious, and not every wave will be the worst case. Surge heights are strongly influenced by proximity to the subduction zone, how much the seafloor lurches, underwater topography, and the shape of the coast. Modelers draw up inundation maps by trying to juggle those factors and predict the way they will interact. In the Northwest, with no recent experience to draw upon, the process is as much art as it is science.

Modelers generally expect higher surges along the Oregon coast, where the water is deeper and the subduction zone more steeply angled. Waves arriving at the Long Beach Peninsula could be bigger than elsewhere in Washington because of an offshore sandbar where the water will pile up. But the Northwest lacks the jagged, narrow bays that so greatly amplified the tsunami in Japan and resulted in the highest waves.

The broad bays more typical of the Washington coast will probably have the opposite effect, dampening the intensity. The tsunami will remain fearsome as it travels up the mouth of the Columbia and the Strait of Juan de Fuca. But most of the punch will be gone by the time it reaches Puget Sound, Portland, and Vancouver. The urban centers can expect higher water than usual, but major tsunami damage is unlikely unless the earthquake shakes loose landslides that trigger local waves.

A whopper on the subduction zone could cause violent sloshing in Puget Sound and Lakes Washington and Union. The phenomenon is called a seiche. The last time one hit the Seattle area, seismic waves from a 2002 quake in Alaska traveled thousands of miles and caused the water in Lake Union to slop back and forth as if in a giant bathtub. The waves fling houseboats like rubber ducks. But the biggest tsunami threat to Puget Sound is from a quake on the Seattle Fault or any of the other shallow faults that pass under the water.

The toll from a Cascadia tsunami will be paid by those who find themselves on the outer coast—in the wrong place at the wrong time. The UW team that's helping Long Beach design its berm estimates the peninsula's likely death toll at more than 2,000. A series of strategically located berms and towers could save about half of those people.

No one comes right out and says it, but it's a given that many fatalities will be people too immobile or infirm to make it to high ground or an evacuation structure. In Japan, where nearly half of those who died in the tsunami were over the age of sixty-five, private enterprise has stepped in with another option. One company is manufacturing yellow fiberglass survival spheres.

Called Noah for the Biblical ark-builder, a standard pod costs about $4,000 and can hold a family of four. Larger versions are also available. The company says it's sold more than six hundred. At least two American firms are tinkering with the idea of marketing something similar to people along the U.S. West Coast.

Absurd as they sound, Bernard thinks the buoyant pods or something similar might be worth a shot. Not a single evacuation structure has yet been built in the United States, which leaves people in Long Beach, Ocean Shores, and equally vulnerable spots with few options for escape. "We need to be thinking about other alternatives," Bernard said, "but we're not even considering it in this country." Maybe scientists and entrepreneurs can come up with better ideas, like tsunami survival suits or specially designed inflatable rafts.

Even without pods, many people in Japan related amazing survival stories in the days after 3/11. One elderly woman filmed as the water engulfed her was able to grab onto a house that floated by and pull herself up on the roof. A man swept to sea was rescued two days later clinging to the remnants of his home. Inside submerged buildings, a few lucky people found air pockets that kept them alive. "There are going to be people who do exactly the right thing and they will die," Corcoran said. "And there will be people who do exactly the wrong thing and they will live."

So much will depend on when the Cascadia quake strikes. On a January day, the biggest crowds on the beach will be gulls and sanderlings. On a weekend in August, Seaside will be wall-to-wall humanity. The magnitude 8.8 megaquake that rocked the coast of Chile in 2010 struck on the last weekend in February, the equivalent of Labor Day across much of South America. Most locals were savvy enough to run to high ground. Many of those who died were urbanites visiting the beach. The waves washed over an island where extended families were camped out to watch the fireworks. Out of nearly a hundred people on the island, all but a handful were killed.

One of the things that shocked the Japanese people most on 3/11 was how their government failed them. Warnings underestimated the earthquake and tsunami size. In many areas the alerts never got through. Emergency responders were slow to arrive in remote coastal villages, leaving people to fend for themselves in the freezing weather. In the Northwest it's going to be much worse, warned Dengler, who spends more of her time these days on public education than on tsunami science. "Japan's systems are far more robust than ours."

For nearly twenty years, Dengler has been surveying residents in Humboldt County, California, about earthquake and tsunami risks. During that time the percentage of people who know about the danger has soared. The majority even understand that the first tsunami wave isn't usually the biggest. But by other measures, the region seems to be moving backward. When Dengler started asking people who they would rely on for help in the immediate aftermath of the disaster, three-quarters said it would be up to them and their neighbors to take care of one another. By 2010 more than half of respondents said they expect the cavalry to swoop in, in the form of an organized government response.

Results like that make Dengler worry she's been wasting her time. A Cascadia earthquake and tsunami will so overwhelm the region's fire departments, police forces, and National Guard units that people should expect to fend for themselves for as much as two weeks. "People still think somebody else is going to tell them what to do, somebody else is going to take responsibility," Dengler said.

But there's one story from Japan that gives Dengler hope as she works to prepare people in the Pacific Northwest. The Japanese call it the miracle of Kamaishi.

In the town where the tsunami flicked aside the $1.6 billion breakwater, a university professor had been working with local schools on an education program that broke the mold in a nation where children are taught not to question authority. Toshitaka Katada had noticed Japan's fear of tsunamis fading as the government erected King Kong–size barriers to protect fishing ports and coastal communities.

People put their faith in the gates and seawalls and the official warning system.

Katada based his approach on psychology. Humans have a built-in bias that makes it hard for them to accept they're in danger, he explained. The alarm sounds but few people bolt immediately. They hesitate. They look around to determine if the threat is real and how others are reacting. Katada taught his students to take the lead, to be the one who runs first. By doing so they could not only save themselves but prompt others to flee. Katada also urged the youngsters not to rely on teachers, scientists, or tsunami evacuation maps. "With nature, anything is possible," he said in one interview. "Nobody can predict what kind of tsunami will come."

On 3/11 the children of Kamaishi took the teachings to heart. The earthquake knocked out alarm systems, but students at the junior high school near the town center evacuated anyway. At the neighboring elementary school, teachers had already herded the kids to the top floor. But when they saw the older students heading for high ground, the younger children and their teachers decided to follow. As they raced along, eighth-graders took second-graders by the hand to help them keep up.

The group arrived at the designated evacuation point and looked behind them. The tsunami was rolling up the river and traveling overland, its path marked by a cloud of dust from demolished buildings. So the students kept going. From the high point where they finally stopped, they watched as the water swallowed up their classrooms and the evacuation site. Every child in school that day survived.

CHAPTER 10:

"IT'S OUR JOB"

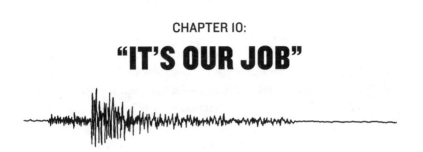

IN 1879 the men of the newly formed U.S. Geological Survey turned heads as they toured the mining districts of the Rocky Mountains. Dressed in snow-white buckskins stitched by London tailors, Clarence King, the first director of the USGS, traveled with a valet and "an apparently inexhaustible supply of fine wines, brandy, and cigars," according to author Wallace Stegner. King's corps of geologists was drawn from Harvard, Yale, and other elite schools. The director himself was a national hero, celebrated for exposing a phony diamond mine that snookered some of America's leading financiers. One contemporary eulogized him as "the best and brightest man of his generation."

In *Angle of Repose*, Stegner described King and his party rolling into Leadville, Colorado, with a train of wagons and mules. They made camp in a stand of aspen and stayed two months to study ore deposits. Stegner's story is fiction, but based on historical accounts. In the novel, as in reality, the USGS men held court in the evenings, dazzling the locals with literate discourse, well-aged liquor, and delicacies prepared by their cook.

Today's USGS rolls with a lot less flash. In 2012, at a workshop hosted by the agency in Seattle, more than a hundred people crammed into a windowless room on the University of Washington campus. Refreshments were Costco bagels, bottled water, and coffee.

The meeting was called to order by Art Frankel, a breed of USGS scientist King couldn't have imagined. Frankel jokes that he can't tell one rock from another. He spends most of his time crunching numbers on a computer and writes code to relax. But Frankel and his colleagues represent a clear line of succession from the gentlemen geologists of the nineteenth century. Instead of mapping minerals, they map earthquakes.

Sizing up seismic risk wasn't codified as part of the USGS mission until Jimmy Carter's presidency, but it has grown into one of the agency's most high-profile jobs. The maps Frankel and his team develop are forecasts of future ground shaking. Hugely influential, the maps form the basis for building codes and shape emergency plans across the country. They're also controversial. Critics accuse the USGS of hyping the danger in some places and low-balling it in others. The grumbling has intensified since devastating quakes in Sumatra, Japan, and New Zealand took many experts by surprise.

Like his USGS predecessors, who foreswore any financial stake in the mineral deposits they uncovered, Frankel tries to steer clear of competing interests and let science be his guide. He organized the Seattle meeting as a forum where earthquake experts and engineers could debate the latest seismic discoveries in the Northwest and come to a consensus on how—or if—they should be factored into the hazard equation.

Among the questions on the table were whether giant subduction zone quakes occur more frequently along the Oregon coast than along the rest of the plate margin and whether the seismic rating in Eastern Washington needs to be dialed up.

Wearing one of the few sport coats in a room dominated by denim and fleece, Frankel urged the participants to be candid. "Improving public safety is what it's all about," he said. "We want your comments. We welcome your participation." But the final responsibility rests with the USGS, as spelled out in the law that added earthquakes to the agency's portfolio in 1977. The same law charged it with doing the research necessary to identify the danger.

That's why USGS scientists have been at the center of almost every seismic breakthrough in the Pacific Northwest, from uncovering the

Cascadia Subduction Zone's true nature to digging into the history of the faults that threaten the region's cities. "The short answer is, it's our job," said David Applegate, associate director for natural hazards. Earthquake programs account for only 6 percent of the agency's budget but attract the lion's share of public attention. After every major quake, USGS scientists are called on to explain what happened and what it means. "When the quake hit," Applegate said, "the world turns to us."

That wasn't the case in 1906, when the great San Francisco earthquake and fire left the city in ruins. The federal agency responsible for monitoring quakes at the time was the Weather Bureau, whose observers were supposed to report all unusual phenomena.

The USGS was interested, of course. The agency's chief geologist, Grove Karl Gilbert, said it was the "natural and legitimate ambition of a properly constituted geologist" to feel an earthquake, visit a glacier and witness a volcanic eruption. When the quake hit, Gilbert was in Berkeley, heading up an investigation of hydraulic mining. His report would help end the ecologically ruinous practice of sluicing away hillsides to get at hidden flakes of gold. The early-morning quake knocked Gilbert out of bed. He caught the first ferry to San Francisco and immediately started documenting the quake and its effects. His photos of the dramatic offset on the San Andreas Fault still appear in textbooks.

But literal earthshaking had not been on the mind of Grove's old friend and former boss, John Wesley Powell, when the latter set out to revolutionize the government's role in science. The American West was being rapidly and, to Powell's mind, recklessly settled. He pressed Congress to establish a corps of professional geologists to survey the vast public domain in a systematic way, identifying land best suited for farming, ranching, and timber growing. Only the federal government could do the job free from the corrupting influence of greed, he argued.

A self-taught geologist and Civil War veteran who lost his right arm to a musket ball, Powell was every bit as famous as Clarence King, the man he anointed to be the USGS's initial leader. Powell's celebrity was sealed in 1869, when he led the first party to navigate the treacherous Colorado River through the Grand Canyon. It was the last major journey of discovery in the continental United States. Powell set out with four wooden rowboats and a rag-tag crew of nine volunteers. Ninety-nine days and a thousand miles later, six starving men paddled out of the unknown. Their adventures were splashed across the front pages of newspapers around the world.

After guiding the creation of the USGS, Powell became its second director in 1881 when King left government service to chase gold in Mexico. Powell soon launched the young agency on perhaps its most ambitious and enduring project: the topographical mapping of the entire United States. Powell promised Congress he would get the job done in twenty-four years. It took more than a century. The fifty-five thousand quadrangle maps that resulted remain the go-to standard for hikers, planners, and resource managers. Powell also foresaw the need for long-term monitoring of waterways, especially in the arid West where the agency pioneered the development of stream gauges. For more than 120 years the USGS has maintained the nationwide network used to monitor floods and water supplies.

But for most of its existence, the USGS's bread and butter was geologic mapping in support of the mining industry. There was no better job for a young graduate than to join the legions of hard-rock men who set off into the mountains with mules and rock hammers and came back with schematics of sandstones, conglomerates, and shales—and, they hoped, clues to the next mother lode.

"Many people in the profession tend to think that a geologist who has not at some point worked for the Survey has not been rigorously trained," John McPhee wrote in *Annals of the Former World*. "Within the profession, the Survey has particular prestige—as much as, or even more than, the geology faculties of major universities, where chair professors have been known to mutter about the U.S.G.S., 'They think they are God's helpers.'" As the nation's needs shifted, USGS scientists shifted their prospecting from gold and silver to oil, uranium, and sources of geothermal power. Survey scientists trained the Apollo astronauts to collect rocks on the moon.

A USGS topographic mapping crew in Washington's Cascade Mountains, 1903.

The esprit de corps that infused the USGS in its early days was the model for the Forest Service, Park Service, and other government agencies "notable for the disinterested effectiveness of their work," Stegner wrote in *Beyond the Hundredth Meridian*, his biography of Powell. With fortunes to be made and speculators jostling for advantage, Powell insisted the USGS be above reproach. The act that created the agency stated that "the Director and members of the Geological Survey shall have no personal or private interests in the lands or mineral wealth of the region under survey." To this day USGS employees and their families are prohibited from holding individual stock in mining, oil, or energy companies.

Earthquake monitoring didn't become a federal concern until the Cold War. Before then, seismic networks were largely makeshift affairs run by universities. But the defense establishment quickly realized that instruments designed to detect vibrations from earthquakes could also detect vibrations from nuclear explosions. After a ban on atmospheric blasts drove atomic bomb testing underground, money poured in to expand seismic monitoring and develop new techniques. Intelligence agencies picked apart seismograms, trying to figure out what the Soviets were up to.

"It was spy versus spy in its perfect form," recalled Allan Lindh, a veteran of the early earthquake programs. Paranoid that the other side was testing bombs on the sly, the federal government asked USGS scientists to figure out if it was possible to conceal an underground blast. They found it could be done if the bomb was set off within seconds of an actual earthquake. So the rush was on to find ways to more quickly spot and measure earthquakes. "That's when we started programming computers to identify earthquakes in real time," Lindh said.

Seismic monitoring in the Pacific Northwest got a boost from the arms race as well as from the need to keep an eye on ground shaking at the Hanford Nuclear Reservation. The influx of money led to better instruments and more sophisticated methods to analyze seismograms. But the notion that it was the federal government's job to understand and grapple with the risks posed by earthquakes didn't get serious traction until Alaska's 1964 megaquake. An American city was destroyed and more than 130 people died, shattering the nation's illusion of seismic invulnerability. Even so it took another decade and another threat from foreign powers to get the USGS program off the ground.

The race this time was to predict earthquakes, and Russia and China seemed to be winning. Soviet seismologists set off a buzz in the early 1970s with claims that they could detect changes in rocks and swelling in the earth's crust preceding big quakes. It made sense. If cracks formed before a quake, the ground would expand. Could this be the Holy Grail earthquake researchers had been dreaming of? Then sketchy reports started trickling in from the city of Haicheng, on China's northeastern coast.

A quake of magnitude 7.3 struck in February 1975, flattening structures for miles. But the death toll was surprisingly low. According to official accounts that reached the West, untold thousands of lives were saved when seismologists predicted the quake and evacuated their comrades to safety. The precursors the Chinese relied on included foreshocks, fluctuations in well water levels, and snakes emerging from hibernation in the dead of winter. Details were murky. Nevertheless, it seemed earthquake prediction was finally coming of age.

Frank Press, the nation's leading seismologist and later science advisor to President Carter, joined in the euphoria. Earthquake forecasts would be routine within a decade, he vowed. The coming revolution was touted in the media. In her book *Predicting the Unpredictable*, USGS seismologist Susan Hough quoted a 1976 article in *People* magazine that captured the optimism: "Earthquake prediction, long treated as the seismological family's weird uncle, has in the last few years become everyone's favorite nephew."

Many within the USGS were more skeptical, but they kept their mouths shut. If not for the buzz over earthquake prediction, Congress might never have adopted the National Earthquake Hazards Reduction Act of 1977. For the first time, the bill gave the responsibility for assessing earthquake hazards to the USGS, along with the money to pay for it.

Prediction research was a big part of the mix, and for a while no idea was too far-fetched. One plan called for triggering a quake with explosives and monitoring it as it unfolded. Geologists were dispatched to find a suitably remote fault in Nevada's Great Basin before the plan was scrubbed.

The highest-profile experiment centered on Parkfield, a tiny town in the cattle country of central California. The portion of the San Andreas Fault that runs through the area seemed to rupture with almost metronome-like frequency—every twenty-two years, on average. The motto on the wall of the Parkfield Cafe advises, "If you feel a shake or a quake, get under the table and eat your steak." When the experiment started in 1985, it had been nineteen years since Parkfield's last quake.

A team of USGS scientists, including Lindh, boldly predicted that cafe patrons should expect to dive for cover by no later than 1992. The researchers wired up the fault and waited to capture the precursor signals that were sure to appear. None did, even when the fault finally ruptured in 2004, a dozen years "late." "What we learned was that we couldn't predict earthquakes," Lindh said. It was a worthwhile lesson. "When people around the world are claiming they can predict earthquakes, it's hard work to prove you can't."

The signal the Russians thought they saw turned out to be a phantom. When Western scientists were finally allowed to investigate the Haicheng prediction, the story they pieced together was more ambiguous than the simple tale of triumph propagated by Chairman Mao's party apparatus. The national government never issued a specific prediction, but several scientists and a regional earthquake observatory did warn that a quake was imminent based mainly on a ferocious swarm of what proved to be foreshocks.

Local officials in some provinces broadcast warnings by loudspeaker and urged people to evacuate. Already rattled by more than three hundred shocks in twenty-four hours, many residents heeded the warning and were safe when their flimsy homes collapsed. But people in other provinces stayed put. Similar swarms had shaken the region in the past and weren't followed by a big quake.

When a major quake struck seven months later in a neighboring province, China's prediction bureau offered no warning. More than a quarter of a million people were killed. The famed Haicheng prediction was "a blend of confusion, empirical analysis, intuitive judgment, and good luck," one analysis concluded.

With earthquake prediction out of reach, the USGS regrouped. If the agency couldn't offer short-term warnings, the experience at Parkfield and other quake-prone regions around the world proved the value of long-term studies. The San Andreas didn't slip on schedule at Parkfield. But it did slip eventually—just as it had before and just as it will again. A better understanding of faults and their behavior became the cornerstone of USGS work, particularly in the Pacific Northwest, the country's newest hot spot for seismic research.

If you spend much time at the USGS offices on the University of Washington campus, you'll hear people asking, "Where's Craig?" The answer is usually a shrug. He might be in Spokane, briefing local leaders on a newly discovered fault that runs through the center of town. He could be in Washington, D.C., cozying up to a congressional committee. Or maybe he's stuck in mind-numbing budget meetings, scrounging for loose change he can parlay into one more lidar survey, one more earthquake trench.

His team calls him their rainmaker. Others credit Craig Weaver with doing more than anyone else to make the Pacific Northwest as earthquake-savvy as it is today. "Craig wants the research to save lives," said Ivan Wong, principal seismologist at URS Corp., a leader in quake-resistant design and construction. "There is no one in the Survey to compare to Craig in terms of what he's contributed to earthquake safety."

Weaver is having none of it. "If I ever sit back and say, 'Oh, didn't I do a good job,' it's time for me to quit," he said, with feeling. "I just want to focus on what's next. Where does that Spokane Fault go?"

As regional seismic hazards chief, Weaver is the face of earthquake research in the Northwest. At press conferences and public meetings, he's the one who translates the science into English. Weaver can talk to building engineers. He can chat with the mayor and bank CEOs. In fact, it's hard to get him to shut up. "Craig can really filibuster," one colleague said, with a mixture of admiration and exasperation.

That relentless dialogue is part of Weaver's plan. He realized early on that earthquake studies would never do any good on the shelf. "Craig decided he didn't want to sit in his office and write scientific papers," said USGS geophysicist Tom Pratt. "He wanted to make sure the science influenced public policy." That's why Weaver made the leap—kicking and screaming at first—from research to management.

Weaver's fingerprints are on almost every major earthquake discovery in the region, though usually behind the scenes. A master of the art of budget mining, Weaver knows how to find the bucks, then get the biggest scientific bang out of them. When the USGS gave the Northwest one of its first funding bumps for earthquake research, some scientists wanted to split the money so everyone got a small piece of the pie. Instead, Weaver orchestrated the blitz of seismic surveys up, down, and across Puget Sound that laid the basis for all the work since.

Lidar coverage in the Northwest is among the most extensive in the nation largely because Weaver helped cobble together a consortium of water districts, county planning departments, tribes, and state agencies to coordinate the work. Each partner pays for the mapping it wants, and the collective was able to negotiate a lower price for the surveys. Everyone shares the data, including geologists on the hunt for faults. "Craig knows how to make things happen," Pratt said. "Not many scientists do."

Because it's run by scientists, the USGS is more egalitarian than most federal agencies. Weaver's office at the UW is one of the worst, tucked away in the basement near the seismology lab. The frontline researchers get the nice views. Management jobs in the USGS are often considered more a burden than a prize. Scientists reluctantly rotate through leadership slots, serving their time like a prison sentence until they can return to research. But Weaver found his niche when he took over Seattle's earthquake program.

A UW graduate, Weaver was one of the USGS's first Seattle-based researchers. He started in 1979 when geothermal energy was in vogue. Weaver's job was to figure out if Cascade volcanoes could be tapped as natural power plants. In the spring of 1980, he and UW seismologist Steve Malone were getting ready to deploy a batch of seismometers to listen for magma movement under the snow-capped peaks. Then Mount St. Helens started clearing her throat. Weaver and Malone quickly changed plans and installed all their instruments around the volcano that was about to make history.

Mount St. Helens's cataclysmic eruption was a sobering experience for the USGS. The agency's monitoring led to life-saving evacuations, but *Newsweek* pointed out the "embarrassing failure" to predict the blast itself. Nor did the USGS adequately warn communities in the path of the smothering blanket of ash. Weaver joined the crush of researchers who swarmed Mount St. Helens for the next several years, fine-tuning their ability to forecast eruptions by tracking the tremors from magma on the move.

Another natural disaster deflected Weaver's career onto the path he's followed ever since. The Bay Area earthquake that interrupted 1989's cross-town World Series convinced the USGS to widen its seismic focus beyond California. Seattle's waterfront viaduct was a dead ringer for the double-decker freeway that collapsed in Oakland, killing forty-two people. The Northwest was just waking up to the threat posed by the Cascadia Subduction Zone, and Weaver was tapped to join, and later lead, an expanded earthquake program.

Watching Weaver work a conference—chatting, laughing, and huddling in the corridor with key players—it seems like he was born to schmooze. But it was an acquired skill. Like his fellow scientists, Weaver loves to natter on about technical details that make other people's eyes glaze over. "You make an idiot of yourself enough times and you finally realize, hey, we've got to change the way we're talking," he said. He learned to boil the message down to its essence.

One of Weaver's first attempts at public outreach was a disaster. Scientists were about to publish evidence for the massive Seattle Fault earthquake a thousand years ago that lifted beaches twenty feet out of the water and sloughed acres of forest into Lake Washington. Weaver didn't alert city officials until the evening before the news broke. "That was clearly not the way to do it," he recalled ruefully.

The USGS already had a reputation for arrogance, and public relations blunders like that didn't help. As in the days of King and Powell, the agency still considers itself the elite of the geoscience world. So it came as a shock in the mid-1990s when Congress, under the leadership of House Speaker Newt Gingrich, targeted the USGS for elimination as part of its cost-cutting "Contract with America."

The public and lawmakers from earthquake-prone states rallied to the agency's defense. Outraged editorials popped up in newspapers across California. Although several USGS programs took deep cuts, the earthquake work emerged largely unscathed. But a bit of the swagger was gone. "They were basically told, 'Make yourself more relevant or you're going to disappear,'" Wong said. "I think that threat changed them." But there are still many problems the USGS is uniquely equipped to address, and delving into earthquake hazards is foremost among them.

University scientists live from grant to grant. They're not likely to devote decades to trenching and tracking faults from one end of Washington State to the other. "Universities want you pulling in money and working on international projects," said USGS geologist Brian Sherrod, who led most of the fault excavations in the Northwest. "We're paid by the taxpayers to work on problems that affect you." Academic geologists might take pot shots at the USGS for being conservative and bureaucratic, but many envy their federal counterparts, too. USGS geologists can devote themselves to research year-round, not just during school breaks.

That sustained focus helped hammer home the Northwest's seismic perils. Duck-and-cover school drills are routine now, and public works departments plan for earthquake upgrades as a matter of course. When Weaver and Frankel briefed the Seattle City Council on upcoming revisions to the seismic hazard maps in 2012, it was clear that years of talking about earthquakes over and over and over had paid off. No one asked what a subduction zone was. Everybody knew about the Seattle Fault. "People have heard it so many times, it's not a foreign concept anymore," Weaver said.

For the sea change, even Weaver might allow himself a small pat on the back—before chasing off after that Spokane fault.

The seismic hazard map scientists gathered to discuss at the Seattle workshop in 2012 represents the synthesis of everything that's known about earthquakes in the Pacific Northwest. But it looks like it was drawn by a first-grader going through a rainbow phase. A thick red band hugs the coast. Next comes a broad stripe of orange that covers Puget Sound and sideswipes Portland. Successive bands of gold and yellow sweep like waves toward the Cascades. On the other side of the crest, green fades into a wide expanse of blue.

The color scheme is straightforward. Red means high hazard. Sky blue, not so much. Almost everything else about the map is incomprehensible to the average person.

The map represents a forecast of how hard the ground could shake in the future—the yardstick engineers use to design buildings. But the map doesn't show what to expect in any particular earthquake—say a full-rip 9 off the coast or a magnitude 6 on the Seattle Fault. What's mapped is a mash-up, the statistical equivalent of dumping all possible quakes into a blender and punching "puree." Instead of forecasting the worst that could happen, the map is a picture of the worst that's *likely* to happen. Unless it's not.

A growing number of critics say the unexpected devastation from recent quakes shows that seismic hazard maps can be misleading or flat wrong. Coastal communities in Japan based their tsunami defenses on government hazard maps that assumed a magnitude 9 quake was impossible in the Tohoku area. The 2008 quake in China's Sichuan Province struck in an area colored green for low hazard on the map. More than eighty thousand people died, including thousands of children crushed when poorly built schools and dormitories collapsed. The quake that knocked Christchurch, New Zealand, to its knees in 2011 was on a fault that didn't even show up on the maps.

Humbling experiences like those have convinced some experts that countries might be better off just planning for the worst, even if it is a statistical long shot. Others argue that the maps are based on such a shaky tower of assumptions that they're no better than educated guesses. "The probability that we got the right answer is very small, but that's not the impression we give with these maps," said Tom Heaton. Among the first scientists to question the old assumptions about the Cascadia Subduction Zone, Heaton now directs the Earthquake Engineering Research Laboratory at Caltech. It makes him nervous that building engineers take the maps as gospel. "It sounds like we've got it all figured out . . . but earthquakes are still a great mystery to us. We get reminded of that when something unexpected happens."

Art Frankel, who is still active in the USGS mapping program after leading it for more than ten years, is well aware of the uncertainties. He ties himself in knots trying to minimize them. But there's also a lot that scientists do know about earthquakes, he pointed out. The maps are the best vehicle anyone has come up with to pull those insights together in a way that can help people prepare. "It allows you to make intelligent decisions," Frankel said.

Seismic hazard maps were the fallback for the USGS after earthquake prediction fizzled. Even though it wasn't possible to pinpoint when and where a quake would hit, it was clear that some areas were at higher risk than others. The earliest hazard maps essentially drew circles around places that had been hit by big quakes in the past. The next generation of maps tried to identify the biggest possible earthquake that could strike an area and estimate how hard it would shake the ground. This "maximum credible earthquake" approach is still used for critical facilities, like dams and nuclear power plants.

But planning for the worst case is costly. If the Seattle Fault unleashes a giant quake every five thousand years, should office buildings and apartment towers that might last a century be constructed like fortresses, just in case? The probabilistic approach the USGS uses was developed to balance cost and benefits.

Frankel and his colleagues feed earthquake scenarios into their computer models, weighting each one based on likelihood. It's kind of like loading the dice to reflect the fact that Mother Nature more often rolls a moderate quake than a monster. In the next fifty years, the scientists estimate it's almost a slam dunk that another deep, Nisqually-style earthquake will hit. A Cascadia megaquake gets about 14 percent odds without factoring in the possibility of more frequent quakes on the southern Oregon coast. A medium-size quake on the Seattle Fault scores a 5 percent probability.

The most commonly used maps account for the lineup of quakes expected to strike in either a 500- or 2,500-year period. The 2,500-year map for the Northwest includes a magnitude 9 Cascadia megaquake and a magnitude 6-plus shallow fault quake. But the USGS considers a massive Seattle Fault quake like the one that struck the region in 900 AD to be a 5,000-year quake—such a long shot that it gets scant consideration.

And therein lies the Achilles' heel of probabilistic mapping: It discounts the rarest quakes, which are also the most deadly. When calamities do strike, scientists dismiss them as "black swans," statistical outliers too far-fetched to consider. But in 2010 Russian scientists compared the ground shaking forecast by hazard maps to levels actually recorded during big quakes around the world. They found that the 500-year maps underestimated the intensity half the time, often by more than a factor of two. "Our crystal ball is proving mostly cloudy around the world," said Seth Stein, a geophysicist at Northwestern University.

Stein argues that the maps are just as likely to overestimate the danger. Business leaders in Memphis cursed a blue streak when the latest USGS maps ranked the earthquake hazard in the Midwest on a par with California. And in parts of California, the hazard calculations yield such high numbers that the state caps them so as not to shut down all construction.

The USGS maps for the Pacific Northwest and the rest of the country have yet to be tested by a really big quake. But so far they've done a good job of forecasting where small quakes will hit. The magnitude 5.8 quake that cracked the Washington Monument in August 2011 may have stunned folks inside the beltway, but it occurred in a seismic hazard area that's been marked on the national map for years.

The maps' shaking forecasts are most accurate in places like California, where quakes are common and there's a lot of data on how seismic waves move through the ground, Heaton said. That's one of the main reasons he doesn't have much confidence in the maps for the Pacific Northwest, where no one knows how the shaking from a megathrust off the coast will ripple across the region. "When there's another big Cascadia earthquake, nobody has any idea what's really going to happen."

Building a map requires one choice after another, with uncertainty at every turn. How often does the Seattle Fault break? What's the biggest possible Cascadia quake? How much will the Seattle basin amplify the shaking?

Frankel and his USGS colleagues try to make conservative choices, within reason. Unlike in Japan where mappers underestimated the subduction zone that snapped in 2011, the Northwest maps allow for magnitudes as high as 9.2 on Cascadia. The scientists add in a background level of hazard to account for undiscovered faults. "Don't think you've seen everything that nature can throw at us," Frankel cautioned the participants at the Seattle workshop.

When he took over the USGS mapping program in 1993, it was an insular operation. Frankel's predecessor scoffed at the notion that the Cascadia Subduction Zone might be active, so he left it off the maps. Decisions that affected businesses and lives across the country were made by a tiny group of experts. One of the first things Frankel did was open the doors to engineers and other scientists, who were starting to wonder what went on behind the curtain. "They basically wanted to be assured that we didn't go in a back room and smoke cigars and draw lines on a map," Frankel recalled.

The Seattle meeting was one of several Frankel and his colleagues convened around the country to gather input on a new set of maps to be issued in 2014. With several recent discoveries to consider, the schedule for the two-day meeting was as packed as the room. Item number one was a question with major implications: how often does the Cascadia Subduction Zone snap?

Oregon State University scientist Chris Goldfinger kicked things off with pictures of the cores he extracts from the seafloor. Goldfinger explained how he distinguishes layers formed by earthquake-triggered landslides. Then he walked the group through his evidence that cores from the southern coast of Oregon contain double the number of earthquake layers as cores from elsewhere. The scientists listened politely as he laid out his interpretation. In addition to serving up a full-rip 9 every 500 years or so, Goldfinger said, Cascadia also produces smaller quakes that rupture only the southern part of the subduction zone. So on average, the region gets a hard pounding every 250 years.

After Goldfinger wrapped up his presentation, Frankel took the podium again. Factoring the additional quakes into the maps would raise the hazard significantly, he explained. Did the other scientists think the evidence was strong enough to justify the change? "Now we get into the making of the sausage," Frankel said. "Let's get the discussion started."

A few years earlier, when Goldfinger first suggested southern Cascadia rips more frequently, he got a chilly reception. A lot of scientists weren't convinced all the layers in his cores were caused by megaquakes. At the Seattle meeting, though, more heads were nodding than shaking. Goldfinger had more data and some of his "extra" quakes seemed to be corroborated by tsunami layers in coastal lakes. Still, Frankel was reluctant to wholly embrace the story. Changing the seismic hazard maps has economic consequences, he explained after the meeting, so it's important to vet new evidence carefully. Frankel was leaning toward a compromise that would factor in only those southern quakes corroborated by tsunami layers.

A lot of hazard mapping comes down to choices like that, which drives the critics crazy. "It's completely guessing in the sense that you can come up with a range of options and you could say they all represent a reasonable interpretation of the data," Stein said. "Which choice you claim is best is based purely on your gut feeling."

Those who aren't in on the map-making process—including the public—don't realize how many assumptions are folded into the process, Stein said. He likens hazard mapping to credit default swaps and the other convoluted financial deals Wall Street cooked up before the 2008 financial meltdown. Few people on the outside understood the risks or even how the deals were structured. "In hindsight, the problem is that present hazard mapping practices were accepted and adopted without rigorous testing to show how well they actually worked," Stein wrote in the journal *Tectonophysics*.

Max Wyss, of the World Agency of Planetary Monitoring and Earthquake Risk Reduction based in Geneva, is among those calling for a return to worst-case scenario planning. "It's a moral question of who do we want to protect," he said. If countries design dams and other critical facilities to stand up to the maximum credible earthquake, why not apply the same standard to the places where people live?

But defining the worst-case earthquake is also fraught with uncertainty. Even if it could be done, it's unlikely societies would accept the cost. What's next, builders might ask? Bracing for an asteroid strike? "It's a very hard issue," Wyss conceded.

If nothing else, he said, the public should have an opportunity to weigh in as it does on air pollution rules, siting of nuclear power plants, and other decisions that affect the collective welfare. Popular opinion can't wish away the threat of earthquakes. But the people of the Northwest have never been asked if they're comfortable with an approach that seeks the sweet spot between cost and benefit, or whether they would prefer to pay extra for an extra margin of safety. "Ultimately, this is going to affect everybody in the Pacific Northwest," Heaton said.

The USGS's job is to do the science. It's up to society to make the call about acceptable risk, Frankel pointed out. But few people are beating down the door to join the conversation. Technically, the USGS workshops are open to everyone, but they're not a genuine forum for the public. Anyone without a PhD would be baffled by discussions about aleatory variability, Gaussian smoothing, and b-values.

The public can weigh in on building codes. But it's been years since the United States was rocked by a big earthquake, and only a few private citizens are motivated to tackle such a dense topic. James Bela is one of them.

The founder of a one-man organization called Oregon Earthquake Awareness, Bela was the sole public representative at the Seattle workshop. He made the drive from his Portland home in a 1968 Dodge Dart with more than half a million miles on the odometer. This time the car didn't die as it had a few months earlier, stranding him at the border after a session on earthquakes in British Columbia. At his own expense, Bela travels to science meetings and building code hearings across the country. At the Seattle workshop, he taped up a homemade poster listing the death toll from major quakes around the world—deaths he believes could have been averted if countries had just prepared for the worst-case quake.

Bela stood alone in the back of the room, videotaping the proceedings and occasionally asking questions or making comments. He urged the USGS not to water down the threat of more frequent quakes on the Oregon coast. He reminded the scientists of the lessons from Japan's 2011 earthquake and other recent seismic surprises. "I think we ought to look at the maximum event to protect public safety," he said.

A former geologist for the state of Oregon, Bela isn't intimidated by the scientific jargon. But that didn't change the fact that nobody took him seriously. Every time he walked to the microphone, there was a sense of eye rolling in the room. What Bela wanted wasn't on the agenda.

CHAPTER II:

SHAKE, RATTLE—PORTLAND, VANCOUVER, AND SEATTLE

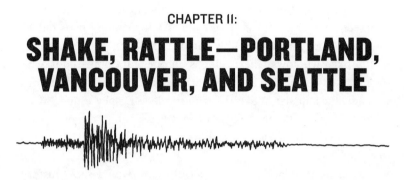

TO APPRECIATE HOW MIRED IN DENIAL many Northwesterners remain about big earthquakes, consider the reaction to a Washington State Department of Transportation (WSDOT) video that simulates the impact on Seattle's waterfront. The animation opens with a panoramic shot across Elliott Bay and zooms in as the initial jolt hits and cars spin slowly out of control.

The Alaskan Way Viaduct, a double-decker monstrosity built in the 1950s, starts to lurch. Thirty-five seconds into the quake, sections of the concrete roadway come crashing down as supporting columns snap and the ground turns to goo. The city's seawall, nearly a century old, slumps into Puget Sound, taking piers, restaurants, and curio shops with it. (Ivar's on Pier 54 remains standing. Apparently, even the WSDOT scrooges couldn't bear to trash the venerable fish house.)

Fires flare from broken gas lines. Half the city goes dark as power poles come crashing down. The simulated quake is like the 2001 Nisqually quake, but bigger—magnitude 7 instead of magnitude 6.8. Its epicenter is ten miles closer to Seattle and the imaginary shaking goes on twenty seconds longer.

WSDOT kept the video under wraps for two years, releasing it only when forced by a public records request. The bureaucrats feared it was too sensational. A lot of people agreed. One letter to the editor dismissed the animation as Disney-caliber fantasy. Others called it a scare tactic. "Perhaps the department wants to bolster a request for funding," one writer sniffed.

Geologists and engineers just shook their heads. They knew the video presented a plausible glimpse of the future, and a sanitized one at that. There's no audio, so viewers don't hear the roar of collapsing concrete, screeching tires, or screams. As the camera pans out for the closing shot, the only visibly damaged building is an office block with broken windows. The skyline is untouched. Compared to what the city would look like after a direct hit from the Seattle Fault or a Cascadia megaquake, WSDOT's video really is Disney-esque. "We're talking about a different ballgame," said Peter Yanev, the outspoken cofounder of EQE, a leading earthquake engineering firm. "It's going to be bad."

A realistic simulation of a powerful quake would show historic buildings collapsing into piles of bricks. No surprise there. Engineers have been warning for decades about the dangers of unreinforced masonry. But people might be shocked to see multistory concrete buildings pancake as shaking severs the flimsy supports that were common until the early 1970s. The tide of liquefied soil that caused the seawall to slump in the WSDOT animation would also undermine the footings of port terminals and industrial tank farms, knocking cranes askew and spilling fuel. An aerial view across the surrounding suburbs would show flattened warehouses and industrial parks, collapsed bridges, and heaved pavement.

But what about the skyline? Will the skyscrapers that dominate the urban core of Seattle—or Portland, or Vancouver—remain upright? The fate of the region's tall buildings has the potential to eclipse all other threats to the built environment. "If a couple of high-rises fall down in Seattle, you could be talking about two or three thousand people," Yanev said. He thinks it's possible, and suggested as much in a 2010 *New York Times* op-ed headlined "Shake, Rattle, Seattle." Many local engineers dismiss Yanev, who is based in California, as an alarmist. But he's not the only one who argues that buildings across the Pacific Northwest could be more vulnerable than most people realize.

To the USGS geologists who prepare the region's seismic hazard maps, the biggest unanswered question is what a Cascadia megaquake will do to tall buildings. But most engineers insist there's no question at all. They're confident modern skyscrapers will do what they were designed to do and roll with the punches. The disconnect is almost as pronounced as the one thirty years ago between the nuclear consultants who insisted the Cascadia Subduction Zone was dead and the geologists who suspected it was alive and poised to kick hard. Tom Heaton was in the middle of the fray then, so there's a kind of symmetry to finding him back at it again.

In the 1980s Heaton was the young hotshot who swept aside the nuclear industry's assertions and zeroed in on the subduction zone's essential nature, finding no reason to dismiss it as harmless. Nearly thirty years later, he's pushing Medicare age, and his wavy hair has faded from blond to white. He still writes music and plays guitar, performing with a Christian band called Leap of Faith. Professionally, he hasn't mellowed a whit. He continues to rankle the establishment, focusing much of his attention these days on the building industry.

When engineers say high-rises in the Northwest are designed for a magnitude 9 quake, Heaton snorts. "As far as I'm concerned, we don't know whether or not tall buildings in Seattle will survive a megaquake," he said. "For anyone to say otherwise is deceptive."

Of roughly 1,300 high-rise buildings in Seattle, Vancouver, and Portland, nearly half were built before 1990. Codes for most urban areas weren't upgraded to account for Cascadia until the mid-1990s. But Heaton isn't convinced even the latest codes adequately consider the unique nature of subduction zone quakes, which rattle tall structures the hardest. No skyscraper in the United States has been through that roller-coaster ride yet. "It's going to be a big experiment, and I'm not sure I want to be there for it," he said.

When Heaton left the USGS almost twenty years ago to take a professorship at Caltech, his mission was to bridge the gap between geologists and engineers. It hasn't gone as well as he had hoped. "I discovered there are no bridges that long. Earth scientists and earthquake engineers are so different I think they must have been born that way."

Engineers crave certainty. Geologists get bored if their work doesn't have an element of mystery. Discovery is messy, full of doubt, debate, and about-faces. Science couldn't progress any other way. If many ideas turn out to be wrong, that's just part of the process. Engineers operate in a higher-stakes world. If they get things wrong, people can die and businesses can be ruined. So when engineers ask geologists what kind of seismic shaking to expect, the last thing they want to hear is, "I don't know."

But Heaton says that's the only honest answer to the question of what will happen when Cascadia quake meets urban core. Of all the seismic hazard maps the USGS prepares, none is more fraught with uncertainty than the forecast for shaking in Seattle during a subduction zone quake. The basin that sits under the city and its suburbs will undoubtedly amplify the shaking, but by how much? Barely? By a factor of two or more? Nobody knows the answer. The other major unknown is how close the quake will come.

The subduction zone's leading edge sits about seventy miles offshore, at the seam in the seafloor where oceanic and continental plates meet. But the three-dimensional interface between the tectonic plates—the fault—is like a giant ramp that extends underneath the Northwest's urban corridor. If the portion of the fault that ruptures is mostly offshore, shaking will be muted by the time it reaches the cities. If the rupture is wider, continuing under the Olympic Peninsula and Oregon's Coast Range, cities will be hit harder. The USGS estimates a wide rupture would intensify shaking in Seattle by about 50 percent over current forecasts and double the level in Portland.

Heaton and a graduate student developed a computer model to simulate the effects of different Cascadia scenarios on hypothetical steel high-rises in Seattle. In the worst-case, widest rupture, all the buildings collapsed. The level of uncertainty is so high that when Heaton served on a federal advisory panel, he argued that the USGS shouldn't produce a hazard map for high-rise designers to use. "For tall buildings in Seattle, we're just shooting in the dark."

High-rises survive earthquakes by being flexible. Designed to cope with strong wind, they have no trouble with moderate ground shaking. People on the upper floors may experience a wild ride, but the structures barely register the motion in their bones. Megaquakes are more dangerous beasts. A magnitude 9 quake doesn't shake the ground that much harder than a magnitude 7, but it shakes a lot longer. In a thirty-second quake, a tall building might whip back and forth ten or fifteen times. In a four-minute quake, the building can gyrate through sixty cycles. Like a paperclip, even steel can bend only so many times before it breaks.

The potential for damage is magnified because the slow, rolling ground motions that dominate in a subduction zone quake can trigger an effect called resonance in tall buildings. The British Army experienced the consequences of resonance in 1831, when a suspension bridge near Manchester collapsed under a detachment of soldiers marching four abreast. The synchronized clomping of 148 boots was perfectly in tune with the structure's natural frequency—the point at which it vibrates like a tuning fork. As they felt the bridge begin to sway, the soldiers stomped their feet harder to amplify the motion. It was hilarious until they found themselves tumbling into the river.

The same thing can happen in an earthquake when seismic waves synchronize with a building's natural frequency. It's as if the building is a swing and the earthquake delivers perfectly timed shoves that send it flying farther and farther. A 1985 subduction zone quake off the coast of Mexico surprised engineers by knocking down new highrises and leaving older, shorter buildings untouched.

Structural engineers try to plan for resonance effects. But the degree to which the basins under Seattle and other cities will amplify the shaking is not factored into building codes, nor is the fact that subduction zone quakes will rock the ground for minutes, not seconds. "Almost none of the buildings in Seattle were designed to withstand three to five minutes of shaking," Yanev said.

Most tall buildings in Japan and Chile weathered recent megaquakes, which is encouraging. But neither country has as many questionable structures as the Northwest, Heaton pointed out. Engineers in Chile and Japan have been designing for great quakes much longer than their American counterparts. Frequent quakes have culled out the weak structure. Chilean laws hold a building's original owner liable for ten years if code violations lead to earthquake damage. The premium on seismic robustness is so high in Japan that owners voluntarily equip their buildings with dampers and isolation bearings. Japanese high-rises also contain more steel, and the codes require sturdier connections. Given a choice, Heaton said he'd much rather ride out a big earthquake in a Japanese building than an American one.

High-rise construction in the Northwest isn't going to stop just because geologists are uncertain what will happen in a megaquake. "We're not going to live in tents," Heaton said. "At the end of the day, we need buildings and we would like those buildings to be well engineered." Given all the uncertainty, Heaton said it behooves engineers to be humble and skeptical: humble about Cascadia's power and skeptical that the USGS or anyone else knows what to expect.

Like Heaton, John Hooper has devoted much of his career to building a bridge between engineers and earth scientists, but from the other side of the gap. His biggest challenge is to drag science into the real world.

As director of earthquake engineering at Magnusson Klemencic Associates, one of the country's premier structural engineering firms, Hooper had a hand in many of the region's architectural landmarks, including Columbia Center—the tallest skyscraper—and the stadiums where the Seattle Mariners and Seahawks play. Designing buildings to handle earthquakes requires a lot of number crunching, but it's not too technically difficult, he said. "If you know the amount of shaking, it's relatively straightforward." Hooper works closely with geologists in the Northwest, so he knows more than most engineers about how the USGS makes the sausage. At the 2012 hazard map workshop in Seattle, he quipped that pure science doesn't seem so pure to him anymore. The geologists laughed. Then Hooper made his pitch for the status quo. "If we're just tweaking something for the sake of change, we don't want that. We'd like to minimize the changes."

Hooper vividly recalls the day Brian Atwater, Craig Weaver, and a team of USGS scientists first met with him and other engineers to brief them on something called the Cascadia Subduction Zone.

Another memorable meeting followed a few years later, when the geologists sprang the news about the Seattle Fault. Hooper used to think he had it easy compared to engineers in California. Now, he envies them. "It's much more complicated here," he said.

With his rapid-fire delivery, Hooper could pass for a New Yorker. He grew up in Everett, though, returning to his home state after graduate school at UC Berkeley. Hooper serves on several of the national committees that develop new building codes and set seismic standards. Since he started in the business more than twenty-five years ago, the changes have been dramatic. "We're constantly, I mean constantly, looking at what we do. We've come from A to Z, but I think there are four more alphabets to go."

Structural engineers take architects' visions and flesh them out to create designs that will stand up to gravity, wind, and seismic forces. Some engineers in the Northwest factor basin effects and duration of shaking into their designs for skyscrapers, even though it's not required, Hooper said. For really big projects, engineers submit their work to other firms for peer review. Significant structures are subjected to simulated earthquakes when they're still on the drawing board. But for nine out of ten new buildings, engineers don't consider what could happen if shaking exceeds the level in the code, derived from the USGS maps. "It's assumed that a building designed to the code will result in acceptable performance," Hooper said.

He's confident few, if any, modern high-rises will collapse in a megaquake. But like a scientist, he never says never. "There's a chance a brand-new building could come down. It's a very low likelihood." Modern building codes are couched in probabilities, not absolutes. The goal is "life-safety:" protecting people from injury or death by preventing collapse. A building that's so damaged it has to be torn down is considered a success as long as all the occupants make it out safely.

"The term 'earthquake-proof' is not in our lexicon," Hooper said. A well-designed building that meets all requirements still stands as much as a 10 percent chance of collapse if it's hit by the maximum earthquake the code considers, roughly a two-thousand-year quake in the Northwest. Slam the same building with something bigger and the risk shoots up. In an off-the-charts event—one that shakes the ground more than twice as hard as the code anticipates—statistics suggest a 50-50 chance of collapse. "That's for a five-thousand- or ten-thousand-year event," Hooper said. "The kind of thing that's just too large to consider."

For older buildings the prospects are worse. But just because a building is old doesn't necessarily mean it's dangerous. So much hinges on design, era, and materials. Long before seismic standards were cranked up, tall buildings in Seattle were built to cope with strong winds and moderate quakes. The Structural Engineers Association of Washington (SEAW) was formed after the 1949 Olympia earthquake and helped institute the region's first seismic codes. With fewer earthquakes Oregon didn't adopt significant seismic standards until 1994.

Cities all along the West Coast share the problem of older steel high-rises, which can be especially vulnerable to quake damage. Most steel-frame office towers and apartments erected between the 1960s and the mid-1990s have flanges fastened with welds rather than with bolts. Welds were cheaper, and lab tests at the time suggested they were stronger.

But after California's 1994 Northridge quake, engineers were shocked to discover fractured welds in more than one hundred buildings, including some still under construction. When they tested the welds in more detail, it became clear they were dangerously brittle. Building codes were changed. But retrofits are costly, and few existing structures have been upgraded. When Heaton and his student simulated the impact of Cascadia quakes on hypothetical high-rises in Seattle, those with brittle welds were more prone to collapse in every scenario.

Hooper works in the real thing. The 514-foot-tall Rainier Tower in downtown Seattle was built in 1977 with a welded steel frame. Perched atop a twelve-story pedestal that looks like a giant golf tee, the skyscraper has always drawn nervous looks from locals. Some call it the wine glass. The Seattle *Post-Intelligencer*'s architecture critic described the tower as both an engineering tour de force and "a teetering colossus that makes any normal human jittery." Hooper's firm did the engineering. He doesn't feel any qualms about reporting for work on the 32nd floor. In a quake the building will sway, but that's what it was designed to do. Hooper was part of a team that investigated brittle welds in California, and he pointed out that no steel buildings collapsed in the twenty-second-long Northridge quake. A building like the Rainier Tower would have to lose more than half its welds to cause major damage, Hooper said. With the amount of steel and number of columns that support the skyscraper, he's betting that's not very likely to happen.

Just as they learned from Northridge, engineers are schooled by every major quake. The SEAW and other groups dispatch teams around the world to study damage and glean lessons that can be applied at home. Codes aren't perfect but they're a lot better than they used to be, said Hooper.

But in order to design buildings for earthquakes, he and other engineers need a starting point. For all their uncertainty, the USGS maps are the only game in town. "We engineers are scratching our heads, asking ourselves, 'Should we believe everything the scientists tell us?' But at some point you've got to believe your smart kid brother."

When Hooper first heard about Cascadia, he was skeptical. The evidence won him over. Despite objections from many in the construction industry, he championed code changes to account for this new seismic threat. Hooper continues to put his trust in science. "There's a handshake and a handoff. But it's not just a blind handoff, like in track and field. We actually look each other in the eye."

Heaton hopes he's wrong, but he can imagine a day when the relationship turns sour. If many new buildings fail when Cascadia lets loose, engineers will point their fingers at geologists and say, "We designed this based on what you told us, and look what happened." Geologists will reply that they were always up-front about what they didn't know. "We'll probably end up in congressional hearings some day," Heaton said. "People will be asking, 'How did it turn out like this?'"

The maxim that new buildings are better took a beating in Chile's magnitude 8.8 megaquake in 2010. Some of the most heavily damaged high-rises were only a few years old. A fifteen-story condominium that toppled onto its side, killing eight people, wasn't even fully occupied yet. In one city close to the epicenter, nearly one in five tall buildings—many of them new—were damaged beyond repair.

Engineers say the surprising failures raise red flags for the U.S. West Coast. "This earthquake caused severe damage to many buildings that are much better than the typical building in Seattle," said Yanev.

Before he sold his company in 2000, Yanev led or directed field investigations of more than ninety earthquakes around the world. Since then, he has traveled the globe as an adviser to the World Bank. In Chile Yanev trekked from leaning apartment towers to cracked hotels and sagging office complexes. Chilean codes generally require stronger construction than do codes in the United Sates. "If our buildings were in Chile, they would be all over the ground," he said.

But in Chile as in the United States, architects and builders have been pushing the boundaries with fewer and thinner shear walls, the structures that protect buildings from damaging side-to-side motion. "Ten years ago most of the big construction companies in Chile were run by engineers who understood the risks. Now they're run by financial people, MBAs who just want to know how much they can shave off the cost," Yanev said. Only a handful of buildings in Chile collapsed, but enough were seriously damaged to leave tens of thousands of people homeless and to throw thousands of businesses into chaos.

Yanev said that the design shift in Chile is similar to what's been going on in California and the Pacific Northwest. Steel construction, considered the most earthquake resistant, is increasingly rare. The typical new high-rise is a slender concrete tower with panoramic windows and few bulky columns to interfere with the views. Earthquake resistance is provided by a heavy central core that contains the elevator shaft. "All the strength is in those four walls." Yanev said. If an earthquake shakes the building hard enough and long enough to damage the core, there's little backup to prevent collapse.

"These concrete buildings scare the living daylights out of me and a lot of other engineers." Many of the new towers are residential. High-ceilinged shops, restaurants, and lobbies on the ground floor, what engineers call a soft story, add to the risk.

U.S. codes used to require more redundancy. Buildings were designed with strong frames and shear walls. If one failed, the other could pick up the load. Now engineers rely on computer simulations to whittle away at the margins and design structures that just meet the minimum standards. "The overreliance on these computer analyses is just crazy," said California-based engineer Kit Miyamoto. "People do these simulations and feel like they know everything."

With five offices in California and one in Oregon, Miyamoto International works on projects around the world. The company designed a 1.2-million-pound seismic damper to protect the Los Angeles airport's famous Theme Building without spoiling its futuristic lines. In Haiti Miyamoto and his team are designing low-cost retrofits for schools and houses damaged in the disastrous 2010 quake. He's on a crusade in the Northwest and in California to convince developers and engineers that it makes good business sense to go beyond the bare-bones seismic code.

To make his case, Miyamoto points to Christchurch, New Zealand. As in Chile few buildings collapsed in the magnitude 6.3 quake that struck in 2011. One that did was the six-story concrete Canterbury Television Building, where more than one hundred people died. Most offices and apartments performed to code, staying upright long enough for occupants to flee. Nevertheless, 80 percent of buildings across a square mile of the city's core were slated for demolition because of damage. Economic losses totaled more than $15 billion.

Superimpose that square mile on downtown Seattle and almost everything from the waterfront to the top of Capitol Hill would be gone. "Looking at Christchurch, you can see what's going to happen to Seattle," Miyamoto said. "I wouldn't be surprised if the city is shut down for more than twelve months." The same could happen in Portland and Vancouver.

Christchurch has top-notch engineers. New Zealand has strict buildings codes and inspectors to enforce them. But just as in the U.S., the codes don't consider the economic impact to communities, businesses, and residents when buildings are rendered unusable. In Chile and Japan, many buildings that rode out the shaking with little structural damage were a shambles inside, with water lines and power supplies severed, ventilation systems wrecked, and expensive finishes shattered. Japanese shelters were filled with high-rise refugees forced to move out of their apartments. Nearly two million people were left homeless by Chile's quake and tsunami, many of them urban condo dwellers. "There's a huge gap between what society expects and what is really practiced by engineers," Miyamoto said. "We need to do better. It's not like we don't know how."

Designing buildings that are seismically sustainable—able to remain standing and usable after a quake—adds only 5 to 10 percent to the total cost. But when engineering firms compete for big jobs, fortunes rise and fall on margins as slim as 1 percent. High-tech businesses like Microsoft and Amazon are among the minority willing to pay extra to ensure their operations won't be disrupted for weeks or months following a big quake. Most new buildings meet the code and nothing more.

Modern building codes may not always be able to achieve even their modest life-safety goals. "It's not like we've got it all solved," said University of British Columbia engineering professor Perry Adebar. Adebar visited Chile and came back concerned about some of the tall buildings in British Columbia's biggest city. The Vancouver metro area has more high-rises than Seattle and Portland combined. Many sit on a river delta and other loose soils guaranteed to amplify shaking.

Adebar noticed that the damaged buildings in Chile all seemed to have six-inch concrete shear walls between rooms, instead of the eight-inch walls that used to be standard. Developers pushed for the switch to cut costs, and building regulators allowed it.

Adebar knew some Canadian buildings have the thinner walls, too. When he got home, he decided to run a series of lab tests to see just how much shaking six-inch walls could take. He used a hydraulic press to squeeze wall sections up to six feet tall, and found they shattered more easily and much more suddenly than expected.

Adebar's experiments set the wheels in motion to change Canada's building codes. But the process will take years and won't do anything to improve existing high-rises. Now Adebar is examining the engineering plans for 350 buildings in Vancouver to figure out how many are at serious risk from thin walls and other design flaws. The provincial government has undertaken similar studies for schools and public structures, but nobody in British Columbia—or Washington or Oregon—is scrutinizing the privately owned high-rises where so many people live and work.

"You've got people with million-dollar condos who have no idea the building they live in is very susceptible to being damaged or potentially collapsing in an earthquake," Adebar said. "There's no process to say, 'This is a bad building.'" Condo owners, apartment dwellers, and businesses assume that if anything was wrong with their buildings, the government would take action. But the only time most jurisdictions inspect or require seismic upgrades on existing buildings is when they undergo major renovations or change use. Most owners don't even know their buildings may be at risk.

Yanev said that's the main reason he wrote his column for *The New York Times*. Practicing engineers aren't eager to talk publicly about problems with buildings they or their colleagues may have worked on. Nearing retirement, Yanev doesn't care. "I have the liberty of seeing the big picture and not worrying about what clients think." After visiting so many scenes of death and destruction around the world, he's got no stomach to see them repeated in his own country. If building owners and others in the Pacific Northwest start pushing now to reevaluate and strengthen dangerous buildings of all types, the region will be much safer when the next big one hits. "What I'm saying is, 'Hey, guys. Some of these buildings are going to collapse unless we do something about it.'"

The most dangerous structures in Portland, Seattle, Vancouver, and scores of smaller cities across the Northwest are concrete buildings constructed before the mid-1970s. Engineers call them nonductile, which means they can't bend without breaking. Their columns lack enough steel reinforcement to keep them from collapsing in a major shake. And when heavy concrete buildings collapse, it can be deadly to anyone trapped inside.

"Those are the buildings that would probably have the highest casualty rate," said Cale Ash, of Degenkolb Engineers in Seattle. "If the columns are overloaded and they start to fail, you could see pancaking." Ash was touring the city's Sodo neighborhood in the fall of 2012, pointing out buildings that probably won't fare well next time the ground starts shaking. He pulled his sedan to a stop in front of a likely suspect, a six-story white building.

Recently returned from an earthquake reconnaissance trip to Christchurch, Ash looks at structures like this one with a more pressing sense of concern. It's often hard to tell from the street which buildings have concrete frames and which of those fall into the high-risk category. The building on First Avenue offers a few clues. The walls still show the marks of the old-fashioned lumber formwork used to cast the concrete. There's a good chance the building also sits on deteriorating wood pilings, Ash said. The ground floor is taller and more open than the upper floors, which further erodes the building's seismic prospects.

In his book *Peace of Mind in Earthquake Country,* Yanev offered a blunt assessment of this type of building: "If you live or work in a pre-1973 un-retrofitted concrete frame structure . . . you are exposing yourself to one of the greatest hazards in earthquake country." His advice: Lobby your landlord to upgrade, or move. But if it's hard for a professional engineer to pick out the most dangerous buildings, it's impossible for the average person. The building's age is the best indicator, but some older buildings are better designed than others. "To know for sure, you really have to look at the drawings and study the construction details," Ash said.

With an estimated forty thousand old concrete buildings across the state, some California cities are compiling inventories and inching toward retrofit requirements. But upgrades can be very costly. There's no similar effort in the Northwest.

The region is also trailing California in tackling the risk posed by old brick buildings, Ash said, driving past rows of masonry warehouses and former factories built in the early 1900s. The only good thing about the structures from a seismic perspective is that they're generally smaller than old concrete buildings so they won't harm as many people when they collapse. Cities like San Francisco and Los Angeles began requiring seismic upgrades on old brick buildings decades ago. Most have been retrofitted or torn down. Some cities post warning signs on those that remain.

In the Northwest, Seattle is leading the way—very slowly—on efforts to mandate retrofits. After several false starts, the city published an inventory that lists more than 800 potentially dangerous brick buildings. Estimates for the State of Oregon range up to ten thousand, with nearly two thousand in Portland alone. A survey in Vancouver identified 8,000 buildings, mostly brick, at risk of catastrophic damage.

Seattle's brick architecture ranges from low-slung mom-and-pop grocery stores to seven-story apartment complexes with ornate parapets and a hundred or more residents. The greatest density is in the historic Pioneer Square neighborhood and the gentrifying industrial center to the south, where Ash pulled up in front of a handsome specimen. The six-story building dates from 1910, but it's clearly been spruced up and houses an artisan soft drink company. "There's diagonal bracing," Ash said, pointing out angled steel beams visible through the lobby windows. If they're sturdy enough, the braces should prevent the vulnerable ground floor from collapsing. Horizontal rows of metal rosettes on the front and back of the building indicate the walls were bolted to the floors to keep them from peeling away during an earthquake.

People who live and work in brick buildings can tell if the structures have been retrofitted by looking for braces and rosettes, Ash said. They can also use the city's list as a starting point. But not all retrofits are created equal. Sometimes a row of rosettes just means the floors were sagging so much that the owner was forced to cinch them to the walls. That might be better than nothing, but it's not a seismic retrofit.

Regulations require at least a basic upgrade only when old buildings change use or are significantly remodeled. The new mandate the city is aiming for would phase in the requirement for all brick buildings. A basic retrofit doesn't bring a building up to current seismic standards, Ash explained, but should strengthen the structure enough to prevent collapse in a moderate earthquake. It also reduces the danger of bricks falling on passersby and parked cars.

There's no guarantee a building with a bare-bones retrofit will survive a more powerful quake. But Ash likes to show photos of two nearly identical brick buildings from Christchurch, just a block apart. The building that hadn't been retrofitted was in ruins. The one that had was still standing, with minimal damage.

Less than half a mile from the soft drink company on First Avenue sits an example of the third type of building no engineer wants be caught in during an earthquake: a concrete tilt-up warehouse. This one is a big-box hardware store. Tilt-ups are common because they go up quickly. Wall segments are poured in place atop a concrete slab, then tilted up into position. If the connections between the wall segments and the roof are weak, the walls can fall like a house of cards.

The good news is that codes have been ratcheted up several times since the mid-1970s. The bad news is that the changes were necessary because tilt-ups seem to get crunched in every major earthquake. The collapse risk isn't high for the newest versions, but the potential for damage is. "So these buildings that have all our food and our home repair supplies could be red-tagged after an earthquake," Ash said, "when you need them the most."

Under Seattle's Aurora Bridge, Carl Barker cocked his head and listened to the whomp-whomp-whomp of traffic speeding by more than 150 feet above. The bridge was getting a seismic retrofit, and Barker could already hear the difference in its vibrato. "It's just a feeling," he said, groping to describe a special sense developed over decades as an engineer for the Washington State Department of Transportation. "I can tell it's stiffer."

Opened in 1932, the bridge arches gracefully over the Lake Washington Ship Canal. Every day almost eighty thousand cars cross the critical link on Highway 99. When crews dug out the abutment at the bridge's south end, they discovered cracks in both girders, probably from previous quakes. Laboratory tests on mock-ups of the aging concrete columns didn't bode well for performance in the next big shake.

As part of the $12.4 million retrofit, the bridge got new expansion joints that allow sections of the deck to slide past each other by more than a foot. Crews sawed through several massive concrete supports and installed shock-absorbing bearings. They excavated around the bridge's footings and added tons of additional concrete. Barker pointed out green-and-black wrappings on several columns. These reinforcing layers are the same type of carbon fiber Boeing uses on the 787 Dreamliner.

The bridge is a historic landmark, so the fixes were designed to blend seamlessly with the original design, Barker explained on a cool day in October 2012. When crews were bolstering the north end, they had to take special care not to damage or block access to the Fremont Troll, a concrete ogre hunkered down with a Volkswagen in its grip.

Barker is satisfied the improvements will do the job. "The bridge shouldn't fall down," he said. But there are five hundred others across Washington that could, and at least that many more in Oregon and British Columbia. The Oregon Department of Transportation (ODOT) says that every bridge connecting the I-5 corridor to the coast is likely to collapse in a Cascadia megaquake, leaving tsunami-ravaged communities cut off from help. In Portland, nine bridges that cross the Willamette River—including the I-405 bridge—were built before modern seismic codes and only a handful have been retrofitted. The most optimistic observation in ODOT's 2009 analysis is that a few segments of I-5 would probably remain passable.

Power, gas, water, and sewer lines are even less equipped than roads and bridges to survive strong shaking. Several high-power transmission lines run through industrial tide flats across the region, where the ground could shift twenty feet or more. Substation transformers that aren't bolted down will be knocked off their foundations.

Many water and sewer lines in the Northwest are buried in river valleys where shaking will turn the ground to jelly. There are still no seismic design requirements for new lines. In Japan, where gas lines are equipped with their own seismometers and automatic shutoff valves, it took three months and the efforts of four thousand extra workers to bring Sendai's service back to full capacity after the 2011 megaquake. "I compare that to what we have here, and I know we have big trouble ahead," said Yumei Wang, geohazards team leader for the Oregon Department of Geology and Mineral Industries.

Wang recently surveyed the tank farms and pipelines that store and deliver 90 percent of Oregon's liquid fuels, from gasoline and diesel to jet fuel. They're all clustered by the Willamette River on the shakiest ground possible. Portland International Airport's only fuel supply arrives via one of those pipelines. "All our eggs are in one basket," she said.

The fact that Wang and others are identifying weaknesses and starting to address them is a remarkable turnaround for a region where emergency managers' worst nightmare used to be a flood. Jim Mullen took over Seattle's emergency department in the early 1990s. As he learned more about seismic hazards, he would pile his staff into the car every Friday to cruise the city and brainstorm scenarios. "We looked at the structures we had and talked about the vulnerability," recalled Mullen, who went on to direct the Washington State Emergency Management Division for nearly ten years. "For me, that was the 'oh shit' moment."

Mullen realized the city didn't have a clue about how to deal with powerful quakes. "We were totally unprepared. Our plans were godawful." Early earthquake drills dissolved into bickering among city departments. In the late 1990s a FEMA-funded program called Project Impact helped get the region moving with enough federal funding to identify problems and get some of the fixes started.

Washington's transportation department was an early adopter. Since 1991 the agency has at least partially retrofitted about four hundred vulnerable bridges, welding steel jackets onto concrete columns and bolting down the decks. The agency's top priority is to create an earthquake resilient route through the Puget Sound corridor. After years of political gridlock, in 2011 the state began dismantling Seattle's decrepit Alaskan Way Viaduct—before the collapse depicted in WSDOT's earthquake animation could come true.

Seattle voters passed a $365 million levy in 2006 that included funding for retrofits on several bridges. Money from another levy is upgrading fire stations so first responders won't be trapped inside damaged buildings. The city strengthened water towers and hardened several fire hydrants to stand up to intense ground shaking. Firefighters also have new pumps and hoses that allow them to pull water directly from lakes, reservoirs, and Puget Sound.

Resilience is the new buzzword in disaster response. It's one thing to survive the immediate crisis but another to bounce back from a blow that could send the entire region into an economic tailspin. Nobody wants to be the next Kobe. The Japanese city was one of the world's largest container ports when it was hit by a shallow magnitude 6.8 earthquake in 1995. Nearly six thousand people died. Rail lines were knocked out and major expressways weren't fully reopened until twenty months later. Some analysts cite the quake as one of the factors that pushed Japan into a decade of decline.

Both Washington and Oregon have embarked on resilience planning. Without those efforts, a Cascadia megaquake could kick off a downward spiral, warned a 2013 Oregon report. "A policy of business as usual implies a post-earthquake future that could consist of decades of economic and population decline—in effect, a lost generation that will devastate our state and . . . affect the regional and national economy," the report concluded.

It's impossible to fix everything at once, Wang said, but there's no better time to start than now. "The scary thing about an earthquake is that it finds the weak links, and it's merciless. It won't say 'I won't bring that building down because there's a bunch of kids in there.'"

When it comes to earthquake preparedness, there's no more emotional flashpoint than schools. No parent wants to put a child in harm's way just by sending him or her off to class. California took that danger to heart nearly eighty years ago. The Long Beach earthquake of 1933 struck on a Friday a few hours after schools had let out. Nearly 250 classroom buildings crumbled or were seriously damaged, and residents shuddered at the close call. Within thirty days the state legislature passed bills requiring earthquake-resistant construction for schools and banning new unreinforced masonry buildings.

School safety in the Northwest remains largely a function of political boundaries. British Columbia launched seismic upgrades more than a decade ago and has committed $1.5 billion to the effort. Half the public schools in Oregon are rated at a high or very high risk of collapse, and the state is only slowly making upgrades. With voter support for levies, the Seattle School District had worked its way through about two-thirds of its dangerous buildings by 2012. Washington has yet to conduct a statewide seismic survey of schools.

The Northwest also falls behind California in grappling with the problem of earthquakes that rip the surface of the ground. In 1971 the San Fernando quake opened a ten-mile-long gash across Southern California and tore apart homes and commercial buildings. Governor Ronald Reagan signed the Alquist-Priolo Act into law the next year, restricting construction near known fault scarps. The law also requires the state to map fault zones, which is fairly easy in California. In the Northwest, it wasn't until the late 1990s that lidar started to peer through the trees and pick out the scarps hidden below.

When Washington's most populous county decided to build a new sewage treatment plant fifteen miles northeast of Seattle in the early 2000s, the hazard posed by surface faults in the Northwest wasn't well-understood. Nobody wants sewage ponds in their backyards, so it took a bruising battle to settle on a location. County officials weren't about to start over, even when USGS scientists cleared their throats and pointed to three places on the property where earthquakes on the South Whidbey Island Fault had broken the surface.

The county commissioned the USGS to excavate one of the scarps, where the scientists found evidence of at least three quakes. As the cost of the project soared to $1.8 billion, engineers seismically strengthened the plant and hoped for the best. So one of the state's costliest public investments now sits on top of the region's biggest shallow fault.

The power of engineering to overcome suspect terrain in the Pacific Northwest was put to its greatest test with the construction of Seattle's two professional sports stadiums. Safeco Field, home of the Seattle Mariners, and CenturyLink Field, where Seahawks fans raise such a din it registers on seismometers, sit side by side on land that didn't exist a hundred years ago.

Photographs from the early 1900s show a broad lagoon fringed by mudflats. Trains chugged across the water on elevated trestles, moving coal, timber, and sacks of flour between mills and ships anchored offshore. When the city decided to level its steep hills, workers sluiced tons of excavated dirt into the lagoon. They tossed in tree stumps, too, along with trash, building debris, and anything else they could lay their hands on. When they were done, the city's waterfront was extended southward by several square miles. The new ground was flat, perfect for building—and about the last place a seismic engineer today would choose for arenas that collectively hold more than one hundred thousand people.

During the Nisqually earthquake, geysers of wet sand sprouted nearby as particles in the already-loose fill rattled apart and water gushed out. Soil turned to thick slurry. Engineers have known for more than a century that reclaimed swamps are among the most dangerous places to build in earthquake-prone territory. Not only is the ground susceptible to liquefaction, but it also shakes harder and longer than more solid soils. The prospects weren't improved by the discovery that the Seattle Fault zone passes directly under the reclaimed land. The fault doesn't break the surface, but there's little doubt the area will heave hard in the next big quake.

Building a stadium under those conditions isn't as tough as building one on the San Andreas Fault—but it comes close, said Martin Page: "That's what made it fun for the engineers." Page works for Shannon & Wilson, the Seattle-based firm that helped design the foundations for both arenas. The next time the ground shakes, he would be pleased to find himself sitting in the stands at either facility. "I think they would be some of the safest places to be during a big rupture on the Seattle Fault, and even in the tsunami that might follow."

To give the arenas a firm footing, Shannon & Wilson relied on a tried-and-true method for building in crappy soil: pilings. Collectively, the stadiums and their associated structures sit on more than 3,700 concrete-filled pilings, each two feet across. The steel piles are embedded in hard-packed glacial till. The ground beneath the ballparks could turn to soup and the structures wouldn't sink or list.

Long before the pile-driving started, the engineers conducted test borings to get a better idea of what lay beneath, Page said. They found a little bit of everything, from stumps and railroad ties to pockets of one-hundred-year-old construction debris. The fill ranges from fifteen to twenty feet thick. Below that are layers of muck, silt, and sand deposited over millennia by the ancient river and its estuary. In many spots the engineers had to bore down ninety feet before they struck solid glacial till.

Pounding a flat-bottom piling that deep is like driving a skinny nine-story building straight into the ground. The tool for the job was a diesel hammer. With a driving ram that can weigh as much as twenty-five tons, the device harnesses the power of exploding diesel fuel to deliver up to fifty blows per minute to the head of a piling. "It's like the difference between driving a railroad spike with a ball peen hammer versus a sledge hammer," Page said. The noisy machines were able to sink a piling in less than half an hour. A few of the steel tubes buckled when they hit buried boulders. When in place, the pilings were packed with steel reinforcing rods and filled with concrete.

Aboveground, both stadiums were built in sections to allow for thermal expansion and differential jiggling during a quake, said John Hooper, whose firm did the seismic engineering. "Safeco Field is really seven different buildings in one," he said. The baseball stadium's retractable roof posed a unique challenge. The engineers installed giant dampers on each of the interlocking sections. "They're like the shock absorbers in your car, only twenty times bigger." An earthquake could hit when the roof is open, closed, or somewhere in between, so the engineers ran computer simulations for multiple configurations.

Safeco Field came through the mild Nisqually quake with no structural damage, though dozens of televisions, interior facades, and light fixtures took a beating. CenturyLink was under construction. The shaking knocked a scaffolding loose and delayed work by three days.

The football stadium's twin roofs were one of the trickiest puzzles the seismic engineers faced. The 720-foot-long canopies arch over the grandstands with no visible supports to block the view. The concrete pylons are tucked out of sight at either end. If the whole stadium torques in an earthquake, the roofs could tear themselves apart.

To keep that from happening, Hooper and his colleagues employed the type of giant ball-bearing systems that many Japanese buildings rest on. This was the first time so-called friction pendulum dampers were used on such a large roof. At CenturyLink Field the bearings essentially allow the roof to float during an earthquake. The ground and the roof supports may shake like crazy, but the roof shouldn't budge. Only one building in Washington incorporates a similar system in its foundation: the State Emergency Management Division's headquarters near Tacoma.

The most recognizable structure in the Pacific Northwest was built long before anyone knew what a subduction zone was, or dreamed that Seattle's hilly landscape harbored tectonic cracks. The Space Needle graced the cover of *Life Magazine* on February 9, 1962, just weeks before the Seattle World's Fair opened. It was constructed in a rush. Engineers were sketching out plans a few steps ahead of workers bolting sections of steel together. Yet the graceful spire is likely to hold up to big earthquakes far better than many modern buildings. "If there's anything left standing in Seattle, the Space Needle will be there," said Gary Noble Curtis, one of the project engineers.

Curtis answered the phone in Pasadena the day the Needle's architects called to recruit his boss, structural engineer John K. Minasian. An expert in tower design, Minasian practiced what he called "sound engineering." That meant being a fanatic for detail. Every calculation was checked, rechecked, and checked again, all by hand or slide rule. "He was very demanding," Curtis recalled. "Everything had to be just so." But after all the numbers were run, Minasian would tug on his ear and explain to his protégés that a design had to sound good, too. What he meant, Curtis said, was that an engineer needs an intuitive sense of the way mechanical stresses will flow through a structure.

Minasian also had a healthy sense of caution, born from investigating tower collapses. Lacking any earthquake hazard maps, he just doubled the existing seismic code. He also upped the wind specs, building for nearly twice the original loads. The result is a much stronger structure than engineers would build today, even with all their knowledge about the seismic risks.

The Needle sits on a thirty-foot-deep foundation of reinforced concrete. For extra strength Minasian insisted on a single, continuous pour. The job took twelve hours and 467 truckloads of concrete. Seventy-two giant bolts, more than thirty feet long and four inches wide, anchor the tower to the foundation. Because the schedule was so tight, Minasian had to order the steel based on back-of-the-envelope calculations. He pulled out a catalog and picked the biggest beams available, Curtis said. "It's probably over-designed by 50 percent." The structure is also highly redundant. If the steel legs fail, the inner core is strong enough to resist earthquake motion, and vice versa.

None of that makes the Needle a fun place to be in an earthquake. The manager of the rotating restaurant likened his experience in the 1965 quake to riding a flagpole. "A couple of Space Needle employees were said to have fled, never to return," wrote Knute Berger in *Space Needle: The Spirit of Seattle*. The women's gymnastic team from Western Michigan University was on the observation deck 520 feet off the ground when the Nisqually quake struck. "Once we realized it was an earthquake, terror kind of ripped through you because you have no control over what's going to happen," the coach told a reporter. The mayor of Issaquah, east of Seattle, clung to a beam and tried not to scream as the saucer tossed from side to side.

But a thrill ride at the top doesn't mean serious trouble for the steel tower. The Needle is so strong it should be able to whip around for the duration of a Cascadia megaquake and then some, Curtis said. "It could do that forever. The structure would take it just fine."

Northwest historian Murray Morgan estimated Minasian's caution boosted the project's cost by $1 million, pushing the final price tag to about $4 million. It probably wouldn't be possible to erect such a strong structure in today's economic environment, Curtis said. No one pressured Minasian and his crew to shave their safety margins. "There was no complaining that we put too much steel in it," he said. "Today, you'd get in big trouble for wasting somebody's money."

CHAPTER 12:

NUTS, BOLTS, AND CHIMNEYS

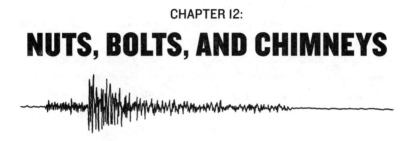

THE DUST HAD BARELY SETTLED from the Nisqually earthquake in 2001 before Derek Booth was cruising the streets of West Seattle. As he drove slowly past Craftsman homes and bungalows built in the Roaring Twenties, Booth counted cracked and crumbling chimneys. The quakes of 1949 and 1965 had rocked this blue-collar neighborhood with surprising force, toppling brick flues like bowling pins. Booth's initial reconnaissance convinced him that the pattern had repeated itself again. This time the University of Washington geologist hoped to get to the bottom of the mystery.

"The working hypothesis was, 'There's something about West Seattle,'" recalled Booth, who splits his time between the UW and the University of California at Santa Barbara. But without a broader survey, he couldn't be certain West Seattle really was hammered harder than other neighborhoods. The city was buzzing with geologists and students, and Booth had no trouble recruiting volunteers to help. In two-person teams, the group fanned out across Seattle and nearby cities. One volunteer would drive at a snail's pace while the other recorded chimney conditions and used a handheld GPS to log coordinates. "We looked at every single chimney we could see from the street. It was a very quick, very crude survey." The scientists were racing to get the job done before homeowners started making repairs.

Within a couple of weeks, Booth and his colleagues had eyeballed 60,000 chimneys, nearly 1,600 of them with obvious problems. Just as he had suspected, West Seattle was a hot spot. "It wasn't just that the people of West Seattle are whiners," Booth said. "They really did have the most damage of anybody." In one narrow zone, almost every other chimney was a mess. Yet just a few blocks over, it was as if the earth hadn't budged. The patchy distribution was nearly identical to what geologists documented after the 1965 quake. "You could try to explain it by saying that maybe some people just had a crappy mason build their chimneys," Booth said. "But unless the same guy did all the chimneys in a three-block area then retired, it just doesn't make any sense."

Chimneys act as crude seismometers, Booth explained. Made up of bricks pasted together with mortar, they're usually the first thing to fail when the ground jerks back and forth. The amount and type of chimney damage in an area is a good indicator of the intensity of shaking. "There are a lot more chimneys than there are seismometers, so that's really useful information." The four real seismometers in West Seattle at the time confirmed the chimneys' informal readings: An instrument close to the area where damage was most severe registered ground motions nearly three times stronger than a seismometer half a mile south. Distance from the quake's epicenter couldn't explain the pattern of damage, nor could the underlying soil. West Seattle sits on the same hard-packed glacial deposits as much of the city and its suburbs.

The scientists also found heavy chimney damage in Bremerton, a Navy town west of Seattle across Puget Sound. As they mapped their observations, the researchers couldn't help but notice that much of the damage lined up on an east-west axis, tracing the route of the Seattle Fault. "We thought, 'Gee, that's interesting,'" Booth said. A powerful quake on the Seattle Fault about 1,100 years ago uplifted beaches in West Seattle and mudflats near Bremerton. But the Nisqually quake originated forty miles south, deep under the delta of the same name. The Seattle Fault didn't move an inch.

Still, Booth and his colleagues suspected that the fault wasn't as blameless as it looked. "It occurred to us that the presence of a major [fault] could certainly influence the way in which earthquake waves from depth might be transmitted up to the ground surface." A few years later another group of scientists confirmed that hunch with a series of experiments. The researchers rolled into West Seattle in a truck mounted with a Vibroseis, a pistonlike device used to shake the ground. By recording the way the signals bounce back, scientists generate a subterranean image. What they saw more than quarter of a mile down was an abrupt step, or fold, in the bedrock. A step marks the edge of the Seattle Fault zone and probably explains why the same part of West Seattle seems to lose chimneys in every major quake.

As seismic waves radiate through the ground, they bend and refract like rays of light when they pass from one kind of rock into another. Scientists think the edge of the Seattle Fault acts like a lens, concentrating and focusing that seismic energy and beaming it straight into West Seattle. Neighborhoods directly in the line of fire shake harder than those a few blocks away. It's a neat solution to a puzzle that has vexed scientists for more than four decades. But what does it mean if you're shopping for a house in West Seattle? "That's a fair question," Booth said, "but I don't want the real estate agents after me. Besides, there's much more to the safety of a house than how hard the ground shakes during a moderate earthquake."

The chimney study is tucked away in a mountain of scientific information Northwesterners can take a shovel to if they want a more complete picture of the seismic risks where they live and work. The problem is that scientists are often more interested in the general than in the particular. The maps of chimney damage in Booth's report don't zoom down to the block level. Nor do research papers on the South Whidbey Island Fault do much for homeowners trying to figure out if a strand runs through their backyards.

Beyond the scientific reports are several resources that do provide practical information for those who know how to interpret them. Geologic maps are available online for many areas. Perhaps the most powerful predictor of earthquake damage is whether a structure sits on solid ground or loose dirt, and the maps can tell you that—as long as you can decipher terms like "advance outwash deposits" (not a bad footing for a house, it turns out). Most people already know if their property is vulnerable to earthquake-triggered landslides. But many cities, including Seattle, offer maps that highlight the risky slopes. In terms of ground shaking from earthquakes, USGS seismic hazard maps are the best guides to what the future may hold. Although the measure of shaking that's mapped is confusing (peak ground acceleration expressed in g-values), the color coding makes it clear which areas are likely to be rattled the hardest.

If you live in West Seattle, you could extract enough information from Booth's paper to roughly determine where your house sits in relation to the epicenter of chimney carnage. But Booth also found clusters of broken chimneys in other parts of the city where the Seattle Fault can't be blamed. The next earthquake may strike from an entirely different direction or on a different type of fault. Tacoma could get the hardest shaking, or Portland.

Given the capricious nature of the threat, geologists, engineers, and emergency managers agree that the best strategy is to assume your house, apartment, business, or condo will get a good shaking one of these days and plan accordingly. "Just do the reasonable, prudent things anybody in a moderate to high earthquake hazard zone should do," Booth advised. "So the chimney falls down? There are worse things that can happen."

It's possible to rebuild an old chimney to modern standards, but the cost is so steep few people bother. Roger Faris got rid of his instead. The old stack teetered over his daughter's bedroom and made him nervous. So Faris dismantled the bricks to below the roofline, replaced the fireplace with a gas-burning facsimile, and installed a stainless steel stove pipe. The rest of Faris's 1906 Craftsman in Seattle's Phinney Ridge neighborhood is equally squared away.

The former barge operator and contractor probably wasn't the first person in Seattle to give his house a seismic makeover, but he was the first to champion the simple fixes that can help people protect their biggest investment. Sitting at his dining room table in 2012, Faris flipped through the 1985 issue of *Fine Homebuilding* that got him thinking about earthquakes. The well-worn magazine fell open to a picture of a two-story California bungalow slumping in on itself like a fallen cake. A quake had knocked the house off its footings and collapsed its lower supports. The article described how to prevent that kind of damage by bolting the house to the foundation and bracing vulnerable spots. Faris followed the step-by-step directions to retrofit his own house, then set out to spread the word.

"You don't need to be very skilled," he said, ducking into the narrow stairwell that leads to his basement. "It's just repetitive tasks." Faris did the seismic work before he Sheetrocked the basement, adding a bedroom and a nook for the ping-pong table. One section of the original wall remains exposed in a storage room.

Faris explained that he started the project by using bolts to fasten the mudsill—the two-by-four that is the base of the house's frame—to the concrete foundation it rests on, but usually isn't attached to, in older homes. "What keeps it there is the force of gravity and friction, the weight of the building just sitting on it," Faris said. An earthquake that shakes the house back and forth can overcome that friction and essentially pull the rug out from under the house. The resulting damage is like totaling a car.

In Faris's basement, the bolts are hidden by plywood panels that are an equally important part of the retrofit. He pointed out how the panels extend from the mudsill to the floor joists above, strengthening what are called the pony or cripple walls. Without plywood bracing, the side-to-side shoving from a quake can cause the pony walls to fall like dominoes.

In 1990, just as awareness of the Cascadia Subduction Zone was dawning, Faris started teaching other homeowners how to do the job themselves. He worked at a cooperative called the Phinney Neighborhood Association, where he taught a wide range of DIY skills and helped pioneer one of the country's first tool lending libraries. The association added retrofit equipment to its collection—tools like air-powered palm nailers for working in tight spaces and rotohammers. "You just pull the trigger and they drill through concrete like butter," Faris said, admiringly.

When the Federal Emergency Management Agency launched an initiative to boost earthquake preparedness in the Puget Sound area, they recruited Faris and incorporated his classes into what was called Project Impact. In a poorly timed move, the Bush administration announced it was cancelling the program on the day of the 2001 Nisqually quake, saying it wasn't effective. Faris begged to differ and along with the City of Seattle helped keep the retrofit classes going. "You don't solve a problem like earthquake preparedness in a few years," he said. "It takes decades."

Nearly six thousand people have attended retrofit classes in and around Seattle, and the approach has spread across the region. Faris passed the teaching baton several years ago, but still makes an occasional guest appearance. "The joy of teaching for me is watching people gain confidence."

Faris's personal preparations go beyond bolts and shear walls, though the retrofit is why he plans on sheltering in his own home after the next big quake. "I have a lot of confidence that this house is not going to collapse and that it's not going to leave its foundation," he said, pulling the lid off a plastic bin stored in the laundry room. Inside are blankets and a sleeping bag. There's a Ziploc bag full of medications, cans of Costco tuna, a can opener, a first aid kit, and a crank radio. "There should be a bottle of wine in here," Faris said, rummaging around. "I need to add that."

After a major earthquake, power and other utilities are likely to be disrupted for an extended period. Emergency managers recommend stashing enough supplies to get through at least three days on your own. On the coast, where a Cascadia quake will be followed by a tsunami, it could be weeks before help arrives.

Several plastic buckets sit by Faris's washing machine, each filled with four gallons of water. Faris keeps these buckets handy, along with several dry-chemical fire extinguishers, to douse any flames that flare up after a quake. The one gap in his preparations is the water heater. It isn't strapped to the wall to prevent it from tipping over. But that's only because the interior wall is too flimsy and Faris hasn't gotten around to rebuilding it yet. The fact that the heater is electric makes the omission a little less risky, he explained. No gas lines will break if it falls. But strapping is still a good idea because the tank can be a source of drinking water.

Faris has another supply, though. Heading outside to his detached garage, he pulled open the door to reveal three thirty-gallon barrels. He adds a few drops of bleach to keep bacteria in check, and tries to remember to dump the stale water and replace it with fresh every six months or so.

On the way to the garage, Faris passed his neighbor's gas meter and pointed out the wrench that dangles from it by a cord. He's got one on his own meter, preset to fit the shutoff valve in case of a post-quake leak. It takes two wrenches to shut off the water at the meter, and those tools hang just inside the garage door for easy access. It's no surprise that Faris's block is one of the city's most prepared. The neighborhood has an emergency plan that includes checking in on elderly residents and conducting sweeps for broken gas lines and water pipes.

Anyone can lay in supplies and plan for disaster, but not everyone is keen to wedge into a crawlspace and drill holes in concrete. FEMA's early support helped Faris and others design a seismic retrofit training course for contractors. "It was sorely needed," said Leif Jackson, one of the early students.

A lot of shoddy retrofits were being passed off as adequate, and Jackson's brother had unwittingly been responsible for at least one of them. On the job for another contractor, he used hurricane straps to fasten a house to its foundation. When he took the retrofit class, he realized the flexible straps might keep the house from blowing away, but they weren't designed to keep it from shifting off the foundation in an earthquake.

"That was really common," Jackson said. "There were no permit requirements and guys would just go to the store and come back with some hardware they thought looked good." A poorly designed retrofit can actually make a house more vulnerable to earthquake damage. Faris and local building officials developed standard retrofit plans for different types of houses, and cities throughout Western Washington imposed permit and inspection requirements. Some jurisdictions in Oregon are following suit.

Fortunately for homeowners, wood-framed construction generally fares well in earthquakes because it flexes with the motion. Scientists who run shake-table experiments have a hard time rattling apart well-built wood frames, even with the power cranked up to maximum. By the late 1970s, building codes required new residences to be braced and bolted to their foundations.

But in Western Washington alone, more than four hundred thousand houses predate those rules. Jackson and his brother did the math and decided to launch a company called Sound Seismic, specializing in retrofits. Two years later the Nisqually quake hit and business boomed. Since then demand has been steady enough to keep at least one crew working full time. Every high-profile quake brings a spike in interest, which tapers off predictably within a few months.

Retrofits aren't cheap. Doing it yourself can cost $1,000 to $2,000 for materials and permits, and the work can consume weekends for a month or more. Hiring a contractor can run anywhere from $4,000 to $15,000, depending on the size and complexity of your house. A lot of people point out that their houses are still standing after quakes in 1949, 1965, and 2001. If the ground doesn't shake harder or longer in the next quake—and if there's no hidden damage from earlier episodes—there's a good chance houses like that will do just fine.

The Nisqually quake lasted about forty seconds. A Cascadia megaquake could have the ground rocking for four minutes or more, longer than it takes to sing the national anthem *twice* at a baseball game. If the next quake strikes on any of the shallow faults that run through the Puget Sound region's biggest cities, the ferocity will be like nothing the region has ever experienced. Nearly ten thousand wood frame buildings were red-tagged in Southern California after the shallow Northridge quake in 1994. The shallow magnitude 6.3 quake that hammered Christchurch, New Zealand, in 2011 damaged 110,000 houses—in a city of 400,000 people.

Even a retrofit doesn't guarantee immunity from damage. Jackson makes sure his customers understand that the work will make their homes more resistant to earthquake damage but won't make them earthquake-proof. That's probably why the insurance company that provides liability coverage for most contractors in Washington won't cover contractors who perform seismic retrofits. "I'm convinced you'll always be better off with a retrofit," Jackson said, "but there's always that potential for a catastrophic event."

In that case earthquake insurance could be the only thing that stands between a homeowner and financial disaster. Jackson doesn't carry it on his own home. Faris used to, but when Allstate bailed out of the earthquake business, he didn't bother shopping for a replacement. Both men admit it's a gamble. With well-fortified homes and the skills to rebuild if necessary, it's a risk they're willing to accept.

Even in California only about 12 percent of homeowners carry earthquake coverage. The Northwest Insurance Council estimates about 12 to 15 percent of homeowners in Washington and Oregon have the policies. "A lot of people have the attitude that it won't happen to me," said the council's president, Karl Newman. Many people may not realize that standard homeowner's insurance doesn't cover earthquake damage—unless the house burns in a quake-triggered fire. Anything else, from total collapse to the destruction of your Ming vase collection, and you're on your own.

Earthquake insurance has its limitations, too. It usually doesn't cover damage from the landslides, floods, broken water pipes, or tsunamis that earthquakes trigger. All those potential disasters require separate policies.

Before they insure an older home against earthquakes, most companies require a seismic retrofit. Adding earthquake insurance in the Northwest can roughly double your homeowner's premiums. But what makes many people balk are the deductibles, which generally range between 10 and 20 percent. If your home is worth $500,000, that means you'd have to pay out of pocket for the first $50,000 to $100,000 of damage. There's a separate deductible for damage to belongings.

After the Nisqually earthquake, very few homeowners filed insurance claims, even though minor dings like broken chimneys were widespread. The cost of fixing the damage didn't approach their deductibles. The fact that the Seattle Mariners play in a stadium named for Safeco Insurance didn't help them, either. With a deductible of $1 million, the team was on the hook for the $400,000 in cosmetic damage caused by the 2001 quake. After the quake, the

Mariners' earthquake premiums were jacked up nearly threefold and the deductible raised to $11 million.

"What earthquake insurance protects against is the big one," Newman said. "For most of us, our home is our most valuable asset. If it's destroyed and you don't have earthquake insurance, where are you?"

The other option is what disaster planners mock as the Air Force One solution: waiting for the president and the federal government to swoop in and shower the region with money.

A major quake in the Northwest will easily make the cut for a federal disaster declaration. After the Nisqually quake, FEMA received forty thousand applications for assistance, more than from all other previous disasters in Washington combined. Checks from FEMA paid for chimney repairs and a slew of other damages. Faris fixed a broken sewer pipe in his yard, then found out his neighbors got grants to cover the same type of damage.

But keep in mind that the average FEMA grant is $5,000, said Denise Everhart, of the agency's Portland office. Most post-disaster federal aid comes in the form of loans. The feds paid out $53 million in grants after the Nisqually quake and $77 million in loans. Individual FEMA grants top out at a ceiling that's adjusted every year. In 2012 it was $31,900. That's the most you could get even if your house was reduced to matchsticks. "We call it home replacement," Everhart said. "But there's no home you can replace for that amount."

Humorist Jack Handey, whose "Deep Thoughts" were a staple on *Saturday Night Live*, once mulled the question of how to respond when the ground starts shaking. "Here's a good joke to do during an earthquake," he suggested. "Straddle a big crack in the ground, and if it opens wider, go, 'Whoa! Whoa!' and flail your arms around like you're going to fall in."

Here's some other advice:

WHAT TO DO BEFORE AN EARTHQUAKE:

- Keep a stash of emergency supplies—water, food, first aid supplies, flashlight, batteries, blankets, warm clothes, a can opener, medications—at your home, in your car, and at your office. Be prepared to fend for yourself at least three days, and possibly much more.

• Your family may not be together when an earthquake strikes, so have a plan to contact one another. Local phone networks often fail, but it may be possible to make long-distance calls. Designate an out-of-state contact to check in with, and have a backup in case that person's not home. Even if phone networks are down, text messages may get through.

• Lower the chances that stuff will break or fall on you during a quake. Secure bookshelves, water heaters, and other major appliances, especially those that use gas. Disconnected gas lines can start fires. Store heavy, breakable, or hazardous objects (like pesticides) on lower shelves.

• Learn how to shut off the gas and water supplies to your house.

• Keep a flashlight, gloves, and shoes near your bed. Floors may be littered with broken glass after a quake.

• If you live in a coastal area susceptible to tsunamis, learn where to go. Be aware of the high ground near your home, office, and other places where you hang out.

WHAT TO DO DURING THE EARTHQUAKE:

• Drop, cover, and hold on.

• If you're indoors stay there. Most injuries occur when objects fall from buildings and hit people. Get under a desk or table, or get on your hands and knees against an interior wall. Experts don't recommend standing in a doorway. Most internal door frames aren't strong, and you're likely to get hit as the door swings. After the quake don't use elevators, which may be damaged.

- If there's no place to take cover, crouch down and cover your head and neck with your arms. In a theater or stadium, stay in your seat, duck down, and cover your head.

- If you're in bed, stay there and cover your head with a pillow. If there's a heavy light fixture dangling above you, lie down next to the bed.

- If you're driving, pull to the side of the road and stop. Don't park under bridges or overpasses and try to get clear of trees, light posts, power lines, and signs. Stay in your car until the shaking stops.

- If you're outside, move into the open. Get as far as you can from buildings, power lines, trees, and anything else that may fall on you.

- If you're surrounded by skyscrapers, duck into a doorway or get as far as possible from the buildings without running into traffic.

- In the mountains, beware of the potential for landslides.

- If you're on the coast, expect a tsunami and head for high ground.

- One way to reduce anxiety is to count. Scientists say counting helps them focus and seems to slow things down. Counting can also give you an idea of what kind of quake you're experiencing. Deep and shallow quakes usually last no more than thirty to fifty seconds. Subduction zone quakes will last several minutes.

- If you're trapped in a collapsed building or under debris, try to avoid inhaling dust. Don't light a match because there could be a gas leak nearby.

WHAT TO DO AFTER THE EARTHQUAKE:

- If you're in a coastal area where a tsunami might strike, head for high ground as soon as the ground stops moving. Don't wait for a siren or official warning.

• If you're indoors, exit the building after the shaking stops.

• Check on your neighbors or help trapped or injured people. In a big quake, emergency services will be overwhelmed.

• Check your house for gas leaks. If you smell gas, shut off the main valve. If you smell other fumes or can't shut off the gas, leave the area. (Don't shut off the gas if it's not leaking since only qualified technicians can restart service.)

• If electrical wiring seems damaged, shut off the power at the control panel. Extinguish small fires if you can do it safely.

• Be alert for aftershocks. Deep quakes under Puget Sound usually have few aftershocks. A Cascadia Subduction Zone quake or a quake on a shallow fault will likely be followed by many aftershocks, some large enough to cause damage.

• Don't use the phone unless you need to. Heavy traffic after a quake often crashes the networks.

• Check for cracks in your home's foundation. Inspect chimneys and check for damage to sewer and water lines.

• Help the USGS track quake impact by reporting your experience at the agency's "Did You Feel It?" site: http://earthquake.usgs.gov/earthquakes/dyfi/

HOW TO SURVIVE A TSUNAMI:

• After the ground shaking stops, immediately head for high ground. Stay away from rivers and streams, which can funnel the waves inland.

• Whether the ground shook or not, if you see the water drawing away from the shore, head to high ground immediately.

- If you can't make it to high ground, take shelter in the tallest, sturdiest building, parking garage, or other structure around you.

- If there are no buildings nearby, climb the biggest tree you can find.

- If you're swept up in the water, try to grab onto something. Many people in Japan survived by climbing onto floating houses. One survivor of the 2004 Indian Ocean tsunami said he swam for his life, looking for smooth water and steering away from obstacles.

- If a tsunami overtakes your car, roll the windows down. The water pressure will make it impossible to open the vehicle doors.

- Get out of the water as soon as you can, so the receding wave won't suck you out to sea. Expect multiple waves that can arrive over a twelve-hour period. The first waves aren't usually the biggest.

See Resources (page 262) for resources to help assess your risk.

CHAPTER 13:

FUTURE SCIENCE, COMING QUAKE

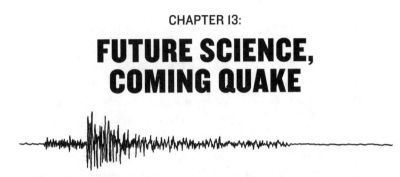

IN HIS OFFICE ON SAANICH INLET, Herb Dragert frowned at his computer screen. It was 1994 and he was monitoring results from the region's first network of continuously operating GPS stations. At a time when many American scientists still thought of the Cascadia Subduction Zone as moribund, Dragert and his colleagues at the Geological Survey of Canada had installed the state-of-the-art satellite instruments to check for signs of life. The Canadians could afford only four stations. Even so they were already compiling the most dynamic view yet of the region's restless nature.

For the first time scientists could actually measure tectonics in action, watching as the ground deformed almost before their eyes. Since the initial station went in on southern Vancouver Island in 1991, the GPS measurements had shown that British Columbia's outer coast was being shoved about four-tenths of an inch northeast every year. To Dragert, that was clear proof the subduction zone was locked and headed for trouble. But now something seemed to be amiss with the network, which was his baby. If the numbers on his screen were right, the station near Victoria had turned on its heel and moved in the opposite direction for about a week. The motion wasn't big. Dragert put it at six millimeters—about a quarter of an inch. But millimeters matter in geodesy, the science of measuring the Earth's surface.

Dragert drove out to Albert Head, the point of land where the GPS antenna was anchored to a granite outcrop. Maybe water and ice had cracked the rock, making the monument unstable. But Dragert didn't see any problems. Follow-up surveys checked the station's position relative to reference points, but still couldn't explain what had happened. "At that point we had to shrug our shoulders and shelve it," Dragert recalled. But he couldn't stop puzzling over that blip.

From the time he joined the government agency in 1976, Dragert had earned a reputation for fastidiousness. When you're trying to size up landforms with enough precision to detect a quarter-inch bulge, it pays to be obsessive about details. Dragert's career paralleled the evolution of geodetic techniques, starting with old-fashioned surveying. One of his first projects compared leveling lines run by highway crews in the early 1900s to modern results. The changes he saw piqued his interest, hinting that over the intervening decades the ground had warped and tilted slightly.

In the late 1970s, Dragert helped pioneer the use of sensitive gravity meters to detect changes in elevation. The measurements were finicky, and the scientists had to run every transect at least eight times with multiple instruments. "Boy, it was labor intensive," Dragert recalled. After all that work, it was often impossible to tell if the gravity fluctuations represented real land-level changes or just the movement of groundwater.

A breakthrough arrived in the 1980s with a method called laser ranging. The logistics weren't any easier, but the technique allowed scientists to measure the distances between mountaintops with near-pinpoint accuracy. Helicopters deposited the scientists and their bulky gear on summits across central Vancouver Island. Sometimes teetering on the brink of a chasm, the researchers set up breadbox-size lasers and banks of parabolic reflectors. They fired off light pulses and timed how long it took the beams to bounce back and forth between peaks.

As the "met" man in charge of collecting meteorological data, Dragert had one of the cushier jobs. While his colleagues hunkered on the mountains, he shuttled back and forth in a helicopter, measuring air temperature, barometric pressure, and humidity. All those factors affect the speed of light and had to be carefully factored into the calculations. At least the weather was always good. The scientists couldn't run their surveys in the rain.

Collecting enough data took an entire field season, but when the scientists finally laid out their results against conventional surveys from the 1930s, there was no doubt about it. The mountaintops were being squeezed together in a northeast direction.

The Geological Survey of Canada is tiny compared with the USGS. But Dragert and others at the agency's West Coast outpost in Sidney, British Columbia, were well ahead of their American colleagues in accepting Cascadia's menace. Tuzo Wilson, discoverer of the Juan de Fuca Plate, was Canadian. John Adams, who was the first to point out that coastal ranges in Washington and Oregon were tilting like those near other active subduction zones, works for the Canadian Survey.

Several Canadians collaborated with the team that discovered magnetic zebra stripes on the bottom of the Pacific, proving that fresh seafloor was oozing up from the depths. Enthusiasm for geology's new paradigm spread quickly at the Canadian Survey, helped along by the organization's small size, recalled Garry Rogers, long-time leader of the Sidney group.

Oceanographers rubbed shoulders with geologists, whose offices were next door to seismologists, geodesists, and computer modelers. Everyone gathered for coffee and bounced around ideas. Years before Brian Atwater started digging in marshes, Rogers was sounding the alarm in British Columbia about possible megaquakes. Atwater's evidence was the smoking gun the Canadians had been waiting for. "Brian had a tough sell in the U.S., but we were totally convinced right away," Rogers said.

Canada's pioneering investment in GPS added to the growing evidence. By 1999, when Dragert noticed another strange blip in some of his measurements, the regional network had expanded to fourteen stations. "Lo and behold, I was looking at the Albert Head station and I thought, 'Hmmm. This looks like what I saw in 1994,'" Dragert recalled. "I immediately checked all of the other sites." Seven contiguous stations arrayed in a broad band from southern Vancouver Island through Washington's Olympic Peninsula had sidled seaward a few millimeters. The stations outside that band hadn't budged. "I said, 'Either somebody is trying to fool me by pushing over every one of those monuments, or we've got something here.'"

Dragert spent nearly a year reanalyzing the data to assure himself it wasn't instrumental glitches or some artifact of the data analysis technique. In 2001 he and two other colleagues set the earthquake world abuzz when they published their interpretation. Deep underground, they argued, the subduction zone that seemed zipped up tight was slipping a tiny bit. The movement had started under Seattle and migrated up to Vancouver Island over about a two-week period. Then it stopped and all the GPS stations reverted to their normal trajectories.

A lot of geologists were suspicious of Dragert's claim. The persnickety Canadian might trust GPS to detect such teeny shifts, but many others weren't so sure. Another line of evidence soon won over the doubters. At a conference in New Zealand in 2002, Dragert chatted with a Japanese scientist who had reported tiny tremors emanating from within the Nankai Trough subduction zone off Honshu's southeast coast. The tremor seemed to migrate over several days, very much like the slip on Cascadia, and at about the same rate. "I've often been credited with an uncanny grasp of the obvious," Dragert deadpanned, "and this ability now came into play." As soon as he got back to Sidney, he started quizzing his colleagues to see if they had seen similar vibrations.

Rogers was the center's senior seismologist. He told Dragert he'd noticed odd vibrations on occasion but wrote them off as unexplained background noise. By this time Dragert and others had compiled a list of multiple slip events over the past several years. Rogers picked a date and went to the room where he stored seismograms in the same flat boxes the photosensitive paper came in. "I found the box, opened up the month, and I flipped to the day," Rogers said. "And there was this funny-looking noise I was talking about."

He tore down to Dragert's office. "It's there! It's there at exactly the same time," he said. Dragert gave him another date; Rogers raced back and pulled out another box. "Every fifteen minutes I'd come tearing back to Herb's office with another match," Rogers recalled. "It was a very exciting afternoon, the kind that makes the hair stand up on the back of your neck." It was as if after listening to human chests for centuries doctors suddenly discovered the heart can beat out a salsa rhythm.

The subduction zone wasn't just slipping—it was chattering under its breath as it did so. Scientists coined the term "silent quake" to describe the process. Stretched over a period of two weeks or more, the subduction zone was unleashing as much energy as a Nisqually-size earthquake. But the motions were so slow and faint that only GPS and the most sensitive seismometers could detect them. Even more remarkable, scientists at Central Washington University reported that silent quakes seemed to occur on a regular schedule, every fourteen to fifteen months. The term Dragert came up with to describe them is "episodic tremor and slip."

A process that releases energy sounds like a good thing, a way to defuse the seismic time bomb. But Dragert and Rogers could see at once that the silent quakes had just the opposite effect. Instead of bleeding off stress, every episode bumps it up and nudges the fault closer to catastrophic failure. "The megathrust earthquake is probably more likely during or immediately after one of these slip events," Dragert said. "It's like tightening a guitar string. It's more likely to break at the time you're adding that extra bit of stress."

The subduction zone's complex geometry accounts for the counterintuitive effect. The portion of the fault that's slipping is twenty to thirty miles down, in a region where the plates are growing increasingly hot and pliable. In Washington that section lines up about midway under the Olympic Peninsula. Scientists have deployed arrays of special seismometers there to better listen in on the faint murmurs.

But the fault's danger zone—the brittle, locked portion that will rupture in a megaquake—is shallower and closer to the coast. That section doesn't budge at all during the silent quakes. So every fourteen months when the subducting plate slips a tiny bit deeper into the Earth, the motion ratchets up the strain on the locked portion. "It's adding another straw to the camel's back," Rogers said.

The discovery was a watershed for earthquake scientists. One of the questions they started asking was whether silent earthquakes could represent something geologists have sought for decades: a harbinger that a big quake could be on the way.

What the world wants most from seismology is what the discipline has never been able to deliver. The quest to predict earthquakes has been such a resounding failure that most seismologists shun the subject like vampires shun sunlight. There's no shortage of people, some crackpots, some serious, who claim the power to foretell based on electrical discharges from rocks, phases of the moon, or radon gas emissions. "It is a holy grail, and it's just a magnet for crappy science," said Tim Melbourne, a geology professor at Central Washington University (CWU) in Ellensburg.

The theories are seductive because many of them have a semblance of validity. The weight of tides and the moon's pull can tug on faults. The most thorough analyses do find a tiny correlation between tides and earthquake rates. The problem with all precursors, however, is lack of consistency. Many big quakes announce their arrival with a burst of foreshocks. Many don't. There's no way to tell the difference until after the fact.

Melbourne was newly arrived at the CWU campus when Dragert discovered Cascadia's slow slip. Swept up in the excitement, he felt a frisson of trepidation every time a new event started. "There was a sense of, Oh my God! The fault is slipping," Melbourne recalled. But the scientists could all see it would be tricky to use the phenomenon to time the next megaquake.

Few experts doubt that a silent quake could be enough to knock Cascadia over the edge. Historic records hint that Chile's 1960 megaquake and several big quakes in Japan were preceded by similar slip. Japan's 3/11 quake was, too, though scientists are still trying to make sense of the complex pattern of foreshocks, slip, and deformation that unfolded in the days before the great earthquake. "The slip almost certainly loaded the region of the fault that subsequently ruptured," Melbourne said. "It's about as close to a smoking gun as you could ever hope to see."

By one estimate the odds of a Cascadia megaquake are thirty to one hundred times higher during slip events. But what should people do with that information? Even when the subduction zone is slipping and chattering, the odds of a megaquake remain small—about one in four thousand, according to the same analysis. It's been more than three hundred years since Cascadia last ruptured, and none of the silent quakes in the intervening years has yet triggered a repeat. Each silent quake may pile on another straw, but scientists have no way of knowing how many straws it will take to break the camel's back.

The Geological Survey of Canada used to post notices on its website when a silent quake was under way and pass on the information to emergency managers. The routine practice led to a nationwide scare when the *Globe and Mail* in Toronto published a story under the headline "Scientists predict monster quake." In those days Dragert and his colleagues thought the patch under southern Vancouver Island and the Olympic Peninsula was the only part of the subduction zone where tremor and slip occurred on a repeating basis. Since then silent quakes have turned up under Central Oregon and Northern California, returning on one- and two-year cycles. So nearly a third of the time, some segment of the fault is slipping. The megaquake could be triggered in any of those regions. "The whole idea that the subduction zone is most likely to fail when you add an increment of stress is still probably right," Rogers said. "It's just not terribly useful because it's happening so often."

But the discovery of silent quakes helped galvanize a new era of investigation in the Northwest. Dragert's four GPS stations have proliferated into an array of nearly five hundred across the region. Instead of providing measurements once a day, the devices now stream data in real time to CWU, where Melbourne oversees the network. Scientists around the world can spot unusual patterns as soon as they appear. The instantaneous GPS reveals changes as small as two centimeters. When Melbourne and his team spend more time crunching the numbers to factor out noise, the resolution zooms down to one millimeter, less than four hundredths of an inch.

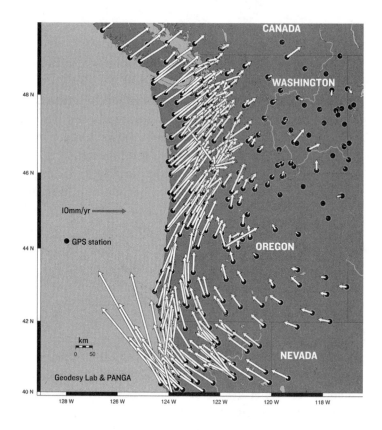

More than 500 GPS stations track the way the Northwest is being shoved and squeezed, setting the stage for future earthquakes.

With that level of precision and coverage, GPS has emerged as one of the most powerful tools in the earthquake arsenal. From his office Melbourne can track the region's slow march to the northeast. On average the Northwest moves about half an inch a year. But the GPS observations clearly show that the motion isn't uniform.

The town of Forks, on the Washington coast, travels a full inch. Across the Cascades in Central Washington the rate dwindles to an eighth of an inch a year. More than any seismogram, GPS illustrates the inevitability of earthquakes. The motion never ceases. The pressure never stops building on the subduction zone, the Seattle

Fault, the Tacoma Fault, the South Whidbey Island Fault. Yearly increments are insignificant but they add up, and add up, and add up. Since the 1700 megaquake, the coast has moved more than twenty-five feet.

The GPS network also provides a new way to tackle old problems. Scientists still can't say for sure how close the Cascadia rupture will come to Seattle and the region's urban corridor. The closer it gets, the more destructive it will be. Earlier research put the locked portion of the fault—the danger zone—well offshore. But GPS measurements, as well as the slip and vibrations under the Olympic Peninsula during silent quakes, suggest that the locked portion of the fault could extend nearly fifty miles closer to Seattle.

For the next generation of Cascadia research, the action is shifting to the seafloor. Several ambitious experiments are under way or in the works to wire up the Juan de Fuca Plate. There's an outside chance the effort could hit the jackpot and detect signs of stirring before the next big quake. More likely, it will succeed in peeling away a few more layers of mystery to give the region a clearer picture of the threat. "The new technology we're tapping into now is unbelievable," said University of Washington marine geologist John Delaney, one of the masterminds behind what he calls underwater observatories.

The inspiration came to him in a Seattle bar more than twenty years ago. Delaney was grousing with a fellow scientist about the limitations of deep-sea research. One of Delaney's interests is black smokers, fantastical chimneys that form where fresh magma superheats seawater. But opportunities to dive to the seafloor in a submersible like *Alvin* are rare and costly. "You might have twenty hours a year to look out the window at unbelievably complicated systems—black smokers, tube worm beds, big fractures," Delaney said, recalling his booze-fueled lament. "And then you come back two years later when you get another grant, and everything is changed and you don't know why or when."

Delaney's friend pointed out that telephone companies had recently laid the first submarine fiber-optic cables from North America to Ireland. Delaney agreed that was cool, then thought a moment.

"There ought to be a way to use that for science," he said. He grabbed a cocktail napkin and sketched out a fiber-optic loop snaking from the coast across the seafloor. The cable could deliver power to instruments on the ocean bottom and transmit data to scientists on land. Most important, the observations would be continuous.

Delaney spent several years expanding and refining the concept. He named it NEPTUNE and patched together an unwieldy string of words to fit the acronym. Then he started pitching the idea to anyone who would listen. Eventually, the National Science Foundation agreed to fund the project and put Delaney and his UW colleagues in charge of building it.

But when the region's first underwater observatory started operating in 2009, it wasn't an American initiative. The five-hundred-mile-long loop of cable starts in Port Alberni on Vancouver Island, and crosses the continental shelf. Branches thread down submarine canyons and cross over the buried seam where the Juan de Fuca Plate meets the continent. The cables extend across the pitted expanse of the abyssal plain before rising onto the Juan de Fuca Ridge, where the steady upwelling of molten rock replenishes the tectonic plate and sets it in motion.

Spanning the entire tectonic plate was always central to Delaney's plans. Canada got on board early and avoided the bureaucratic and budget battles that delayed Delaney's progress at home. Cable for the first American observatory was finally laid off the Oregon coast in 2011. The footprint looks a lot like Delaney's napkin sketch, with cable extending from Pacific City to Axial Seamount, the most active underwater volcano in the north Pacific. The first instruments will be installed in 2013 and full operations are scheduled to start in 2014.

Both observatories are multipurpose. Cameras allow biologists and school kids alike to spy on crabs, cod, and octopuses. Oceanographic instruments track temperatures and salinity and tackle climate change questions. But getting a better handle on Cascadia is a prime objective. "The great subduction zone earthquakes of the world occur in the ocean," said Kate Moran, director of NEPTUNE Canada. "For the first time now, we're putting very, very sensitive instruments close to the location where these earthquakes take place."

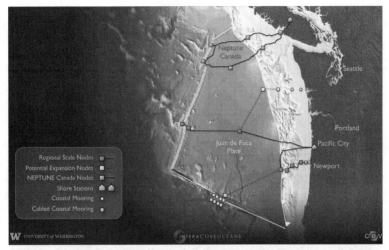

Underwater observatories off the Northwest coast are taking studies of subduction zone quakes to the source. NEPTUNE Canada and the National Science Foundation-funded Regional Scale Nodes off Oregon include seismometers and instruments to measure seafloor deformation and will expand in the future.

Permanent seafloor seismometers can detect tiny quakes invisible to land-based instruments. A grid of ocean pressure sensors deployed off Vancouver Island is already helping assess the size of incoming tsunamis and fine-tune warnings. Similar instruments will sit on the seafloor off Oregon. Delaney's not satisfied, though. He's already pushing for the next big thing: a dense web of sensors to run the length and width of the subduction zone and take its pulse constantly.

Lack of good seafloor monitoring cost Japan dearly during the 3/11 quake. Pressure sensors on the seafloor would have allowed scientists to quickly size up both the earthquake and the tsunami by estimating displacement. Instead, warnings based solely on seismometers underestimated the disaster in the crucial first minutes.

Japan also missed precursory motion on the seafloor. After-the-fact analyses showed that the underwater fault had been slipping for several days. Following a large foreshock, that motion seems to have accelerated two days before the main rupture. If sensors had detected the slip early, would the Japanese have been alarmed enough to raise the alert level? It's hard to say. Most episodes of slow slip don't trigger big quakes. But more extensive monitoring could have alerted Japan to the fact that dangerous levels of strain were building up offshore in a region where most seismologists didn't believe a magnitude 9 quake was possible.

"I don't think there is any magic bullet that will unambiguously identify an upcoming rupture," said Jeffrey McGuire of Woods Hole Oceanographic Institution. "But I do think there are time periods when large ruptures are more likely than others, and it is a realistic goal for our community to get much better at putting quantitative, probabilistic assessments [on] those risks."

Japan is determined not to miss any possible red flags the next time. The government pledged $400 million for a cabled network of sensors off the Tohoku coast. More than 150 instrument packages, each containing a seismometer and water pressure gauge, will stand constant watch. A similar network is already in place along the Nankai Trough south of Tokyo where Japanese scientists have long anticipated a major quake. Japan is also boosting its investment in underwater GPS to monitor the way the seafloor deforms as pressure builds. If subduction zones tip their hand at all before they rip, the warning signs are most likely to show up in unusual warping or motion on the ocean bottom, things GPS is well-suited to spot.

In the near term, the Northwest's best chance of detecting any unusual movement on the Cascadia Fault could be a pair of sensors McGuire and his colleagues plan to plug into NEPTUNE Canada by 2014. Called tiltmeters, the instruments will be able to detect motion of less than half an inch on the fault and track the buildup of strain. Based on the same principle as a carpenter's level, tiltmeters are often used on land to monitor the way volcanoes inflate and deflate with the movement of magma. Underwater robots will place the instruments directly above the subduction zone in a one-thousand-foot-deep borehole. "The location is great for studying subduction zone earthquakes," McGuire said. The meters could help determine which parts of the fault are primed to rupture and put better estimates on the size of the next Cascadia tsunami.

Other scientists are working to bring seafloor GPS to the Northwest. The technique was pioneered off Vancouver Island but is so costly and cumbersome only the Japanese have embraced it. Satellite and radio signals can't penetrate water, so conventional GPS technology doesn't work under the ocean. The Japanese rely on a two-step process. Acoustic transponders on the seafloor send signals to a ship. Instruments on the ship calculate the transponders' positions while GPS fixes the ship's location.

To detect changes in the seafloor, the ship must return to the same spot repeatedly. Setting up a single station on the ocean bottom can cost $120,000. But the real expense is ship time, at up to $50,000 a day. Japan enlisted its Coast Guard to take the readings. American researchers are searching for lower-cost alternatives.

Scientists from the Scripps Institution of Oceanography are exploring the use of buoys and robot gliders to collect data beamed up from the seafloor. Delaney's dream is a web of interconnected acoustic sensors spaced about a mile apart. The network could continuously monitor conditions along the length of the subduction zone. "That would be a very big deal," Delaney said. "It would give us the ability to detect the early onset of major deformation events."

So far, though, intensive GPS monitoring of faults on land hasn't yielded advance notice of earthquakes. When the massively wired Parkfield section of the San Andreas Fault finally broke in 2004, neither GPS, tiltmeters, nor seismometers dropped any hints. Pessimists say earthquakes may be inherently unpredictable. Optimists, like Harold Tobin, argue that scientists may have been looking in the wrong place. "We've had a hundred-plus years of seismology, but all those instruments are on the surface," he said. "Earthquakes don't happen on the surface. They happen kilometers down in the Earth."

Tobin is going deep. The University of Wisconsin geoscience professor is leader of the first project to drill into a subduction zone. His earliest experience with seafloor drilling was off the coast of Oregon. As a graduate student, Tobin participated in expeditions that augered holes up to 1,500 feet into the Cascadia fault system. But those projects barely scratched the surface. Tobin wanted to burrow down to the zone where earthquakes are born. The only nation willing to finance an undertaking of that magnitude was Japan. "Earthquakes are their greatest national security threat," he said. "The way the U.S.

thought of terrorists after 9/11 is how Japan thinks of earthquakes and tsunamis all the time."

No existing research ship was powerful enough to handle the job, so Japan built its own at a cost of half a billion dollars. Called *Chikyu*, which means "Earth," the vessel features the same kind of drilling technology used by the oil industry. Daily operating expenses range between $200,000 and $400,000. "It's not an exaggeration to say that every few days is a million dollars," Tobin said. Since the ship started drilling off Japan's coast in 2007, it has set several depth records. The goal is to reach 3.5 miles down, into the zone where one plate grinds past another. It will be the deepest research borehole in the ocean and the first time science has reached into the living heart of a subduction zone.

The target is the Nankai Trough, which has so much in common with Cascadia that Tobin calls them sisters. "We're going to learn a lot from this, and much of that will translate directly to understanding the hazard and the science of the Cascadia Subduction Zone." Tobin and an international team of collaborators will pack the hole with instruments to measure temperature, strain, creep, and fluid behavior. They're already poring over miles of core to better understand the way rocks change and break during an earthquake. In one set of cores from the fault zone, researchers found a thin band where rock had been heated to nearly six hundred degrees by the frictional heat of a past quake.

Theory predicts that earthquakes start with small ruptures that propagate and cascade, but no one knows the steps or how long the process takes. "We don't know enough yet to even know if precursory signals exist, but it's worth looking," Tobin said. "We need to have long-term monitoring before an event, then be there during the event." He doesn't expect the instruments or boreholes to survive the next great Nankai quake, but he hopes to collect data up until that instant. Then he would be happy to move on. "I would love to do this in Cascadia, too."

While subduction zone studies in Japan promise insights for the Pacific Northwest, the Italian city of L'Aquila provides an example of what can go wrong when it comes to sharing those insights with the public. In a case that made seismologists around the world shudder, six scientists and a government official were convicted of manslaughter there in 2012.

Most news coverage of the trial cast the scientists as scapegoats, prosecuted because they couldn't predict an earthquake that killed 309 people and left the lovely, medieval city in ruins. But the charges had nothing to do with earthquake prediction. The scientists were hauled into the dock because they failed to adequately communicate seismic risks to frightened residents in a community that had been rattled by hundreds of small tremors.

The accused were members of a science advisory panel convened in March 2009 to assess the likelihood of a damaging quake. Wire-tapped conversations later revealed that the meeting was largely a public relations ploy to quell panic over the earthquake swarms and a local man's prediction that a massive shock was imminent.

After less than an hour's discussion, the panel members dismissed the prediction as bogus and agreed among themselves that small quakes were not necessarily a precursor to anything bigger. Then the scientists left town without issuing a statement. It fell to the bureaucrat on the panel to answer questions from the press.

Bernardo De Bernardinis, deputy chief of Italy's Civil Protection Department, told journalists there was no danger because "there is an ongoing discharge of energy." De Bernardinis even endorsed a television reporter's suggestion that residents should relax with a glass of wine. The deputy chief suggested a Montepulciano. When the magnitude 6.3 quake struck a week later at 3:32 AM, most residents were in bed. Many told the court De Bernardinis's reassuring statement convinced them not to sleep outdoors, as was traditional when small quakes rumbled the region. The victims were crushed or buried in rubble. After a lengthy trial, the court sentenced all seven defendants to six years in prison. (The Italian justice system allows for multiple appeals, and it's not clear whether any of the men will serve time.)

Watching the case unfold from Seattle, John Vidale felt uneasy. One of these days, the Cascadia Subduction Zone could start acting up. Maybe a magnitude 6 quake will pop on the plate interface. Perhaps an episode of slow slip under the Olympic Peninsula will continue for months instead of weeks, potentially raising the risk of a major quake. As director of the Pacific Northwest Seismic Network at the University of Washington, Vidale will be among the first to know if anything unusual is afoot. So he finds it easy to put himself in the shoes of the Italian scientists.

Vidale's not worried about going to jail. Scientists who advise the U.S. government are generally shielded from liability. But the rest of the L'Aquila scenario could play out in the Northwest, with a spooked public demanding answers from seismologists who have no real way of knowing what the Earth is going to do next.

"If strange things are happening, we will just have to be transparent and try not to say more than we know," Vidale said. He's also determined to avoid the missteps of the Italian experts, who were accused of providing "inexact, incomplete, and contradictory information."

There was no basis for De Bernardinis's claim that the city was safe because small quakes were bleeding off energy. "That was just stupid," said one American seismologist. "You never say there's no danger." The scientists on the panel knew De Bernardinis was wrong but didn't step forward to correct him. Nor did the experts remind residents about the region's history of deadly quakes or caution people who lived in ancient stone buildings. And although the scientists were technically correct that swarms of small quakes do not usually presage anything bigger, they failed to provide the one piece of useful information seismology can offer in a situation like that: earthquakes *can* trigger other earthquakes. The odds of a big quake striking L'Aquila were still low in the spring of 2009, but they were higher than usual because of the recent tremors.

The question of what to tell the public if Cascadia starts to rumble is already on the agenda of the National Earthquake Prediction and Evaluation Council (NEPEC); yes, there really is such a thing. NEPEC was established in 1976 to advise the USGS at a time when routine quake predictions seemed just around the corner. They weren't, and the council went dormant for more than a decade until the USGS revived it in 2006. Much of what the council does now is debunk earthquake prediction claims, whether from spiritual channelers in Taos or retired engineers in Pomona. NEPEC's other job is to help the Survey grapple with questions of risk, communication, and forecasting, the very issues at center stage in L'Aquila.

Vidale serves on the council, which has drafted statements that could be issued after a moderate quake on the subduction zone. "The likelihood of an earthquake being followed by a larger event is elevated over the background rate for a period of three to ten days," reads one version. Beyond that, there won't be much more scientists can say, except to remind people what a Cascadia megaquake could do and offer generic preparedness advice. It will be up to political leaders and emergency managers to decide whether any action is warranted, Vidale said.

Tom Jordan, director of the Southern California Earthquake Center, is pushing for a more systematic approach. He calls it operational earthquake forecasting and says the goal should be to emulate meteorologists. "We need to be producing something like seismic weather reports every day," Jordan said. He's convinced seismologists already have many of the tools they need to calculate the odds that an earthquake will strike in the near future. The main risk factors are the occurrence of other earthquakes in the vicinity and the level of stress on the target fault.

Jordan chaired a commission that examined the L'Aquila incident and advised the Italian government on how to respond the next time earthquake swarms or small quakes strike in seismic hot spots. A version of what the commission proposed is already in place in California, Jordan said. The state's earthquake prediction council, on which he serves, advises the governor when tremors pop up near faults that may be primed to rupture.

For example, at about the same time foreshocks started rattling L'Aquila, a swarm of fifty small earthquakes shook the shores of the Salton Sea east of San Diego. The area lies near a portion of the San Andreas Fault that hasn't ruptured since 1680. Residents were awakened before dawn on March 24 by a magnitude 4.8 shock, the region's biggest since record keeping began. Within a few hours, Jordan and the other members of the California Earthquake Prediction and Evaluation Council (CEPEC) met by teleconference and crafted a statement: "CEPEC believes that stresses associated with this earthquake swarm may increase the probability of a major earthquake on the San Andreas Fault to values between 1 and 5 percent over the next several days." Numbers that low would never justify an evacuation, Jordan said. Nor did the alert cause an exodus from the lightly populated valley. Emergency managers weren't impressed by a 5 percent risk, but some took advantage of the incident to emphasize the value of earthquake kits. The San Andreas didn't rip.

If the Italians had offered a similar assessment, coupled with a cautionary statement about central Italy's seismic danger, criminal charges would probably have never been filed, Jordan said. "In some sense you have to empower people to do what they think is the right thing to do." By laying out what they knew and didn't know, the California scientists let residents decide whether or not to act. "The anger you see in L'Aquila is over the fact that people felt they were deprived of important information."

The public appetite for seismic information is growing. More than twenty thousand people a day visit the Pacific Northwest Seismic Network's website and a community of enthusiasts dissects the data posted online. When the network sought 90 homeowners to install and maintain seismometers in their basements and garages, nearly two thousand people volunteered. Vidale and his colleagues started a blog and Facebook page in 2011, and they've been fielding a steady stream of questions and comments ever since.

Jordan sees regular earthquake forecasts as another way to communicate with the public and help counter misinformation floating around in cyberspace. But his approach hasn't gained much traction. Weather forecasts can help you decide whether to carry an umbrella or plan a hike. Most people have no idea how to react to a forecast that calls for a 1 percent chance of an earthquake. Some seismologists question the probability calculations. Compared to weather forecasters, scientists who study earthquakes remain virtually in the dark about what the next week—or the next ten years—will bring. It's easy to crank out numbers, but it's impossible to validate them.

Vidale puts more stock in a type of alert that can guarantee a quake is on its way. There's a catch, of course. The earthquake early warning system he and others hope to implement along the West Coast would offer at most five minutes notice that the ground is about to shake. In some areas the window could be as slim as fifteen to thirty seconds. That's because the technology doesn't kick into action until the earthquake is already under way. The system is designed to detect the first seismic waves to arrive and sound the alarm before more destructive pulses hit.

Half a minute isn't enough time to jump in your car and evacuate to Idaho. But it would allow you to climb off a ladder, duck under a table, or put down your scalpel if you happen to be performing surgery. Japan completed a $1 billion early warning system in 2007 and has issued alerts for more than a dozen strong earthquakes since then. Many Japanese businesses and industries are hardwired to automatically shut down machinery, recall elevators, and switch to backup power the moment the warnings arrive. Schools broadcast the alerts over their public address systems and students dive for cover. The system's biggest test came on 3/11. Before the worst shaking hit, twenty-seven bullet trains slowed to a stop without a single derailment. Warnings went out to people all along the coast and, coupled with tsunami warnings, saved thousands of lives. "Japan showed that early warning has a lot of value," Vidale said. Mexico, Taiwan, and Romania have similar systems in quake-prone urban areas.

The approach works for two reasons. Seismometers closest to an earthquake's source detect the motion first and can relay information faster than the seismic waves travel through the ground. The fact that earthquakes send out several different types of seismic waves can also provide a short warning window. The fastest waves to spread are called p-waves. They zip through the ground at up to 17,000 mph and are responsible for the first, small spike that appears on a seismogram. P-waves are less destructive than the slower-moving secondary waves and surface waves that follow on their heels.

At sites distant from a quake's origin, the lag between the arrival of p-waves and the most damaging motion can stretch to minutes. In a Cascadia megaquake, the strongest shaking won't hit Seattle until two to five minutes after the start of the rupture. In California, where cities are riddled with fault lines, warning times would be much shorter. The West Coast warning system that Vidale and his colleagues hope to build would also be tied into GPS stations. With instantaneous measurements of how far the ground has moved, GPS can judge the size of big earthquakes much less ambiguously than seismometers can.

Scientists are testing a prototype system in California. Bay Area Rapid Transit trains are already programmed to shut down automatically. The Northwest network is still in its infancy. Vidale and other scientists are testing the software on their own computers, and so far, it's worked well with small quakes. Their next step is to see how businesses, utilities, and government agencies could use the warnings. A full-scale system like Japan's, which includes public notification, is years down the road.

It all depends on money, Vidale said. Japan invested heavily in its system, but the U.S. government hasn't been as willing to open the vault. Much of the initial work is being funded by a $6 million grant from the Gordon and Betty Moore Foundation in Palo Alto. A pioneer of the semiconductor industry, Gordon Moore is the cofounder of chipmaker Intel. But it's unlikely he or any other billionaire will be willing to pay the $200 million or so it would cost to roll out a coastwide network.

CHAPTER 14:

INEVITABLE, INSCRUTABLE

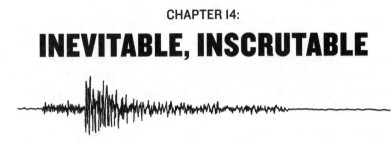

THE PACE OF GEOLOGIC DISCOVERY in the Pacific Northwest has been breathtaking. Brain Atwater published the first definitive evidence of ancient megaquakes in 1987. Five years later, scientists pieced together the story of the Seattle Fault and a powerful earthquake that tore through the heart of Puget Sound. By 2005, maps were crowded with new fault lines turning up on lidar surveys, and scientists were using GPS to watch in real-time as the region's tectonic train wreck unfolded. Findings continue to pour in. From hidden faults east of the Cascades to subterranean rumblings that might presage the next subduction zone quake, there's no shortage of surprises.

People who live in the Northwest might be forgiven for saying, "enough already."

The human mind has a tendency to wander after one too many worst-case scenarios, and earthquakes are the toughest natural disaster to wrap the brain around anyway. Hurricanes, forest fires, and floods follow seasonal schedules. There's usually enough warning time to board up the windows, stack sand bags, and evacuate. Earthquakes operate on a time scale that's both inevitable and inscrutable. Another Cascadia megaquake will strike. It could be ten minutes from now, or it could hold off until today's toddlers are great-grandparents.

When he took over FEMA in 1993, James Lee Witt grappled with the question of how to make American communities more resistant to rare catastrophes. The standard approach to disaster management at the time was reactive: Wait for nature to wreak havoc, then open the federal wallet to fix the mess. Witt thought it made more sense to invest up front and reduce damage in the long term. He picked the Puget Sound area to be part of Project Impact, an initiative launched in 1997. The goal was to help the region size up its earthquake risk; identify the most vulnerable bridges, buildings and economic links; and develop plans to strengthen them before the next quake hits. The program expanded Seattle's home retrofit classes and other education efforts. It brought together people who usually didn't talk to each other, like highway officials, seismologists, port commissioners, business owners, and hospital administrators.

"The reason we focused on this program was that we could no longer continue the damage-rebuild-damage-rebuild cycle," Witt recalled. "We knew that if we raised public awareness about the way we dealt with disaster that it would catch on—and it did."

When the Nisqually quake struck in 2001, one reason the damage wasn't worse were steps taken under Project Impact, like bolting down television monitors and bookshelves in daycare centers and classrooms. Seattle's mayor said at the time that he was convinced the number of casualties would have been far higher if the work hadn't been done.

Project Impact lasted only four years, but Witt's philosophy inspired many of the efforts today to brace the region for coming quakes and allow it to recover as quickly as possible. The resilience planning projects in Washington and Oregon are translating three decades' worth of scientific research into detailed scenarios of expected damage and impacts on the people of the Northwest and the wider economy.

The findings are both chilling and encouraging: Chilling in the extent of the damage and how long it could take to fix, but encouraging in the way so many players have come together to map out a way forward.

In Oregon, where most of the state's gasoline, diesel, and jet fuel are concentrated in vulnerable facilities and pipelines near the Willamette River, a Cascadia megaquake could disrupt supplies for weeks or months. Natural gas lines pass through the same area, and high-voltage transmission towers sit near the water's edge, where soil liquefaction is expected to cause the ground to shift twenty feet or more. Oregon's resilience plan, released in February 2013, estimates electrical service in Portland and surrounding areas will be knocked out for one to three months, while it could take up to a year to fully restore water supplies and repair damaged sewer pipes and waste treatment plants. In tsunami-ravaged coastal areas it could be six months before power is restored to pre-quake levels.

Washington's plan estimates it will take one to three months to fully restore telephone and Internet services, and up to three years to rebuild damaged power transmission lines. Some petroleum refineries and transmission pipelines could be closed for a year or more.

In the aftermath of the quake, simultaneous damage to so many crucial lifelines and services across Washington, Oregon, Northern California, and British Columbia is likely to lead to a kind of paralysis. Without gasoline, crews won't be able to repair buckled roads and bridges. Until roads and bridges are repaired, it will be difficult to fix downed power lines and damaged electrical substations. And without electricity, it won't be possible to bring telephone and Internet services back online. A lack of power also means no ATMs at a time when many banks will be closed because of earthquake damage. If outages persist for even a month, warns the Oregon plan, many businesses will leave the area.

Experiences in Japan and Chile prove that planning and preparation can minimize the downtime and gridlock. After its 2010 megaquake and tsunami, Chile was able to restore most electrical power, telephone, and Internet services within two weeks. Commercial airline flights resumed in ten days. In Japan, electrical power was almost back to normal within ten days of the 2011 megaquake and tsunami, though shutdowns at nuclear power plants required homes and businesses to cut back on energy use for several months. Most Japanese cell phone towers were operational again within three weeks of the quake.

The Northwest isn't close to that level of preparedness, but the region is making progress. For example, fuel companies with storage facilities and pipelines in Oregon agreed to evaluate their seismic risk and start upgrades. And the utility that owns the high-voltage transmission towers on the banks of the Willamette plans to strengthen them.

It's great to see the Pacific Northwest taking earthquake risk so seriously, said Witt, who left FEMA in 2001 and now runs a consulting firm that helps businesses and governments plan for disaster. Witt also launched an advocacy group called ProtectingAmerica.org, along with former Coast Guard Commandant and Deputy Secretary of Homeland Security James Loy. Their goal is to reduce the economic ripples from catastrophes like a Cascadia megaquake and tsunami. "In a major subduction zone quake, not only will the direct damages to structures and infrastructure be enormous, the long-term economic impact could alter our entire economy," Witt said. The damage to roads, utilities, and productivity will reverberate across the nation.

The cost will be too much for the Northwest to absorb. Much of the loss won't be insured, because policies are so costly many people don't bother with them. Witt's solution is a law that would create a national catastrophe fund. His logic is the same as for Project Impact: It's better to prepare ahead of time for those bad days that will surely come. "The economic devastation from major disasters can be minimized if we begin to strengthen our financial infrastructure now," he said.

The federal government would administer the fund, but the money wouldn't come from the Treasury. Insurance companies would chip in a portion of the premiums they collect. The fund would be tapped to backstop states and insurers after calamity strikes. The system as Witt envisions it would actually reduce the cost of insurance because the amount companies chip in would be less than what they now pay for reinsurance to protect themselves against financial calamity. Interest that accrues on the fund would be plowed back into equipment and training for first responders and public education. "The law would protect taxpayers from the inevitable after-the-fact bailouts we use today to help communities recover from natural catastrophes."

For an example of the time-honored approach, consider the aftermath of Superstorm Sandy. The cyclone lashed the northeastern United States just before Halloween 2012. Millions of homes lost power, thousands of buildings were destroyed, and more than 130 people died. At a time when Congress was locked in a wrestling match over federal deficits and spending, the lawmakers voted to appropriate $50 billion in federal aid. The scenario is repeated over and over. Including the Sandy funds, the federal government has given states $300 billion for disaster recovery since 1992.

Another aspect of Witt's crusade is a push for better building codes. There's no more effective way to reduce earthquake deaths than good construction. The 2010 Haiti earthquake proved it by killing 200,000 people when shoddy buildings collapsed. The recent megaquakes in Chile and Japan proved it with low death tolls due to structural damage.

In the United States, the development of building codes is a process largely left up to engineers. But many of them wish the public would weigh in more to help define acceptable levels of risk. Are the residents of Seattle or Portland or Vancouver comfortable with new buildings that have a 10 percent chance of collapse at the maximum level of shaking the codes consider? Is it OK that many of the structures that survive a major quake will have to be torn down because they're so damaged?

"Why should a bunch of structural engineers in a conference room be making those decisions?" asked Peter Yanev, author of the "Shake, Rattle, Seattle" op-ed in *The New York Times*.

One of the reasons nuclear power plants are built to such strict standards is that the public demands it. Realistically, there won't be an outcry for changes in American building codes until another major quake strikes. "The public doesn't perceive this as a big issue—yet," said Yanev. Incremental steps to strengthen the buildings that pose the greatest risk are possible, though, like Seattle's proposal to require retrofits on brick buildings.

Both Oregon's and Washington's resilience plans recommend measures to mandate seismic upgrades to schools and hospitals. Oregon's plan goes even further, calling for a statewide push to identify and fix vulnerable, critical buildings like medical facilities and the emergency responder headquarters. A 2011 FEMA analysis estimated that nearly 900 fire stations and 150 police stations across the Northwest would be destroyed by a Cascadia megaquake. Damage to hospitals would result in the loss of up to 5,000 beds, at a time when as many as 30,000 injured people would be clamoring for treatment.

As an incentive to retrofit old buildings, Oregon's plan advocates mandatory disclosure of seismic risk during real estate sales. The state plan also proposes a seismic rating system for buildings to inform people about the risks where they live and work and encourage owners and builders to go beyond the minimum code for new structures.

Over the coming years, science will undoubtedly yield new insights into the seismic forces that shape the region, and how they are likely to play out in the future. But unless geologists find a way to predict earthquakes, the new discoveries are more likely to be incremental than revolutionary. In many ways, geoscience has done its part for the Pacific Northwest.

On the flanks of Mount Hood in 2011, Ian Madin reflected on decades of progress, even as he pushed the research forward with another trench on another fault. As chief scientist for the Oregon Department of Geology, Madin loves the thrill of finding something new. But he's convinced the best investment the region can make now is to use whatever breathing room nature provides to create communities that will be able to bounce back after the Big One strikes. "Let's fix the most important highway corridors so that within 24 hours we can reach communities on the coast," he said. "Let's make sure we have hospital facilities that will be functional. Let's make sure schools and police stations will still be standing."

While Madin spoke, a backhoe clawed at the ground, lengthening the trench across the newly discovered fault. "This is exciting stuff for a geologist, but it's just adding detail to a big picture that's pretty clear by now," he said.

"We already know what we need to do. Now we just have to do it."

ACKNOWLEDGMENTS

PARTWAY THROUGH THE RESEARCH for this book, I realized I needed to visit the Niawiakum River. In all my years of reporting on earthquake science in the Pacific Northwest, I had never seen the little river on Willapa Bay where so many discoveries were made.

I didn't want to bug Brian Atwater again. He had already hauled me along on multiple field trips and sat patiently through more interviews than any one person should have to endure. But I did ask his advice on the best vantage points.

I should have known better.

It wasn't long before Brian and I were headed out for another day-long excursion.

Throughout this project, Brian was unfailingly generous with his time and expertise. The book would not have been possible without his help. Equally crucial was the assistance of dozens of other scientists, emergency managers, and experts.

Chris Goldfinger had the *Pacific Storm* detour into Newport so I could join the cruise and get a feel for seismic fieldwork at sea. Dave Yamaguchi let me tag along as he schooled a group of teachers on subduction zone quakes and the Copalis ghost forest. He spent hours on other occasions explaining the life of samurai in eighteenth-century Japan and the intricacies of tree-ring dating. Ian Madin welcomed me at his trench on Mount Hood, and Brian Sherrod opened my eyes to the evidence of giant earthquakes on Alki Beach, in my own neigh-borhood of West Seattle.

Patrick Corcoran toured me around the northern Oregon coast and convinced me to always have an escape plan when I visit the Northwest seashore. Stephanie Fritts introduced me to the special perils faced by the people of Washington's Long Beach Peninsula, and the pragmatic way in which they're tackling them.

I'm grateful to everyone who appears in these pages—and many who don't—for taking the time to share their knowledge and insights. Several people went far beyond what I had any right to expect. I lost track of how many conversations and e-mail exchanges I had with Tom Heaton, who responded graciously even in the midst of a long-awaited sabbatical. Tom Pratt and Ralph Haugerud both offered pri-vate tutorials on aspects of earth science and Northwest geology I was struggling to understand.

Tim Walsh, of Washington's Department of Natural Resources, was always there to answer questions and clear up confusion. And if John Vidale charged for every question he fielded, I would be more indebted to him than I already am.

John Vidale and Craig Weaver reviewed the entire manuscript and helped weed out errors. Several others were kind enough to review individual chapters. The mistakes that remain are my own doing.

Thanks to Hal Bernton and Patti Epler for their comments, inspi-ration and suggestions on the journalistic side of the equation. Jerry Holloron, best copy editor I've ever worked with, undertook a final check of the manuscript just days before deadline. Thanks also to Gary Luke at Sasquatch Books, for luring me into the project.

I'm grateful to my editors at *The Seattle Times*, who never com-plained when I asked for time off—and who let me come back to the job I love when the book was done. A grant from the National Asso-ciation of Science Writers arrived at the perfect time and helped pay my travel expenses.

Finally, I'm lucky to have a friend like Carmen Dybdahl. Not only did she track down and process most of the illustrations for the book, she also reviewed and proofed the manuscript, offered suggestions, dug up obscure facts, and never wavered in her support and encouragement.

SOURCES

INTRODUCTION: A WARNING FROM THE PAST

For information about Native American life on the West Coast of North America in 1700:
Ludwin, Ruth, University of Washington, and Alan McMillan, Simon Frasier University, conversations with author.

Losey, Robert J. "Native American vulnerability and resiliency to Cascadia earthquakes," *Oregon Historical Quarterly*, 2 (2008): 108.

On the casualty/damage estimates for Oregon:
Wang, Yumei. "The first statewide earthquake risk assessment using HAZUS-estimated losses in Oregon." Presented at the American Society of Civil Engineers Technical Council on Lifeline Earthquake Engineering, Seattle, WA, 1999.

Oregon Seismic Safety Policy Advisory Committee. *The Oregon Resilience Plan*, Report to the 77th Legislative Assembly, Draft. February 2013. http://www.oregon.gov/OMD/OEM/osspac/docs/Oregon_Resilience_Plan_draft.pdf

For Professor Cobb's words:
Cobb "Promotional Ad," *The Outlook: An Illustrated Weekly Journal of Currently Life* 231 (June 1921): 128.

Ellensburg Daily Record, November 13, 1939.

For Eldridge Moore's quote:
McPhee, John. *Annals of the Former World*. New York: Farrar, Straus and Giroux, 1998.

CHAPTER I: QUIET AS KANSAS

Ratcliff, Stan, and Daniel Pope, conversations with author, auction at Satsop Nuclear Plant, October 2011.

Information on WPPSS, the region's nuclear history and early thinking about the Cascadia Subduction Zone:
Pope, Daniel. *Nuclear Implosions: The Rise and Fall of the Washington Public Power Supply System*. New York: Cambridge University Press, 2008.

Pope, Daniel. "Environmental Constraints and Organizational Failures: The Washington Public Power Supply

System," *Business and Economic History* 19 (1990).

Connelly, Joel, "Locals rejected plans for nuke plant on fault line," *Seattle PI.com*, March 15, 2011. Accessed December 2012, http://www.seattlepi.com/default/article/Locals-rejected-plans-for-nuke-plant-on-fault-line-1191350.php.

Welch, Bob. "Memories of a nearly nuclear coast." *The Register-Guard*, March 12, 2011.

"Preliminary Safety Analysis Report." *WPPSS Nuclear Project No. 3*, 1974.

"Final Safety Analysis Report." *WPPS Nuclear Project No. 3*. 1983.

For information on the history of earthquake theories and the development of plate tectonics:
Kious, W. Jacquelyne and Robert I. Tilling. "This Dynamic Earth: The Story of Plate Tectonics," USGS, January 2013, http://pubs.usgs.gov/gip/dynamic/dynamic.html#anchor10790904.

Bryson, Bill. *A Short History of Nearly Everything*. New York: Broadway Books, 2003.

Hough, Susan Elizabeth. *Earthshaking Science: What we Know (and Don't Know) about Earthquakes*. Princeton: Princeton University Press, 2002.

Zeilinga de Boer, Jelle and Donald Theodore Sanders. *Earthquakes in Human History: The Far-Reaching effects of Seismic Disruptions*. Princeton: Princeton University Press, 2005.

Pringle, Patrick, Centralia College, Tom Heaton, and Hiroo Kanamori, conversations with author.

Heaton, Thomas H. and Hiroo Kanamori. "Seismic potential associated with subduction in the Northwestern United States." *Bulletin of the Seismological Society of America* 74, (1984): 933-41.

CHAPTER 2: WRITTEN IN MUD

Atwater, Brian, Kery Sieh, Wendy Grant Walter, Boyd Benson, John Shulene, Carrie Garrison-Lacey, Frances Demarco, and Dave Yamaguchi, conversations with author.

For studies providing the first hints of activity in Cascadia:
Ando, Masataka and Emery I. Balas. "Geodetic evidence for aseismic subduction of the Juan de Fuca Plate." *Journal of Geophysical Research* 84, (1979): 3023-28.

Reilinger, Robert and John Adams. "Geodetic evidence for active landward tilting of the Oregon and Washington coastal ranges." *Geophysical Research Letters* 9, (1982): 401-3.

Adams, John. "Active deformation of the Pacific Northwest continental margin." *Tectonics* 3 (1984): 449-72.

Doig, Ivan. *Winter Brothers: A Season at the Edge of America*. San Diego: Harcourt Brace & Company, 1980.

For studies documenting Atwater, Yamaguchi, and other's research on the NW coast:
Atwater, Brian F. "Evidence for great Holocene earthquakes along the outer coast of Washington State." *Science* 236 (1987): 942-44.

Atwater, Brian F. and David K. Yamaguchi. "Sudden probably coseismic submergence of Holocene trees and

grass in coastal Washington State."
Geology 19 (1991): 706-9.

Atwater, Brian F., Minze Stuiver and
David K. Yamaguchi. "Radiocarbon
test of earthquake magnitude at the
Cascadia Subduction Zone." *Nature*
353 (1991): 156-8.

Atwater, Brian F. "Geologic evidence
for earthquakes during the past 2000
years along the Copalis River, southern coastal Washington." *Journal
of Geophysical Research* 97 (1992):
1901-19.

Nelson, Alan R. et al. "Radiocarbon
evidence for extensive plate-bound-
ary rupture about 300 years ago at the
Cascadia Subduction Zone." *Nature*
378 (1995): 371-4.

Atwater, Brian F. et al. "Summary of
coastal geologic evidence for past
great earthquakes at the Cascadia
Subduction Zone." *Earthquake Spec-
tra* 11 (1995): 1-18.

Atwater, Brian F. and Eileen
Hemphill-Haley. "Preliminary estimates of recurrence intervals for
great earthquakes of the past 3500
years at the northeastern Willapa Bay,
Washington." *U.S. Geological Survey
Open-File Report 96-001* (1996).

Atwater, Brian F. et al. "Earthquake
recurrence inferred from paleoseismology." *Developments in Quater-
nary Science.*1 (2003): 331-350.

CHAPTER 3: PARENT QUAKE, ORPHAN TSUNAMI

For information about the life and
work of James Gilchrist Swan:
McDonald, Lucile. *Swan Among
the Indians: Life of James G. Swan.*
Hillsboro: Binfords & Mort Publishers, 1972.

Swan, James G. *Northwest Coast: Or,
Three Years' Residence in Washington
Territory.* Seattle: University of Wash-
ington Press, 1969.

For Native American earthquake tra-
ditions and stories:
Riebe, Viola, Robert Dennis, and Vicki
Ozaki, conversations with author.

Heaton, Thomas H. and Parke D.
Snavely, Jr. "Possible tsunami along
the Northwestern coast of the
United States inferred from Indian
traditions." *Bulletin of the Seismological Society of America* 75 (1985):
1455-1460.

McMillan, Alan D. and Ian Hutchin-
son. "When the mountain dwarfs
danced: aboriginal traditions of pale-
oseismic events along the Cascadia
Subduction Zone of Western North
America." *Ethnohistory* 49 (2002): 1.

Ludwin, Ruth et al. "Dating the 1700
Cascadia earthquake: Great coastal
earthquakes in native stories." *Seismological Research Letters* 76 (2005):
140-8.

Younker, Jason T. "Weaving long
ropes: Oral tradition and understanding the great tide." *Oregon Historical
Quarterly* 108 (2007): 193.

Phillips, Patricia Whereat. 2007. "Tsunamis and floods in Coos Bay mythol-
ogy: great Cascadia earthquakes and
tsunamis along the Oregon Coast."
Oregon Historical Quarterly 108
(2007): 181.

Byram, R. Scott. "Tectonic history
and cultural memory: catastrophe
and restoration on the Oregon coast."

Oregon Historical Quarterly 108 (2007): 167.

For information about Japanese history and earthquake monitoring:
Roberts, Luke S, UC Santa Barbara, and Kenji Satake, conversations with author.

Goldfarb, Lyn and Deborah Desnoo. 2004. "Japan: Memoirs of a Secret Empire." *PBS* video, 2004. http://www.pbs.org/empires/japan.

Atwater, Brian F. et al. "The Orphan Tsunami of 1700: Japanese clues to a parent earthquake in North America." USGS, 2005, http://pubs.usgs.gov/pp/pp1707

Satake, Kenji et al. "Time and size of a giant earthquake in Cascadia inferred from Japanese tsunami records of January 1700." *Nature* 379 (1996): 246-249.

Kanamori, Hiroo and Thomas H. Heaton. "The wake of a legendary earthquake." *Nature* 379 (1996): 203-4.

Yamaguchi, David K. et al. "Tree-ring dating the 1700 Cascadia earthquake." *Nature* 389 (1997): 922.

Jacoby, Gordon C., Daniel E. Bunker and Boyd E. Benson. "Tree-ring evidence for an A.D. 1700 Cascadia earthquake in Washington and northern Oregon." *Geology* 25 (1997): 999-1002.

CHAPTER 4: A VIEW FROM THE SEA

Goldfinger, Chris, and Gary Griggs, conversations with author.

Study on ocean cores:
Griggs, Gary B.. "The first ocean evidence of great Cascadia earthquakes." *Eos* 92 (2011): 325-6.

For background on underwater landslides and the Grand Banks earthquake:
Heezen, Bruce C. and Maurice Ewing. "Turbidity currents and submarine sumps, and the 1929 Grand Banks earthquake." *American Journal of Science* 250 (1952): 849-873.

Nisbet, Euan G and David J.W. Piper. "Giant submarine landslides." *Nature* 392 (1998): 329-330.

"The 1929 Magnitude 7.2 "Grand Banks" earthquake and tsunami." *Natural Resources Canada.* http://www.earthquakescanada.nrcan.gc.ca/hist-tor/20th-eme/1929/1929-eng.php

For John Adams's analysis of underwater landslides:
Adams, John. "Paleoseismicity of the Cascadia Subduction Zone: Evidence from Turbidites off the Oregon-Washington Margin." *Tectonics* 9 (1990): 569-583.

For additional information on Goldfinger's research:
McCaffrey, Robert and Chris Goldfinger. "Forearc deformation and great subduction earthquakes: Implications for Cascadia offshore earthquake potential." *Science* 267 (1995): 856-859.

Goldfinger, Chris et al. "Deep-water turbidites as Holocene earthquake proxies: The Cascadia subduction zone and Northern San Andreas Fault systems." *Annals of Geophysics* 46 (2003): 1169-1194.

Kelsey, Harvey M. et al. "Tsunami history of an Oregon coastal lake reveals a 4600 year record of great earthquakes on the Cascadia Subduction Zone." *GSA Bulletin* 117 (2005): 1009-1032.

Goldfinger, Chris et al. "Turbidite event history—Methods and implications for Holocene paleoseismicity of the Cascadia Subduction Zone." USGS, 2012, http://pubs.usgs.gov/pp/pp1661f/.

For seafloor secrecy:
Spinrad, Rick, conversation with author.

Jeremy Legget, "The depths of secrecy—Just when you thought the Cold War was over, the US Navy tries it again," *The Guardian*, December13, 1988.

William J. Broad, "Map makes ocean floors as knowable as Venus," *The New York Times*, October 24, 1995.

Doel, Ronald E., Tanya J. Levin and Mason K. Marker. "Extending modern cartography to the ocean depths: Military patronage, Cold War priorities, and the Heezen-Tharp mapping project, 1952-1959." *Journal of Historical Geography*, 32 (2006): 605-26.

CHAPTER 5: SEATTLE'S FAULT

Daněs, Frank, Professor and Wayne Gilhamn, conversations with author.

For other work and adventures of Daněs:
Daněs, Zdenko Frankenberger. *"Memories of an Adventurer"* (unpublished manuscript, 2011).

Daněs, Z.F. et al. "Geophysical investigation of the southern Puget Sound area, Washington." *Journal of Geophysical Research*. 70 (1965): 5573-80.

Bucknam, Bob, and Brian Sherrod, conversations with author.

For a summary of the archaeological and geological findings of the tsunami at West Point:

Lape, Peter et al., "The Archaeology of West Point," The Burke Museum, accessed January 2013, http://www.burkemuseum.org/westpoint/.

For information about the underwater forests of Lake Washington and the case of John Tortorelli see:
Williams, Pat, and Brendan Buckley, conversations with author.

McKnight, Edwin F. T. "The Origin and History of Lake Washington." B.S. thesis, University of Washington, 1923.

Williams, David, B. *The Seattle Street-Smart Naturalist*. Portland: West-Winds Press, 2005.

Hopkins, Jack, "Log salvager sank too low, prosecutors say; trial focuses on trees under Lake Washington," *Seattle Post-Intelligencer*, January 13, 1995.

Hopkins, Jack. "Salvager convicted of stealing Lake Washington logs," *Seattle Post-Intelligencer*, February 17, 1995.

P-I Staff. "Prison term for theft from sunken forest," *Seattle Post-Intelligencer* April 15, 1995.

Washington vs. John Tortorelli, Supreme Court of Washington, En Banc, No. 71251-4, April 10, 2003.

For the *a'yahos* and their possible connection to Seattle Fault earthquakes:
Ludwin, R.S. et al. "Serpent spirit-power stories along the Seattle Fault." *Seismological Research Letters*. 76 (2005): 426-31.

For studies that proved an earthquake on the Seattle Fault 1,100 years ago along with a commentary from John Adams:

Adams, John. "Paleoseismology: A search for ancient earthquakes in Puget Sound." *Science* 258 (1992): 1592-3.

Bucknam, Robert C., Eileen Hemphill-Haley and Estella B. Leopold. "Abrupt uplift within the past 1,700 years at southern Puget Sound, Washington." *Science* 258 (1992): 1611-1614.

Atwater, Brian F. and Andrew L. Moore. "A tsunami about 1,000 years ago in Puget Sound, Washington." *Science* 258 (1992): 1614-7.

Karlin, Robert E. and Sally E.B. Abella. "Paleoearthquakes in the Puget Sound region recorded in sediments from Lake Washington, USA." *Science* 258 (1992): 1617-20.

Schuster, Robert L., Robert L. Logan and Patrick T. Pringle. "Prehistoric rock avalanches in the Olympic Mountains, Washington." *Science* 258 (1992): 1620-1.

Jacoby, Gordon C., Patrick L. Williams and Brendan M. Buckley. "Tree ring correlation between prehistoric landslides and abrupt tectonic events in Seattle, Washington." *Science* 258 (1992): 1621-3.

For the 1995 earthquake on or near the Seattle Fault:
Dewberry, Shawn R. and Robert S. Crosson. "The M 5.0 earthquake of 29 January 1995 in the Puget lowland of Western Washington: An event on the Seattle Fault?" *Bulletin of the Seismological Society of America* 86 (1996): 1167-72.

For the Seattle Fault quake scenario:
"Scenario for a Magnitude 6.7 Earthquake on the Seattle Fault," Earthquake Engineering Research Institute and the Washington Military Department Emergency Management Division, accessed January 2013, http://www.eeri.org/projects/earthquake-scenarios/seattle-fault-scenario/.

CHAPTER 6: SEEING THE FAULTS FOR THE TREES

For information on lidar and aeromagnetic surveys and their use to find and investigate faults in the Pacific Northwest:
Berghoff, Greg and David Harding, NASA, conversations with author.

Haugerud, Ralph, Craig Weaver, Ian Madin, Rick Blakely, Tom Pratt, conversations with author.

For additional information:
Harding, David J. and Gregory S. Berghoff. "Fault scarp detection beneath dense vegetation cover: Airborne lidar mapping of the Seattle Fault zone, Bainbridge Island, Washington State." *Proceedings of the American Society of Photogrammetry and Remote Sensing Annual Conference*, Washington, D.C., May 2000.

Nelson, Alan R. et al. "Late Holocene earthquakes on the Toe Jam Hill fault, Seattle Fault zone, Bainbridge Island, WA." *Geological Society of America Bulletin*. 115 2003: 1388-1403.

Haugerud, Ralph A. et al, "High-resolution lidar topography of the Puget lowland, Washington—A bonanza for earth science," *GSA Today*, June 2003, http://earthweb.ess.washington.edu/~bsherrod/brian/Haugerud_etal_GSAToday_LiDAR_Bonanza.pdf.

Sherrod, Brian L. et al. "Holocene fault scarps near Tacoma, Washington, USA." *Geology* 32 (2004): 9-12.

Blakeley, Richard J. et al. "Connecting the Yakima fold and thrust belt to active faults in the Puget lowland, Washington." *Journal of Geophysical Research: Solid Earth* 116 (2011): B07105.

Sherrod, Brian L. et al. "Finding concealed active faults: Extending the southern Whidbey Island fault across the Puget lowland, Washington." *Journal of Geophysical Research* 113 (2008): B05313.

Yeats, Robert S. and Craig Weaver. "Surface faulting: A new paradigm for the Pacific Northwest." *Seismological Research Letters* 75 (2004): 467-9.

Wells, Craig, and Tim Melbourne, conversations with author.

For information on tectonic motions in the NW:
Wells, Ray E., Craig S. Weaver and Richard J. Blakely. "Fore-arc migration in Cascadia and its neotectonic significance." *Geology* 26 (1998): 759-62.

White, Randall, and David Hill, USGS, conversations with author.

For links between earthquakes and volcanic eruptions see:
Linde, Alan T. and I. Selwyn Sacks. "Triggering of volcanic eruptions." *Nature* 395 (1998): 888-90.

Hill, David P., Fred Pollitz and Christopher Newhall. "Earthquake-Volcano Interactions." *Physics Today*, November 2002.

CHAPTER 7: THE EARTHQUAKE THAT WOULDN'T STAY PUT

Hooper, Margaret, William Bakun, Bob Royer, Eric Cheney, and Ivan Wong, conversations with author.

For information on the earthquake and nuclear investigations:
Splawn, A.J. *Ka-mi-akin: Last Hero of the Yakimas*. First edition copyright by Mrs. A. J. Splawn: 1917.

Milne, W.G. 1956. "Seismic activity in Canada west of the 113th meridian, 1841-1951." Ottawa: Publications of the Dominion Observatory, 1956.

Bechtel, Inc. "Investigation of the December 14, 1872 earthquake in the Pacific Northwest." *Skagit Nuclear Power Project, Preliminary Safety Analysis Report,*1975.

Woodward-Clyde Consultants. "Review of the North Cascades earthquake of 14 December, 187." *WPPSS Nuclear Power Projects 1 and 4, Preliminary Safety Analysis Report* 1976.

Weston Geophysical Research, Inc. "The 1872 earthquake, significant data and conclusions." *United Engineers and Constructors, Inc.* 1976.

Coombs, Howard A. et al. "Report of the review panel on the December 14, 1872 earthquake, in Washington Public Power Supply System." *WPPSS Nuclear Project No. 1, Preliminary Safety Analysis Report*, 1976.

Malone, Stephen D. and Sheng-Sheang Bor. "Attenuation patterns in the Pacific Northwest based on intensity data and the location of the 1872 North Cascades earthquake." *Bulletin of the Seismological Society of America* 69 (1979): 531-46.

Weichert, Dieter. "Omak Rock and the 1872 Pacific Northwest earthquake." *Bulletin of the Seismological Society of America.* 84 (1994): 444-50.

Madole, Richard F., Robert L. Schuster and Andrei M. Sarna-Wojcicki. "Ribbon Cliff landslide, Washington and the earthquake of 14 December 1872." *Bulletin of the Seismological Society of America.* 85 (1995): 986-1002.

Bakun, William H., Ralph A. Haugerud, Margaret G. Hopper and Ruth S. Ludwin. "The December 1872 Washington state earthquake." *Bulletin of the Seismological Society of America* 92 (2002): 3239-58.

Royer, Bob. "The Earthquake That Wouldn't Stay Put," *Cascadia Courier*, accessed January 2012, http://www.thecascadiacourier.com/2011/04/earthquake-that-wouldnt-stay-put.html.

Vidale, John, conversation with author.

Spall, Henry. 1980. "An interview with Charles F. Richter. USGS Earthquake Hazards Program," *Earthquake Information Bulletin* 12 (1980): 1, http://earthquake.usgs.gov/learn/topics/people.php?peopleID=23.

Scheid, Ann. "Oral History: Charles F. Richter -- How it was." *Engineering & Science.* (1982): 24-8.

Strauss, Stephen. *The Sizesaurus.* New York: Kodansha America, Inc., 1995.

Udias, Agustin and William Stauder. "The Jesuit Contribution to Seismology." *Seismological Research Letters* 67 (1996): 10-9

Levinson, Bill, "Time to dump the Richter Scale," *San Francisco Chronicle*, October 17, 1999.

"USGS Earthquake Magnitude Policy," 2002, http://earthquake.usgs.gov/aboutus/docs/020204mag_policy.php, October 2012.

Zannos, Susan. *Charles Richter and the Story of the Richter Scale.* Delaware: Mitchell Lane Publishers, 2004.

Hough, Susan Elizabeth. *Richter's Scale: Measure of an Earthquake; Measure of a Man.* Princeton: Princeton University Press, 2007.

Bodin, Paul, 2012. "How earthquake magnitude scales work," *Seismo* (blog), *Pacific Northwest Seismic Network*, 2012, http://www.pnsn.org/blog/2012/02/16/how-earthquake-magnitude-scales-work.

CHAPTER 8: IT CAME FROM THE DEEP

Davis, Carol and Bill Steele, University of Washington, conversations with author.

For information about the Nisqually earthquake:
Sorensen, Eric, "Shaken, but OK," *The Seattle Times*, March 1, 2001.

Jamieson, Robert L "6.8 Shocker," *The Seattle Post-Intelligencer*, March 1, 2001.

Cat Le, Phuong, "Mud engulfs home, dams river," *The Seattle Post-Intelligencer*, March 1, 2001.

Anderson, Ross, "The tower is collapsing!," *The Seattle Times*, March 3, 2001.

Ostrom, Carol and David Postman, "Why it's called the miracle quake," *The Seattle Times*, March 4, 2001.

Scott, Alwyn and Monico Soto, "How high-tech giants fared," *The Seattle Times*, March 4, 2001.

Sitt, Pam, "What readers told us about quake experiences," *The Seattle Times*, March 18, 2001.

Norris, Bob, "Narrative of strong ground shaking and liquefaction on Harbor Island during the Nisqually earthquake." *USGS Nisqually earthquake information page*, August 2012, http://www.ess.washington.edu/USGS/DOCS/quakestory.html.

Staff of the Pacific Northwest Seismograph Network. "Preliminary report on the Mw=6.8 Nisqually, Washington earthquake of 28 February 2001." *Seismological Research Letters*, 72 (2001): 352-61.

Filiatrault, Andre, et al. "Reconnaissance report of the February 28, 2001 Nisqually (Seattle-Olympia) earthquake." *University of California Structural Systems Research Project Report*. 2001.

Frankel, Arthur D, David L. Carver and Robert A. Williams. "Nonlinear and linear site response and basin effects in Seattle for the M 6.8 Nisqually, Washington, earthquake." *Bulletin of the Seismological Society of America*, 92 (2002): 2090-109.

Montgomery, David R., Harvey M. Greenberg and Daniel T. Smith. "Streamflow response to the Nisqually earthquake." *Earth and Planetary Science Letters*. 209 (2003): 19-28.

Gilmore, Susan, "Big outpouring helped our region rebuild; Nisqually earthquake: 5 years later," *The Seattle Times*, Feb. 28, 2006.

Creager, Ken, Steve Kirby, and Cliff Frohlich, conversations with author.

For background on deep earthquakes: Frohlich, Cliff. "Kiyoo Wadati and early research on deep focus earthquakes: Introduction to special section on deep and intermediate focus earthquakes." *Journal of Geophysical Research*. 92 (1987): 13,777-88.

Frohlich, Cliff. "Deep Earthquakes." *Scientific American*. 1989.

Frohlich, Cliff. "The nature of deep-focus earthquakes." *Annual Review, Earth and Planetary Science*. 17 (1989): 227-54.

Kirby, Stephen H, Emile A. Okal and E. Robert Engdahl. "The 9 June 94 Bolivian deep earthquake: An exceptional event in an extraordinary subduction zone." *Geophysical Research Letters*, 22 (1995): 2233-6.

Kirby, Stephen, Kelin Wang and Susan Dunlop, editors. "Seismic structure, intraslab earthquakes and processes and earthquake hazards." *The Cascadia Subduction Zone and Related Subduction Systems*. USGS Open-file report 02-328, 2002.

Preston, Leiph A., et al. "Intraslab earthquakes: dehydration of the Cascadia slab." *Science* 302 (2003): 1197-200.

Frohlich, Cliff. *Deep Earthquakes*. Cambridge: Cambridge University Press, 2009.

Davis, Carol, conversation with author.

For information about the 1949 and 1965 Puget Sound earthquakes:
"Earthquake listed as major; 5 dead; damage in millions," *The Seattle Daily Times*, April 13, 1949.

"Quake-loosened cliff plunges into sound near Tacoma," *The Seattle Daily Times*, April 16, 1949.

"Waltz with death atop Narrows Bridge," *The Seattle Daily Times*, April 14, 1949.

"Quake laid to shift in Olympics fault," *The Seattle Daily Times*, April 14, 1949.

"Quake hits Seattle: City lists 2 dead; Damage widespread, mostly minor," *The Seattle Daily Times*, April 29, 1965.

"Epicenter of earthquake set in Mason County," *The Seattle Daily Times*, April 29, 1965.

"Earthquake damage in state estimated at $12.4 million," *The Seattle Daily Times*, April 30, 1965.

Lange, Greg, "Earthquake hits Puget Sound area on April 13, 1949." *HistoryLink.org*, http://www.historylink.org/index.cfm?displaypage=output.cfm&file_id=2063, January 2013.

Lange, Greg, "Earthquake rattles Western Washington on April 29, 1965," *HistoryLink.org*, http://www.historylink.org/index.cfm?DisplayPage=output.cfm&file_id=1986, January 2013.

CHAPTER 9: RUN FOR YOUR LIFE

Okawa, Kamaishi, Lori Dengler, and Megumi Sugimoto, conversations with author.

For news accounts of the Japanese earthquake and tsunami:
The Yomiuri Shimbun. "Terrifying moments before tsunami revealed," *Daily Yomiuri Online*, August 24, 2011, http:// www.yomiuri.co.jp/dy/national/T110823005568.htm, October 2012.

Gilhooly, Rob. "Parents unable to let go, continue search for missing kids," *Japan Times Online*, October 13, 2011, http://www.japantimes.co.jp/text/nn20111013f1.html, October 2012.

Kenyon, Paul. "Japan Tsunami: The Survivors' Stories." *BBC News Panorama Documentary* video. 2011. http:// www.youtube.com/watch?v=tU1dLutdRAM, October 2012.

"Miracles of Kamaishi as a result of following 'Three principles of evacuation'." *MSN Sankei News* video. April 13, 2011. http://www.seedsasia.org/eng/projects-japan.html, January 2013.

Harding, Donald & Ben. "Tendenko: Surviving the Tsunami." *Witness, Al Jazeera English* video, 2011. http://www.youtube.com/watch?v=wymX-0J4G8r8, October 2012.

Harding, Donald & Ben. "Tsunami Survival Strategy Interview with Prof. Katada." *Al Jazeera English*, 2011. http://vimeo.com/31601481, October 2012.

Gilhooly, Rob. "Time has stopped for parents of dead and missing children," *Japan Times Online*, March 11, 2012, http://www.japantimes.co.jp/text/nn20120311f3.html, October 2012.

Corcoran, Patrick, Stephanie Fritts, Eddie Bernard, Vasily Titoy, Lori Dengler, Tim Walsh, Bob Freitag, Rob

Witter, and Harvey Kelsey, conversations with author.

For descriptions of the Cape Mendocino, California earthquake of 1992:

USGS. "Cape Mendocino, California Earthquakes of 1992," USGS, http://earthquake.usgs.gov/earthquakes/states/events/1992_04_25_26.php, January 2013.

Feldman, Paul and Jennifer Warren, "6.9 quake rocks N. California Coast" *Los Angeles Times*, April 26, 1992.

"Earthquake Notebook," *Orange County Register*, April 26, 1992.

Reinhold, Robert. "Amid quake's aftershocks, affirmations in California," *The New York Times*, April 27, 1992.,

Oppenheimer, D., et al. "The Cape Mendocino, California, earthquakes of April 1992: Subduction at the triple junction." *Science* 261 (1993): 433-8.

Thompson, Jerry. "Shockwave: Surviving North America's Biggest Disaster," *Omni Films* and *CBC*, 2009, http://www.cbc.ca/documentaries/doczone/2009/shockwave/, January 2013.

Priest, George R., et al. "Confidence levels for tsunami-inundation limits in northern Oregon inferred from a 10,000-year history of great earthquakes at the Cascadia Subduction Zone." *Natural Hazards* 54 (2010): 27-73.

Imamura, Fumihiko and Suppasr Anawat. "Damage due to the 2011 Tohoku earthquake tsunami and its lessons for future mitigation." *Proceedings of the International Symposium on Engineering Lessons Learned from the 2011 Great East Japan Earthquake*, March 2012, Tokyo, Japan.

Wood, Nathan and Christopher Soulard. "Variations in community exposure and sensitivity to tsunami hazards on the open-ocean and Strait of Juan de Fuca coasts of Washington." *USGS Scientific Investigations Report*, 2008.

Wood, Nathan. "Variations in city exposure and sensitivity to tsunami hazards in Oregon." *USGS Scientific Investigations Report*, 2007.

Project Safe Haven: Vertical Evacuation on the Washington Coast, https://catalyst.uw.edu/workspace/wiserjc/19587/116498, January 2013.

CHAPTER 10: IT'S OUR JOB

Weaver, Craig, Allan Lindh, Ivan Wong, David Applegate, Tom Pratty, Ralph Haugerud, Steve Malone, and Susan Hough, conversations with author.

Stegner, Wallace. *Beyond the Hundredth Meridian: John Wesley Powell and the Second Opening of the American West*. Boston: Houghton Mifflin, 1953.

Stegner, Wallace. *Angle of Repose*. New York: Doubleday, 1971.

Rabbitt, M.C. 1989. "The United States Geological Survey: 1879-1989," *U.S. Geological Survey Circular 1050*, 1989, http://pubs.usgs.gov/circ/c1050/index.htm, January 2013.

Wallace, Robert E., and Stanley Scott. "Earthquakes, minerals and me: With the USGS, 1942-1995." *USGS Open File Report*, 1996.

Gohn, Kathleen K.,"Celebrating 125 Years of the U.S. Geological Survey," *Circular 1274*, USGS, 2004, http://pubs.usgs.gov/circ/2004/ 1274/, January 2013.

Ulin, David L. *The Myth of Solid Ground: Earthquakes, Prediction and the Fault Line Between Reason and Faith*. New York: Penguin Books, 2004.

"125 Years of Topographic Mapping," *USGS*, http://nationalmap.gov/ustopo/history.html, January 2013.

Wang, Kelin, et al. "Predicting the 1975 Haicheng Earthquake." *Bulletin of the Seismological Society of America*, 96 (2006): 757-95.

Hough, Susan. *Predicting the Unpredictable:The Tumultuous Science of Earthquake Prediction*. Princeton: Princeton University Press, 2010.

For information on seismic hazard mapping:
Frankel, Art, Tom Heaton, Seth Stein, Max Wyss, and James Bela, conversations with author.

"United States National Seismic Hazard Maps," USGS, http://pubs.usgs.gov/fs/2008/3017/pdf/FS08-3017_508.pdf.

Stein, Seth. "Code Red: Earthquake Imminent? Understanding Earthquake Hazard Maps." *Earth Magazine*. January 2009.

Stein, Seth, Robert Geller and Mian Liu. "Bad assumptions or bad luck: Why earthquake hazard maps need objective testing." *Seismological Research Letters*, 82 (2011): 623-6.

Kerr, Richard. "Seismic crystal ball proving mostly cloudy around the world." *Science*, 332 (2011): 912-3.

Lay, Thorne. "Why giant earthquakes keep catching us out." *Nature*, 483 (2012): 149-50.

Achenbach, Joel, "Unexpected quakes shake geologists' faith," *The Washington Post*, March 10, 2012.

Achenbach, Joel, "Disaster struck, but not where it was expected," *The Washington Post*, March 12, 2012.

Stirling, Mark W. "Earthquake hazard maps and objective testing: The hazard mapper's point of view." *Seismological Research Letters*, 83 (2012): 321-2.

Wyss, Max, Anastasia Nekrasova and Vladimir Kossobokov. "Errors in expected human losses due to incorrect seismic hazard estimates." *Natural Hazards*, 62 (2012): 927-35.

Stein, Seth, Robert J. Geller and Mian Liu. "Why earthquake hazard maps often fail and what to do about it." *Tectonophysic*, 562-563 (2012): 1-25.

CHAPTER II: SHAKE, RATTLE— PORTLAND, VANCOUVER, SEATTLE

"Alaskan Way Viaduct-Earthquake Simulation, Washington State Department of Transportation, *YouTube*, http://www.youtube.com/watch?v=hos_uIKwC-c, January 2013.

For information on how buildings and other structures in the NW are likely to perform in future earthquakes:
Yanev, Peter, Tom Heaton, John Hooper, Perry Adebar, Kit Miyamoto, Cale Ash, Carl Barker, and Yumei Wang, conversations with author.

Wang, Yumei and J.L. Clark, "Earthquake damage in Oregon: Preliminary estimates of future earthquake losses," *Oregon Department of Geology and Mineral Industries*, 1999, http://oregongeology.com/sub/earthquakes/SP29SUMMARY.pdf, January 2013.

Heaton, Thomas H. "Will performance-based earthquake engineering break the power law?" *Seismological Research Letters*, 78 (2007): 2.

Lewis, Don. "Statewide seismic needs assessment: Implementation of Oregon 2005 Senate Bill 2 relating to earthquakes and seismic rehabilitation of public buildings," *Oregon Department of Geology and Mineral Industries*, 2007m http://www.oregongeology.com/sub/projects/rvs/OFR-O-07-02-SNAA-onscreen.pdf, January 2013.

Cheek, Lawrence. "Architectural bummers: These local designs are simply dispiriting," *Seattle Post-Intelligencer*, Sept. 25, 2007.

Anagnos, T. et al. "Los Angeles inventory of nonductile concrete buildings for analysis of seismic collapse risk hazards." The 14th World Conference on Earthquake Engineering, October, 2008, Beijing, China.

Heaton, Tom and Jing Yang, "Simulated deformations of Seattle high-rise buildings from a hypothetical giant Cascadia earthquake," *Seismological Society of America*, 2009, http://heaton.caltech.edu/, January 2013.

Yang, Jing. "Nonlinear response of high-rise buildings in giant subduction earthquakes." PhD diss., California Institute of Technology, 2009, http://www.thesis.library.caltech.edu/1298, October 2012.

"Seismic Vulnerability of Oregon State Highway Bridges," Oregon Department of Transportation, 2009, http://www.ftp.odot.state.or.us/Bridge/bridge_website_chittirat/2009_Seismic_Vulnerability_final.pdf, January 2012.

Yanev, Peter "Shake, Rattle, Seattle," *The New York Times*, March 28, 2010.

"Earthquake preparedness: Activities completed and future efforts," City of Seattle, 2010, Available: http://www.seattle.gov/emergency/docs/CityofSeattleEarthquakePreparednessActivitiesCompletedandFutureEffortsJune2010v2.pdf, January 2013.

Adebar, Perry, "Earthquake alert: How safe are the high-rise buildings in B.C.?," *The Vancouver Sun*, Feb. 5, 2011.

"Report on the 2010 Chilean earthquake and tsunami response," American Red Cross Multidisciplinary Team, *USGS*, 2011, http://pubs.usgs.gov/of/2011/1053, January 2013.

Jones, Lucy, "Lessons for the next big one," *Los Angeles Times*, April 8, 2011.

Adebar, P. and A. Lorzadeh. "Compression failure of thin concrete walls." 15th World Conference on Earthquake Engineering, Lisbon, Spain. 2012.

Wang, Yumei, Steven F. Bartlett and Scott B. Miles. "Earthquake risk study for Oregon's critical energy infrastructure hub: Final report to Oregon Department of Energy & Oregon Public Utility Commission." *Oregon Department of Geology and Mineral Industries*, 2012.

Mahin, Stephen A., "Lessons from steel buildings damaged by the Northridge earthquake," *National Information Service for Earthquake Engineering*, http://nisee.berkeley.edu/northridge/mahin.html, January 2012.

"Washington State's Bridge Seismic Retrofit Program," *WSDOT*, www.wsdot.wa.gov/eesc/bridge/preservation/pdf%5CBrgSeismicPaper.pdf, January 2013.

For information on the construction of sports stadiums and the Space Needle:
Hooper, John, Martin Page, and Gary Noble Curtis, conversations with author.

Gurtowski, Thomas M. "Finding a firm footing." *Daily Journal of Commerce*, June 17, 1999.

Magnusson, Jon D. "Soft soil makes for tough design." *Daily Journal of Commerce*, June 27, 2002.

Page, Martin. "Driven piles make stadium strong." *Daily Journal of Commerce*, June 27, 2002.

Murray, Morgan. *Century 21: The Story of the Seattle World's Fair, 1962*, Seattle: University of Washington Press, 1963.

Spector, Robert. *The Space Needle: Symbol of Seattle*. Seattle: Documentary Media LLC., 2006.

Berger, Knute. *Space Needle: The Spirit of Seattle*. Seattle: Documentary Media LLC., 2012.

CHAPTER 12: NUTS, BOLTS AND CHIMNEYS

For information on analyses of chimney damage:
Booth, Derek, conversation with author.

Booth, Derek B. et al. "Chimney Damage in the Greater Seattle Area from the Nisqually earthquake of 28 February 2001." *Bulletin of the Seismological Society of America*. 94, 3 (2004): 1143-58.

Stephenson, William J. et al. "Toward resolving an earthquake ground motion mystery in west Seattle, Washington State: Shallow seismic focusing may cause anomalous chimney damage." *Geophysical Research Letters*. 33 (2006).

For retrofitting advice:
Faris, Roger, and Leif Jackson, conversations with author.

Yanev, Peter I & Andrew C.T. Thompson. *Peace of Mind in Earthquake Country: How to Save Your Home, Business, and Life*. San Francisco: Chronicle Books 2008..

For information on earthquake insurance:
Newman, Karl, conversation with author.

Hunsberger, Brent, "Earthquake insurance is not a shaky investment," *The Oregonian*, March 14, 2010.

Pender, Kathleen, "New options for quake insurance," *The San Francisco Chronicle*, July 10, 2012.

Matheny, Keith, "Very few people have earthquake insurance, even in California where the risk is high," *USA Today*, Oct. 19, 2011.

For tips on tsunami survival:
Atwater, Brian, et al. "Surviving a Tsunami—Lessons from Chile, Hawaii and Japan," *USGS Circular*, 2005, http://pubs.usgs.gov/circ/c1187/, October 2012.

Tabor, Damon, "A Tsunami Hits the Northwest," *National Geographic Adventure Survive Almost Anything*, 2009, http://adventure.nationalgeographic.com/2009/08/survival/tsunami/3, October 2012. Chapter 13: Future Science, Coming Quake

For information on using GPS to monitor ground motions and the discovery of silent earthquakes:

Dragert, Herb, Garry Rogers, Tim Melbourne, and John Vidale, conversations with author.

Dragert, Herb, Kelin Wang and Thomas S. James. "A silent slip event on the deeper Cascadia subduction interface." *Science*, 292 (2001): 1525-8.

Miller, M. Meghan et al. "Periodic slow earthquakes from the Cascadia Subduction Zone." *Science*, 295 (2002): 2423.

Rogers, Garry and Herb Dragert. "Episodic tremor and slip on the Cascadia Subduction Zone: The chatter of silent slip." *Science*, 300 (2003): 1942-3.

Hirn, Alfred and Mireille Laigle. "Silent heralds of megathrust earthquakes?" *Science*, 305 (2004): 1917-8.

Mazzotti, Stephane and John Adams. "Near-term probability of a great earthquake on the Cascadia Subduction Zone." *Bulletin of the Seismological Society of America*, 94 (2004): 1954.

Brudzinksi, Michael R. "Do faults shimmy before they shake?" *Nature Geoscience*, 1 (2008): 295-6.

Vidale, John E. and Heidi Houston. "Slow slip: A new kind of earthquake." *Physics Today*, 2012.

For seafloor monitoring, drilling and underwater observatories, and precursors to 2011 Tohoku quake:

Delaney, John, Kate Moran, William Wilcock, Jeffrey McGuire, Tim Melbourne, and Harold Tobin, conversations with author.

Delaney, John R. *Understanding the planetary life support system: Next generation science in the ocean basins.* Unpublished manuscript.

NEPTUNE Canada, http://www.neptunecanada.com, January 2013.

"The National Science Foundation's Ocean Observatories Initiative," *Ocean Observatories Initiative*, http://www.oceanobservatories.org, January 2013.

Tobin, Harold J. and Masa Kinoshita. "NanTroSEIZE: The IODP Nankai Trough Seismogenic Zone Experiment." *Scientific Drilling*, 2 (2006).

Kinoshita, Masataka, et al. "The Seismogenic Zone Experiment." *Oceanography*, 19 (2006): 28-38.

Wilcock, William et al. "The deployment of a long-term seafloor seismic network on the Juan de Fuca Ridge." *Oceans*, 2007.

Lubick, Naomi. "Danger Zones." *Nature* 476 (2011): 391-2.

Yagi, Yuji. "Enhance ocean-floor observation, in Rebuilding Seismology." *Nature*, 473 (2011): 147-8.

Newman, Andrew V. "Hidden depths." *Nature*, 474 (2011): 441-3.

Scherwath, Martin et al. "Seafloor seismometers monitor Northern Cascadia earthquakes." *EOS*. 92 (2011): 421-40.

Okada, Tomomi et al. "Shallow inland earthquakes in NE Japan possibly triggered by the 2011 off the Pacific coast of Tohoku earthquake." *Earth Planets Space*, 63 (2011): 749-54.

Miyazaki, Shin'ichi, Jeffrey J. McGuire and Paul Segall. "Seismic and aseismic fault slip before and during the 2011 off the Pacific coast of Tohoku earthquake." *Earth Planets Space*, 63 (2011): 637-42.

Nishimura, Takuya, Hiroshi Munekane and Hiroshi Yarai. "The 2011 off the Pacific coast of Tohoku earthquake and its aftershocks observed by GEONET." *Earth Planets Space*, 63 (2011): 631-6.

Kerr, Richard. "New work reinforces megaquake's harsh lessons in geoscience." *Science*, 332 (2011): 911.

Lay, Thorne and Hiroo Kanamori. "Insights from the great 2011 Japan earthquake." *Physics Today*, 2011.

Sato, Mariko et al. "Displacement above the hypocenter of the 2011 Tohoku-Oki earthquake." *Science*, 332 (2011): 1395.

Monastersky, Richard. "Tsunami forecasting: The next wave." *Nature*, 483 (2012): 144-6.

Kanamori, Hiroo. "Putting seismic research to most effective use." *Nature*, 483 (2012): 147-8.

Kerr, Richard A. "A tantalizing view of what set off Japan's killer quake." *Science*, 335 (2012): 272.

Kato, Aitaro et al. "Propagation of slow slip leading up to the 2011 Mw 9.0 Tohoku-Oki earthquake." *Science*, 335 (2012): 705-8.

For background on the L'Aquila earthquake and trial:
Jordan, Tom, and John Vidale, conversations with author.

Hall, Stephen S. "At Fault?" *Nature*, 477 (2011): 264-69.

Ropeik, David, "The L'Aquila verdict: A judgment not against science, but against a failure of science communication," *Scientific American* (blog), October 22, 2012, http://blogs.scientificamerican.com/guest-blog/2012/10/22/the-laquila-verdict-a-judgment-not-against-science-but-against-a-failure-of-science-communication, January 2013.

Jordan, T.H. "Lessons of L'Aquila for operational earthquake forecasting." *Seismological Research Letters*, 84 (2013): 1-4.

For information on earthquake early warning:
Jordan, Thomas H. and Lucile M. Jones. "Operational earthquake forecasting: Some thoughts on why and how." *Seismological Research Letters*, 81 (2010): 571-4.

Allen, Richard, "The essential lessons from the Japan earthquake for the U.S.," *Scientific American* (blog), March 12, 2011.

Hoshiba, Mitsuyuki et al. "Outline of the 2011 off the Pacific coast of Tohoku Earthquake—Earthquake early warning and observed seismic intensity." *Earth Planets Space*, 63 (2011): 547-51.

Vidale, John. "Earthquake early warning in the PNW," *Seismo Blog*, 2011, www.pnsn.org/blog/2011/12/01/earthquake-early-warning-in-the-pnw, January 2013.

Allen, Richard. "Seconds before the big one." *Scientific American*, 2011.

Allen, Richard M. and Alon Ziv. "Application of real-time GPS to earthquake early warning." *Geophysical Research Letters*, 38 (2011): L16310.

"BART installs quake early-warning system," *The Associated Press*, September 28, 2012.

CHAPTER 14: INSCRUTABLE, INEVITABLE

Witt, James Lee, Peter Yanev, and Ian Madin, conversations with author.

McCarthy, Francis X. and Natalie Keegan. "FEMA's Pre-Disaster Mitigation Program: Overview and Issues." Congressional Research Service 7-5700, RL34537, 2009.

ProtectingAmerica, http://www.protectingamerica.org/, January 2013.

Witt, James Lee and James M. Loy, "U.S. needs a disaster insurance fund," *Newsday*, March 31, 2011.

For quake impact estimates:
"Washington State Emergency Management Council: Seismic Safety Committee," *Resilient Washington State*, November 2012, http://www.emd.wa.gov/about/SeismicSafety Committee.shtml, February, 2013.

"Draft Analytical Baseline Study for the Cascadia Earthquake and Tsunami." *Department of Homeland Security, National Infrastructure Simulation and Analysis Center*. 2011.

RESOURCES

MORE INFORMATION ABOUT EARTHQUAKE PREPAREDNESS

FEMA, http://www.ready.gov/earth quakes.

"What to do in an Earthquake," *California Department of Conservation*, http://www.consrv.ca.gov/index/ Earthquakes/Pages/qh_earthquakes_ what.aspx.

"Are you prepared?," *72 hours.org*, http://72hours.org/.

"Preparedness," *Washington State Emergency Management Division*, http://www.emd.wa.gov/prepared ness/prep_index.shtml.

The Great Washington ShakeOut, http://www.shakeout.org/washington.

EARTHQUAKE SCIENCE, STORIES, AND IMPACTS

Yeats, Robert S. *Living with Earthquakes in the Pacific Northwest*, second edition. Corvallis: Oregon State University Press, 2004.

Musson, Roger. *The Million Death Quake: The Science of Predicting Earth's Deadliest Natural Disaster.* New York: Palgrave McMillan, 2012.

Thompson, Jerry. *Cascadia's Fault: The Coming Earthquake and Tsunami that could Devastate North America.* Berkeley: Counterpoint Press, 2011.

Nance, John J. *On Shaky Ground.* New York: William Morrow and Company, Inc., 1988

Sieh, Kerry and Simon LeVay. *The Earth in Turmoil: Earthquakes, Volcanoes and their Impacts on Humankind.* New York: W.H. Freeman, 1999.

For magnitude comparisons:
"Earthquake size comparison calculator," *USGS Earthquake Hazards Program*, http://earthquake.usgs.gov/ learn/topics/how_much_bigger.php.

RESOURCES ON TSUNAMI

"Oregon tsunami inundation maps and evacuation," *Oregon Department of Geology and Mineral Industries*, (brochure), http://www.oregongeology .com/sub/earthquakes/coastal/Tsu mapsbycity.htm.

"Washington tsunami inundation maps and evacuation," *Washington Department of Natural Resources*, (brochure), http://www.dnr.wa.gov/ResearchScience/Topics/GeologicHazardsMapping/Pages/tsunamis.aspx.

"California tsunami inundation maps," *California Department of Conservation*, http://www.conservation.ca.gov/cgs/geologic_hazards/Tsunami/Inundation_Maps/Pages/Statewide_Maps.aspx.

"British Columbia tsunami notification zones," *Emergency Management B.C.*, http://embc.gov.bc.ca/em/hazard_preparedness/Tsunami_Preparedness_Information.html.

SEISMIC HAZARD MAPS

"USGS Seismic Hazard Mapping Project," *USGS*, http://earthquake.usgs.gov/hazards/.

For buildings and bridges: "Seismic Retrofit Program," *WSDOT*, http://www.wsdot.wa.gov/Bridge/Reporting/SeismicRetrofitProgram.htm.

"Unreinforced Masonry Buildings," City of Seattle, http://www.seattle.gov/dpd/Emergency/UnreinforcedMasonry/Buildings/default.asp.

IMAGE CREDITS

Page vi: North America Map © 2013 Digital Vector Maps

Page xi: Map by Guillaume Del'Isle, from University of Washington Libraries, Special Collections Division, UW23622z

Page 7: U.S. Geological Survey

Page 8: U.S. Geological Survey

Page 12: U.S. Geological Survey / *The Orphan Tsunami of 1700*

Page 23: Roy D. Hyndman; Reproduced with permission from Natural Resources Canada, courtesy of the Geological Survey of Canada

Page 28: U.S. Geological Survey

Page 31: U.S. Geological Survey

Page 35: U.S. Geological Survey

Page 48: Satake et al, 2003. JGR 108:2325

Page 53: Brian Atwater, U.S. Geological Survey

Page 60: Adams, John. 1990. Paleoseismicity of the Cascadia Subduction Zone: Evidence from turbidites off the Oregon-Washington margin. Tectonics, 9:569-583. Reproduced with permission from Natural Resources Canada, courtesy of the Geological Survey of Canada

Page 66: Oregon Department of Geology and Mineral Industries

Page 90: Puget Sound Lidar Consortium

Page 94: Mark Nowlin, The Seattle Times

Page 120: Carmen Dybdahl and Fred Matamoros

Page 129: U.S. Geological Survey

Page 149: U.S. Geological Survey / *The Orphan Tsunami of 1700*

Page 165: A.E. Murlin, USGS

Page 224: Tim Melbourne, Pacific Northwest Geodetic Array, Central Washington University

Page 227: Courtesy of Ocean Observatories Initiative Regional Scale Nodes program and the Center for Environmental Visualization, University of Washington

INDEX

Note: Graphics are indicated by *italics*.

ABOUT THE AUTHOR

SANDI DOUGHTON is an award-winning science reporter for *The Seattle Times*. She has been covering earthquake research in the Pacific Northwest for more than twenty years. She lives in West Seattle, not far from the Seattle Fault.